CONTENTS

LIST OF FIGURES

PREFACE

Most libraries do not have a human resources professional on staff. In small and many medium-sized libraries, librarians with little or no training in managing employees hire, evaluate, discipline, and terminate employees as part of their regular duties as an information professional.

Managing human resources without having a background in the field can be challenging and scary. I once fell into this category myself. I have met many others in the same boat in the human resources workshops I run. Invariably, workshop attendees have many questions. How can an institution attract good candidates for an open position in an atmosphere of librarian shortages? What are the legal implications of disciplining or terminating a problematic employee? Should the organization monitor employees' Internet activity? Librarians are searching for answers—more specifically, answers that apply to libraries rather than to large institutions or for-profit corporations. In *Managing Library Employees: A How-To-Do-It Manual*, I try to provide answers to the most common and the most confusing library human resources questions.

Managing Library Employees covers the practical side of human resources, the everyday situations that come up sooner or later in most organizations. It explores the range of essential HR functions from basic employment practices such as hiring, compensation, and benefits to timely topics such as workplace violence, Internet misuse, and human resources software programs. Legal issues are also a primary focus; in addition to the chapter on employment law, other chapters touch on topics such as sexual harassment, designing a lawful and properly documented disciplinary procedure, and identifying potential problem spots before they turn into a lawsuit.

The aim of *Managing Library Employees* is to provide a basic orientation in human resources management for librarians. While the information will be helpful to readers in libraries of all types and sizes, the focus is on the concerns of small- to medium-sized organizations, since individuals in these settings are most likely to have little background in human resources. Where applicable, *Managing Library Employees* discusses how budgetary and staffing limits affect human resources practices and how to work around these problems.

Being a successful human resources manager requires a change in perspective. Coworkers and employees become the manager's internal customers, and need to be treated like other customers: with respect, care, fairness, and objectivity. *Managing Library Employees* aims to help the reader cultivate this new outlook and handle challenges with confidence.

ORGANIZATION

The chapters are arranged roughly in the order in which the topics might be encountered. Though a librarian just starting to take responsibility for human resources tasks or wishing to get an overall view of the field will want to read the book in order, the question-and-answer format also makes it easy to flip between topics as a question comes up.

Chapter 1, "Library Human Resources Management: Introduction and History," defines basic HR terms and provides a general overview of the current state of both the human resources field in general and library human resources in particular. It describes the demographic makeup of today's librarians and investigates possible solutions to anticipated staffing shortages.

Chapter 2, "Laws Affecting the Management of Library Personnel," covers key human resources–related legislation: Title VII, the Family and Medical Leave Act (FMLA), the Americans with Disabilities Act (ADA), HIPAA, and others. It outlines steps that libraries should take to ensure that they are in compliance with these regulations.

Chapter 3, "Recruitment and Selection of Library Staff," focuses on hiring employees, whether professional librarians, student workers, or volunteers. In this chapter, you will also find advice on creating a job description and interviewing, including what interview questions are considered unlawful.

Chapter 4, "Training, Retention, and Professional Development," discusses ways to support new and longtime employees, from orientation to mentoring. Chapter 5, "Compensation and Benefits," examines salary systems and the range of benefits that your institution might consider offering. Even those libraries whose salaries and benefits are determined by city, state, or university systems will profit from being aware of other options. This chapter also touches on unions and collective bargaining.

Chapter 6, "Evaluation and Performance Appraisal," introduces different methods of evaluation, including how to evaluate individuals in team-based organizations. Chapter 7, "Problem Employees and Marginal Employees," clarifies the difference between these two groups and advises readers on how to diplomatically and effectively address performance issues. Absenteeism and bullying are also covered here.

Chapter 8, "Conflict Resolution/Management, Progressive Discipline, and RIF," delves into the most difficult HR tasks. Suggested steps in discipline, handling conflict, and termination are outlined in order to ease these processes.

Chapter 9, "Communication: Verbal, Written, and Electronic," covers the three primary types of communication and how they operate in the workplace environment. Communication with management is often the number one concern for employees. Chapter 10, "The Role of Technology in Human Resources Management," considers the impact of technology in the library environment, especially human resources information systems (HRIS).

Chapter 11, "Managing Change," offers strategies for dealing with a society where change is constant and unavoidable, and touches on technostress, a collection of symptoms that show the effect of change and technology on workers.

At times, even those of us with both experience and education in human resources may feel that we are simply muddling along. People are unpredictable, relationships change, and today's diverse workforce creates an even greater number of opportunities for both positive developments and interpersonal problems. During tough periods, a solid base of human resources knowledge can guide your decisions and restore your professional confidence. I hope this book will be one of the touchstones that helps you through the sometimes perplexing but equally rewarding world of human resources management.

ACKNOWLEDGMENTS

First, I would like to acknowledge Elizabeth Lund, editor for Neal-Schuman, who was an immense help and support as I worked through this text. I would like to acknowledge Paul Seeman who believed in my concept and supported approval for my book proposal. Next, Teresa McCurry, colleague and team member, who faithfully read each draft chapter and encouraged me. I would like to also acknowledge Polly Boruff-Jones and the BAT (Business Administration Team) who agreed to pick up some of my responsibilities while I took my sabbatical. Finally, I would like to acknowledge my children, Jill Pursell and Jeffrey Stanley, for their moral support. Most of all, I would like to acknowledge my husband, Michael, whose faith, humor, and love helped me make it through the process.

1 LIBRARY HUMAN RESOURCES MANAGEMENT: INTRODUCTION AND HISTORY

Many librarians are thrust into the role of human resources manager or professional without any background or training in HR. That is how it happened to me, too. Over a decade ago, the associate director at our library retired and I was asked to fill in for the human resources activities, basically the recruitment of librarians, for our organization. This role was only supposed to last six months until the director retired and then I was to return to my public services role full time. During this six-month period, I was to divide my time equally between the public services role and the administration role.

As I began this role, I faced many fears as well as many challenges. First of all, I had the challenge of learning all of the aspects of recruiting librarians, which included learning all of the policies and procedures that are under the faculty governance of our institution. The librarians at Indiana University Purdue University Indianapolis (IUPUI) are part of the Indiana University system and have tenure-track positions. One of my greatest fears was that I would make errors in the process that could result in some sort of lawsuit for the university. I also worried that since I was junior to many of my colleagues, they would resent my new role in administration.

Immediately, we began a search for three librarian positions. I found that everyone involved was willing to support and help me through the process. The Dean of Faculty's Office, which oversees this process, worked diligently with me while I learned all of the appropriate forms and steps for faculty recruitment. Since the Affirmative Action Office was also involved, they, too, worked with me to make sure that I complied with all of their regulations and procedures. My colleagues and other staff members were gracious and willing to assist me through the process and we successfully hired the three new individuals without any consequential errors or problems. By the time this was done, I felt firmly established and confident in this new role. The new director was on board and the position had developed into a full-blown human resources position responsible for all positions in the library, not just recruitment of librarians. A search was conducted and I was successfully appointed as the full-time human resources librarian. The struggle of learning and conquering all of the various aspects of human resources was one of my greatest challenges but has also become one of the most rewarding experiences in my library career.

I share this with you so that you will realize that although this role may seem like a monumental task at first, you can be successful in transitioning from a librarian to human resources professional. This book is designed to help you through that process.

A BRIEF HISTORY OF HUMAN RESOURCES MANAGEMENT

The one constant in any organization is its workforce. Without the workforce, organizations would cease to exist. The makeup of this workforce may continually be changing and the challenge for any organization is managing this change. Libraries are no different from other organizations in this respect. What may be different for libraries is who is designated to manage the intricacies of personnel matters within the organization. For many smaller libraries, this might well be the director or library head. In larger systems, there might be a human resources administration unit that handles all of the personnel issues. Whoever is responsible for these tasks has one of the most important job responsibilities—managing the human factor. Everyone in the organization should be responsible in managing human resources, but it is truly the primary role of the human resources professional.

Managing the human factor may include job analysis, creating job descriptions, recruitment, selection, compensation packaging, training, adherence to personnel laws, professional development, performance reviews, discipline, policies and procedures, consultation, conflict resolution, and termination or discharge of employees. All of these activities fall under the purview of the human resources department or human resources professional.

Terms centered on personnel and human resources change continuously, especially in today's world, where technology has such a great impact. "Human resources" itself is a phrase coined in recent years to reflect the old practice of personnel management. Another closely related term expressing some of the same responsibilities is "the management of organizational behavior." Organizational behavior has been described as the study of the many factors that have an impact on how individuals and groups respond to and act in an organization (George and Jones, 2000). Organizational behavior management is typically touched upon briefly in the library management classes of the library science programs. It is rare to find library programs that focus specifically on human resources management in any great detail.

Much of the research surrounding organizational behavior has targeted the way in which the characteristics of an individual (personality and motivation) affect how well they do their jobs by matching people to jobs, through job design, and by effective career management. All of these factors can help raise an employee's motivation level and satisfaction with the job. Job satisfaction usually tends to better production and thus leads to a more effective organization.

In today's age of competition, managing human resources is critical for the survival of an organization. IBM, along with a consulting firm, conducted a worldwide survey in 1991 of nearly 3,000 human resource managers and CEOs. This study indicated that about 70 percent of human resource managers see the human resources function as critical to an organization's success (Overman, 1992). Interestingly enough, the CEOs' responses were very similar.

A review of how human resources began is a good first step in understanding the impact of its management. Most disciplines have an element of research or studies that trace the history of the discipline. Human resources is no exception. One of the best known early developments in this arena is the work of Frederick Taylor around the turn of the century. In this early study, focus was placed on the individual for the purpose of motivating, controlling, and improving productivity of the entry level employees. Taylor was the initiator of scientific management (George and Jones, 2002). He set out to systemize the study of workflow organization by breaking tasks into minute detail and devising ways to speed up their accomplishment. He believed that management tried to push workers to achieve output without an objective yardstick to measure a proper day's work. He tried to devise a system to resolve this problem. This was one of the first time and motion studies done in industry. Taylor's work was criticized by many for putting too much emphasis on the individual and defeating the collective power of work groups. Nonetheless, Taylor's principles of scientific management prompted a crusade for efficiency in the 1920s and the 1930s.

The next key study shifted the focus from individual to group but again placed emphasis on productivity. This study was conducted by Elton Mayo, who focused on the social organization of the workplace and the human needs of the workers. Mayo was invited by the Western Electric Company to inspect some experiments being undertaken at the company's Hawthorne Works on the outskirts of Chicago. This factory had almost 25,000 workers and was the main manufacturing plant for the Bell Telephone System in the United States. Mayo's efforts included changing group composition and incentives. They also experimented with some environmental changes such as lighting and physical arrangement. One discovery of this experiment was termed the "Hawthorne

Effect." This refers to a temporary increase in employee productivity in response to personal attention by supervisors and the opportunity to participate in new programs. Mayo felt that singling out certain groups of employees for special attention had the effect of pulling previously indifferent individuals into cohesive groups with a high degree of group pride which resulted in higher work productivity (Stueart and Eastlick, 1981). This is similar to the way that teams functions today. While this study, too, was highly criticized, the importance of the Hawthorne studies is significant. They indicated that workers did respond to managerial efforts to improve the working environment and that the informal group can become a positive unit helping management to achieve its goals. This also was the first time that behavioral scientists went into the industry environment and actually observed workers, setting new standards for management research.

In the 1950s and the 1960s, the focus moved to the selection and development of individuals. The work expanded to include performance appraisal and training, with the spotlight on individual performance in an organization as a measure of success.

All of this research was in fields termed "organizational behavior" or "industrial behavior." It was not until the 1970s that the term "human resources management" made its first appearance. This term included a broader focus than the earlier research, encompassing heath and safety issues (Poole and Warner, 1998).

In the early 1980s, organizational strategy along with international and domestic competition for companies began to impact human resources management. Other concerns of organizations, such as structure, size, culture, products, and life cycles, began to creep into the role of human resources management. Much of this appeared under the guise of personnel management theory. With this global outlook, goals changed as well. While the practice of recruiting, retaining, and motivating employees is still important, it is important primarily as the key factor in achieving bottom line organizational goals.

In the past two decades, with the explosion of technology, human resources managers have seen a change in their roles. The implementation of human resource systems altered their daily work activities. Human resource managers must now focus on aligning the HR systems and the workforce into a strategic business process. Human resource professionals will need to play a role of strategic partner to line management. Key in this planning will be the significance of differentiating employee performance and how this affects the overall organization's performance and success. According to a 2006 HR Practices report, HR professionals are providing information on an organization's overall compensation structure, analyzing industry best practices, developing pay philosophies, and designing compensation plans for executives (Meisinger, 2006). This is a clear demonstration of the strategic role of today's human resource professionals.

This brief history is to give a bird's-eye view of the discipline and how it developed. Many human resources professionals have become generalists and are engaged in practices promoting broad concepts and team focus rather than concentrating on the individual. Of course, with these changes, as with any change, come new debates. There is probably not one single answer to the role of the human resources manager and the discipline will continue to evolve and change as new forces impact the lives of organizations.

HUMAN RESOURCES MANAGEMENT ACTIVITIES

The activities of a human resources department or unit might include: 1) review and analysis of the organization's environment, 2) planning for human resources needs, 3) providing recruitment, selection, interviewing and hiring for the organization, 4) training and continued professional development, 5) appraising employee behavior or training others to evaluate, 6) compensating employee behavior, 7) improving the work environment, and 8) establishing and maintaining effective work relationships. Not every human resource individual will perform all of these activities, but the trend is heading in this direction.

Human resources departments in effective organizations, especially in highly competitive environments, must assume many roles in the organizational structure. These roles will affect the organization's productivity, enhance the quality of work life in the organization, help the organization comply with all of the required laws and regulations related to human resources management, and improve workforce flexibility and efficiency.

In the past, the human resources department played a limited role in the overall picture of the organization. Due to the impact that human resources now has on the effectiveness and success of an organization, that role has become very diverse in nature and is an important aspect of the face of the organization. Although the human resources department may delegate some of the human resources tasks to line managers or supervisors, it is still their responsibility to ensure that these activities are implemented fairly and consistently across the organization.

The human resources unit can demonstrate its contribution to the organization in many ways, including partnering with the other members of the organization and being involved in the strategic planning. Human resources professionals are taking on a more strategic role in the organization, developing the ability to take advantage of the strengths of the employees and making the workforce an asset to the organization. It will be the responsibility of the human resources professionals to recruit and retain highly skilled employees capable of ongoing innovation and able to effectively deal with constant change.

KEY TERMS IN HUMAN RESOURCES

As in any field, human resources management has developed its own language. In this book, some basic human resources terminology will be used. The following terms are some of the more frequently used ones.

Background checks provide history about a potential employee from sources outside of previous employment. Criminal records, motor vehicle records, and credit reports may be part of a background check.

Compliance refers to management's responsibility to maintain agreement with the federal and state employment regulations and their changes.

Employee benefits are all benefits and services other than wages, provided to employees by the employer and may include social insurance programs, health and life-related insurance coverage, retirement plans, and education assistance programs.

Employee identification number (EIN) is a number issued by the IRS to any organization with employees.

Employee policy and procedure manual spells out what the organization expects of its employees and what they can expect in terms of benefits and other topics related to employment. New employees are usually given a copy of this manual or handbook upon hire and are generally required to sign a receipt acknowledging that they have received it.

Exempt employees are employees who receive their full salaries for the work week no matter how many hours they have actually worked. There are strict guidelines set out by the federal government to determine whether an employee is exempt or not.

Headhunters are recruitment firms that search for individuals to fill specific positions for organizations for a fee, most often used in executive position searches.

Illegal interview questions are questions at an interview that do not directly relate to the candidates' qualifications or abilities to perform the job. Such questions include marital status, religion, race, age, and so on.

A **job description** is a detailed listing of the duties to be performed by the individual filling the position and includes the required skills, education, certification levels, and other criteria directly related to the job. (Also called a "position description.")

A **mentor** is an individual either formally or informally designated to coach or provide practical information for another individual, usually a new employee.

Orientation is the beginning period of an employee's life with an organization. There is usually a designated time period for the orientation which usually includes instruction and training as needed.

Outsourcing is the hiring of outside consultants, freelancers, or companies to provide services that in the past have been provided by employees.

Overtime refers to any hours worked by a nonexempt employee above the forty-hour work week.

Performance review or evaluation is the process of assessing an employee's performance within a given period of time and provides an opportunity for feedback, questions, setting new goals, and suggestions for improvement.

A **Personnel Policy and Procedures Manual** provides employers, human resources personnel, and supervisors with a systematic approach to administering personnel policies and practices. It is typically distributed only to management representatives and human resource professionals.

Probationary period is a length of time during which both the employer and the new employee have a chance to see whether the employee is right for the position and vice versa. Before the period is completed, the employee is either let go or hired on an official basis.

Progressive discipline is a series of steps to correct unacceptable behavior or performance by an employee. These steps usually include an oral warning, a written warning, suspension, and eventual termination should behavior not improve.

Recruitment is the process of advertising, searching, and identifying possible applicants for a specific position or vacancy within an organization.

Telecommuting allows employees to work from a location other than the place of business, usually from their homes through computer access.

PAST TRENDS IN LIBRARY STAFFING

To best understand where libraries are now, let us review the recent past. In 1975, the Bureau of Labor Statistics (BLS) published a study entitled *Library Manpower: A Study of Demand and Supply.* This study was conducted because of concerns raised by the library community that an apparent oversupply of librarians were competing for a limited number of vacancies. This study reported that in 1970, 115,000 librarians were gainfully employed in American libraries. The study forecasted that between 1970 and 1985 168,000 new librarians would be needed. Of these, 47,000 would be for new positions and 121,000 to replace those who had left the field because of retirement, or for a variety of other reasons.

The Bureau went on to project that to meet the demand, an average of 9,000 new professionals would have to enter the profession each year and an additional 2,200 librarians would enter the field annually, after absences. BLS predicted that the 168,000 vacancies in the 15-year period would be somewhat in balance; however, they did caution that for new entrants and nongraduate-degree librarians, job prospects would be limited. In 1970, the average age of librarians was 45 years of age. That would mean that half the librarians in the United States would reach the traditional retirement age of 65 by 1990.

Another study was conducted in the 1980s by the King Research Group for the National Center for Educational Statistics and the Office of Library and Learning Technologies (King Research, 1983). This study was conducted to project the supply and demand of professional libraries through 1990. This project did not have access to the latest 1980 census data so the baseline census data on the number of librarians in 1980 was not included in the report. In the King report, a decline in the total number of graduates of accredited master's degree programs was reported. Declines in the total number of persons graduating with undergraduate degrees in library science, nonaccredited master's degrees, and school library certificates were also documented. The King researchers reported a dramatic 35 percent decline in graduates of library and information science education programs between 1977 and 1982 alone (King Research, 1983). The King study recommended that library schools examine the potential for the training of information professionals for nonlibrary settings, knowing the traditional job opportunities for librarians would be in short supply.

One year later, the Census of Population publication, "Earnings by Occupation and Education," provided confirmation that actual librarians in number were nearly 50,000 higher than that of the King data (US Bureau of the Census, 1984). This data also revealed that between 1980 and 2000, approximately 70,000 librarians would reach retirement age or would have retired. Another 70,000 would leave the labor force for other reasons. All of the library education programs would not be able to produce enough graduates over this 20-year period just to replace the numbers of librarians who appeared most likely to retire. Many of the individuals entering the library school programs are entering into a second career. Often, they have tried one field and have decided to try another field where they feel that the combined fields of their previous career and the library field will result in a better fit. This results in an older age group entering the library field at a time when many of the senior librarians are looking to retire.

The average age of librarians has remained remarkably constant at 45 years of age. What changed in the late 1980s, however, was the average age of students enrolled in LIS programs and the age at which librarians chose to leave the profession. Information from the 1990 census reveals that librarians were retiring at 63 years of age and fewer librarians were working after age 65. The 9,000 librarians who were 65 or older in the 1980s had shrunk to just 4,000 in the late 1990s (Matarazzo, 2000). Matarazzo indicates that the average age of students enrolled in programs of library and information science is 36 years, much older than graduate students in other master's degree programs. In the last 40 years, librarianship has had three periods of shortages and two corresponding periods of what seemed to be an oversupply of professional librarians.

We are still in a period of shortage today. In 2003, Laura Bush called on the Institute of Museum and Library Services (IMLS) to help recruit a new generation of librarians through a special funding initiative. The 21st Century Program since that date has funded 1,537 master's degree students, 119 doctoral students, 660 preprofessional students, and 378 continuing education students (ALA, 2007). Although we are making some progress in recruiting new librarians, I feel that we will still fall short of the goal needed to replace the "boomers" as they begin retiring in the next five to ten years. In our library alone, we have had five librarians retire in the past five years, three more to retire within the next two years, and at least three others who will reach retirement age within seven to ten years.

The recurring pattern in the field of feast and famine of professional librarians also affects the role of the library human resources professional. It will be the role of the human resources personnel to find these replacements, to make sure that these librarians and other library staff members have the appropriate skills and training to accomplish their tasks, to ensure that assessment and performance reviews are conducted, to conduct discipline and/or termination procedures, and to be engaged in the strategic planning of goals and objectives for the organization. The library human resources professional will wear many hats and fill many challenging roles. In order to see how complex their roles are, we have to look at the many faces of librarianship and how they affect the management of human resources.

THE FACE OF LIBRARIES

Some of these faces differ depending on the type of library. Each type of library has a different need and role for its staff members. Libraries are typically broken down into public libraries, academic libraries, school libraries, and special libraries (which include corporate libraries and specialized professional libraries, i.e., medical, law, pharmaceutical, and so on). The overall mission of most libraries is expressed as a variation on the theme of excellent service in the provision for the needs of the community they serve. Their communities differ greatly and the communities' needs also vary, impacting the type of services provided.

WHAT DOES THE STAFF OF PUBLIC LIBRARIES LOOK LIKE IN THE 21ST CENTURY?

A public library serves all age groups, all economic groups, all racial and gender groups, and is primarily funded by local government (Moorman, 2006). Most public libraries offer the following types of services: material checkout and return, collection development, adult and children's services, and outreach services.

Below is a detailed statistical report from the National Center for Education Statistics on staffing in public libraries. As it indicates, many of the public libraries do not have a full-time professional librarian. The smaller and rural public libraries are dependent upon the paraprofessional to fill these roles. This is an important issue for the library human resources professional who must find qualified individuals to handle these many responsibilities. While many of these paraprofessionals can learn many of the aspects of library service on the job, they are not trained to the same extent as the professional librarian. On top of this, public library use continues to grow with number of visits per year to US public libraries increasing 61 percent in the period 1994–2004. Circulation increased 28 percent over the decade and was up 2.3 percent in 2004 from 2003.

The report indicates that public libraries had a total of 130,102 paid full-time equivalent (FTE) staff in fiscal year 2000, or 12.23 paid FTE staff per 25,000 population. Of these, 23 percent, or 2.78 per 25,000 population were librarians with the ALA/MLS. Ten percent were librarians by title but did not have the ALA/MLS and 67 percent were in other positions. Only 44 percent of all public libraries, or 4,034 libraries, had librarians with the ALA/MLS. The ALA/MLS is defined as librarians with master's degrees from programs of library and information studies accredited by the American Library Association.

In a survey conducted by the American Library Association in 2002, 55.5 percent of the 9,074 public libraries have no ALA/MLS librarians. Of libraries serving fewer than 1,000 individuals, 96.9 percent have no ALA/MLS librarians, 2.4 percent have less than 1, and 0.7 percent have between 1 and 1.99 ALA/MLS librarians (Lynch, 2003; Chute, 2002). Currently, ALA does not have standards or guidelines on what the balance should be between professional staff and support staff. The Public Library Association focuses on the planning process that recognizes the needs and interests of specific communities rather than on setting national standards (Lynch, 2003).

Smaller public libraries face the same challenges in hiring and staffing as their larger counterparts, but typically have more limited resources. Staffing for the small library will likely include some mix of professionals and paraprofessionals (Bliss, 2006). Changes in the roles of today's librarians from the traditional model of library staff must be considered when recruiting and hiring library employees. For instance, reference librarians may be expected to do Web work and/or training and children's librarians may be expected or asked to do community outreach programs. The increasing demands from the public for the most up-to-date electronic library services add additional challenges for smaller libraries. In addition, the smaller public library must adhere to the policies of its governing authority, usually a board of trustees, who may or may not be aware of staffing issues facing these smaller libraries. In smaller libraries, whether independent or not, the board of trustees cannot be ignored when hiring (Bliss, 2006). In many cases, state library associations have resources to aid the hiring library manager in developing or updating personnel policies. The small library manager should visit as many of these association sites as possible, as guides when creating policies and procedures.

PROFESSIONAL POSITIONS

When filling professional positions (those which require a master's degree in library or information science), one of the first places to search is in the latest crop of MLIS graduates. Sending your position announcement to library schools is one way of attracting these new graduates. Most library schools will post this information to their student listservs at no charge. It is important to seek recruitment from both unemployed and currently employed personnel. Professional publications are a good source both for advertising positions and for seeing who might be in the market for a position. Costs will be involved and will, no doubt, have to have board approval, but in the long run will be worthwhile.

The "2000 Report to the Executive Committee of the Public Library Association" indicates that there is still a shortage of librarians available in the field of public librarianship. This report could be useful in convincing the library board of the need for greater advertisement to reach potential applicants. Other Web sources can be used to solicit applicants for your vacant positions—*Library Journal* classifieds, the American Library Association Web site, the Public Library Association Web site, and so on. The fee for posting job notices will vary. Another useful resource is the Placement Center established at ALA Conferences (Losinski, 2005). These resources are useful for all types of libraries but particularly for smaller public libraries.

The following is a small selection of possible online places for recruitment of librarians.

American Library Association—www.ala.org/ala/education/empopps/employment.htm
Placement Services—www.ala.org/ala/hrdr/placementservice/currentconference.htm
Jobs in Libraries and Information Technology—www.ala.org/ala/lita/litaresources/litajobsite/litajobsite.cfm
American Association of Law Libraries—www.aalnet.org
Special Libraries Association—www.sla.org
Chronicle of Higher Education—http://chronicle.com
Jobs for Librarians and Information Professionals—www.lisjob.com
Library Associates Recruitment—www.libraryassociates.com/index.html
Library Job Postings—www.libraryjobpostings.org/

Figure 1-1. Web Site Resources for Library Recruitment

PARAPROFESSIONALS

Recruiting for paraprofessionals is a much harder challenge, especially for the smaller library. The United States Bureau of Labor Statistics indicates that the pay for these positions tends to be so low that obtaining quality employees can be difficult. In addition, recruitment for paraprofessional positions often does not include widespread advertising. Small public libraries with limited advertising funds tend to use public postings within the library itself or advertising in local newspapers as the most common means of finding support staff. With low pay being a challenge, it is especially important that library staffers be offered continuing education in the field (Farley, 2002). This will help balance the compensation in a small way. There are numerous opportunities for continuing education from professional organizations at the national, state, and regional levels. Often, financial support will be provided by the organization for those needing it. Several state libraries also offer continuing education models. Distance learning opportunities are also provided through satellite teleconferencing, videoconferencing, and online learning.

Paraprofessionals are often the first face seen in the public library. These individuals attend to the Circulation desk activities. They will be responsible for checking materials in and out of the library, processing interlibrary loan requests, collecting overdue fines, and answering the telephone. Many users in libraries assume that all personnel behind a desk in a library are professional librarians. It is important that these individuals demonstrate a professional manner and handle the users as a professional. The library human resources professional will need to make sure that they hire individuals who can acquire these skills and successfully perform their duties.

CHILDREN'S LIBRARIANS

Another face of the public libraries is the children's librarian. Almost all public libraries have active programs for children as part of their customer focus. The term "children's librarian" is not as straightforward as it may seem. The position may carry responsibilities far beyond services for children. In most cases, the term relates to a "person who is responsible for the provision of library services to children and teenagers in a range of 0–18 years of age" (Fisher, 2000). Often, children's librarians are called upon to do reference desk coverage, interlibrary service duties, and technology access for the general public in addition to their services for children.

While this range of duties can be positive, sometimes it can be overwhelming. The workload of children's librarians can be very broad, and they are often expected to be "masters" of everything. Turnover tends to remain high as many of the positions are filled by entry-level librarians or paraprofessionals who may either move on or "burn out" under the stress of the workload.

HOW DO SCHOOL LIBRARIES DIFFER FROM PUBLIC LIBRARIES?

It is estimated that there are more than 94,000 school library and media centers located in 95 percent of public schools and 86 percent of private schools. More than 66,000 librarians and 99,000 support staff work in school library media centers. Although this seems like a great number, about 25 percent of all schools do not have a school librarian (Tabs, 2004).

Many school librarians who entered the field in the 1960s are near retirement. Many states require districts to hire only certified staff, but with the diminishing number of librarians who fit that category, administrators are forced to hire noncertified staff and, in some cases, have dismantled the library program entirely (Everhart, 2006). If vacant school library positions are unfilled too long, principals may choose to phase librarians out and spend these resources elsewhere.

A survey by the National Center for Education Statistics conducted in 1999/2000 reported data on traditional public school and private school library media centers nationwide. Public schools were more likely than private schools to staff the library media center with paid professional staff members . Among the public schools, only 42 percent employed professional library staff with an MLS or related degree. Seventeen percent of private schools with a library media center had paid professional staff. High schools with a library media center were more likely than elementary schools or combined schools to employ a professional librarian. Among public schools with a library media center, 52 percent of high schools had a school librarian with an MLS or related degree in 1999–2000, compared to 39 percent of elementary schools. Public schools were more likely to employ a full-time, state certified library media specialist than private schools. Public schools were more likely to employ at least one library aide or clerical staff than the private schools. A larger proportion of private school library media centers relied on adult volunteers. These figures show the lack of professional staffing in a great percentage of our public and private school systems. The situation has not improved much since the 1991 survey. Another survey will be conducted in 2007/2008 and perhaps this survey will be more hopeful.

Respondents to the 1991 survey from over half of the states, in both rural areas and inner cities, reported librarian shortages ranging from moderate to extremely severe. Reasons cited for this shortage included retirements, limited access to library education, stricter certification rules, workloads, and the increased emphasis on standards and test scores. Several states have raised the certification requirements bar for prospective librarians (Everhart, 2000). With many library school closings, the access to library education has decreased, which also impacts the number of certified librarians available. In addition, most school library media specialists must have dual certification (library media and another teaching area).

School districts are using a number of methods to cope with the librarian shortage. One common method is to assign a teacher who agrees to work toward library media certification, usually at the pace of six credits per year. This is known as emergency or provisional certification. Other states have allowed public librarians and other college graduates to work in school libraries but may not require that they seek certification. One of the worst situations allows individuals without any college degree to lead library programs.

In some cases, the school librarian in a metropolitan area may be responsible for several schools within a district. This puts a strain on the school librarian. They cannot be at each school every day and ensure that all of the library programs are taking place. They may spend one or two days a week per school, and the rest of the time the library is under the direction of a paraprofessional who may not even have an undergraduate degree.

The shortage of school librarians nationwide is reaching a crisis stage. Many states are enhancing the appeal of this type of librarianship by offering financial assistance for students enrolling in library science programs. Even so, the school librarian role is difficult to fill. Often during budget crunches, this is one of the positions that is first eliminated. This greatly impacts the work of the human resources personnel in charge of finding librarians to fill current and future school library vacancies.

One program that has been instituted in Indiana, with the support of the Indianapolis Foundation, provides financial support for existing teachers to complete the library media specialist program. This program is a collaboration between the Indiana University School of Library and Information Science based in Indianapolis and falls under the "grow your own" philosophy. School library human resources professionals can check with their closest library science program to see if this is an option that they could use to attract potential school librarians. Potential sources of funding might be found in the community.

HOW DO SPECIAL LIBRARIES DIFFER FROM OTHER LIBRARIES?

The face of the special libraries is greatly different from the traditional public library, school library, or academic library. Special libraries can encompass medical and dental libraries, law libraries, corporate libraries, and special collection type libraries, i.e., museums or national archives. The library may range from a one-person library to one that is fully staffed by a number of librarians. Most special librarians have additional education or certification in the specialty area. It is difficult to pinpoint the exact number of special librarians because of their vast differences; however, at the 2006 Special Libraries Association Annual Conference, there were 5,844 participants, surpassing the 5,283 in attendance at the 2005 Toronto conference (DiMattia, 2000). The American Library Association stated that as of December 2003, there were 8,300-plus special libraries in the United States, but these numbers do not include government and armed forces libraries, or those special libraries in public and academic libraries (Moorman, 2006).

Special libraries have staffing concerns of their own. Libraries close or expand, staff members shift to different positions in the larger organization, and special librarians move around in their local special library community. Knowing what skills are becoming more valued and required in the field and following trends in the education of new librarians helps to identify areas for staff development.

The individual responsible for hiring the special librarian will have to be cognizant of the special skills required to fulfill this type of position. Each special library will have its own unique skill set requirements depending upon the type of library and the clientele that it serves. The HR professional should survey the library users to see what type of information is needed and record past experiences with the library services. It is very important for the person responsible for recruitment to verify applicants' experience and skill sets as well as their references.

With the variety of libraries that fall under the term "special libraries," it is difficult to project the future and future trends for these libraries. Many special libraries require a second degree beyond the MLS, such as a law degree for law librarians or a science degree for those in a clinical or laboratory library. It is easy to see that filling these special needs may prove to be as difficult as filling positions in the school, public, or academic arena.

WHAT IS THE FACE OF ACADEMIC LIBRARIES TODAY?

The face of academic libraries in this century is much different than in the past. Many libraries have been forced to cancel journal subscriptions, which impacts the collection available for users. Services for the academic libraries have changed as well. Undergraduate students are more likely to visit the library through virtual means rather than actually visiting the library in person. With Google and Wikipedia access, the students feel that they can find all of the information they need without the help of the library. Libraries will have to move to the model of being the link between the user and the resources they need. There will still be some linkage to print collections, especially those that are specialized or unique, but the majority of needs will be satisfied by the digital formats.

The librarian of the future will assume roles totally different from the traditional subject librarian or bibliographer often found in academic libraries. Librarians and other library staff members will become navigational guides and help users make discerning choices among available resources in the public domain on the Internet as well as the resources subscribed to by the library. Librarians may be called upon to do more in-depth consultations to assist users through the mire of information they have gathered electronically. Librarians must be knowledgeable of the variety of databases and resources available and keep current in all aspects of technology to guide their users. Librarians and staff will share some of the responsibility that used to be solely under the domain of faculty—fostering skills of inquiry in students and providing the tools necessary to evaluate and assess the quality of information found—and must also partner more with faculty ("Changing Roles of Academic and Research Libraries," 2006).

It is clear that the library staff must acquire a mix of skills. Librarians and staff must develop strong technical skills. In addition, librarians must attain the necessary skills of pedagogy in the use of instructional technology. The library human resources professional will need to make sure that training and development practices are in place to ensure that these librarians can meet the challenge of their new roles. We will discuss training issues in a later chapter.

Academic libraries are no different from public, school, and special libraries when it comes to the graying of the profession. Many academic librarians will retire within the next five to ten years and the new crop of librarians replacing them will need to be ready to take the helm. Many of these new librarians will already have more technical skills than their predecessors, but will not have the historical knowledge that the aging librarians possess. It will be the responsibility of the human resources professional to match skills and knowledge to support these new roles in a digital information age. Human resources professionals will also have to convince administrators that salaries for library staff members need to be raised to meet the competition. Traditionally, library salaries have been much lower than their faculty counterparts. With the increasing demand for technical skills, instructional skills, and assessment skills, the librarians of the future will need to be compensated for their abilities. The investment academic libraries make in a position search is substantial.

A survey done over a decade ago found that a typical entry-level position search in an academic library takes an average of five months, with an additional month to hire and place the chosen candidate (Raschke, 2003). Costs of conducting a search can range anywhere from $1,200 to $13,300, depending on the situation and the intensity of the hiring process. It takes an enormous amount of time to recruit, interview, and hire academic librarians. When positions remain open for long periods, existing staff have to cover for the vacant position. Library human resources professionals need to review and determine how this process can be made more effective and efficient to save time and money for the organization.

Most paraprofessionals in an academic library are required to have an undergraduate degree. They will be involved in activities such as copy cataloging, reference desk activities, interlibrary service activities, acquisitions, and digital or technological activities. Their responsibilities may cross over into activities that have traditionally belonged solely to the librarian. In larger academic libraries, technology specialists will be responsible for hardware and software applications and will require advanced degrees.

In addition, numerous student assistants help in the daily functions of shelving, attending at the circulation desk, pulling materials for interlibrary services, checking bibliographic citations for acquisitions, and simple data entry for various areas in the library. While the human resources professional may not be responsible for hiring these student employees, they will be needed to resolve any personnel issues that may arise when dealing with students.

THE ROLE OF TODAY'S LIBRARY HUMAN RESOURCES PROFESSIONAL

For the past several decades, the focus of concern has been technology. One researcher claims that the focus now should be centered on managing people to provide the highest level of service (Ward, 2000).

The term "human resources" has been widely adopted by corporations and organizations in recognition of changing legal requirements, ethical issues, and changing expectations of the work environment, both societal and cultural (Jin, 2006). Previously, the function of the human resources professional was process implementation. Now, HR professionals focus on the staff as a main resource of the library organization. They are part of the strategic planning of the organization and demonstrate to administration how human "resources" will affect future services and goal attainment.

The library human resources professional has the responsibility to hire qualified librarians and staff, provide training and continuing education for these individuals, offer them support, promotions and recognition when they make progress, monitor discipline procedures, and evaluate them on a regular basis.

Good library management results in work efficiency including both quantity and quality. Some library services are quantitative such as library visits, circulations, interlibrary loans, reference questions, classes taught, workshops offered, materials purchased and cataloged, print journals received, electronic databases and times they have been accessed, and electronic materials acquired and processed. Other library attributes are not quantitative such as staff knowledge, skills, work attitude, and eagerness to serve. Most libraries keep very accurate counts of their quantitative measures. A library is usually not aware of the qualitative measures until there is a problem. When these problems appear, the human resources professional is usually called in to address them and make sure that procedures are followed. This could lead to progressive discipline procedures or simply retraining depending on the extent of the problem and what is necessary to resolve the issue.

Library staff members have professional development needs and their own individual career goals. The human resources professional can assist them in determining what type of workshops or courses they need to achieve these goals. Management needs to be understanding and supportive by providing time and financial support when appropriate. Library human resources professionals can also make sure that individuals are recognized for their contributions and achievements. Often, administration is not as sensitive to individual needs and it will be the human resources professional's obligation to make sure that the recognition occurs.

Many of you who are reading this book may find yourself in the position of serving the human resources function with little or no training in this capacity. I was lucky in that my employer offered a "Human Resources Certificate" program in their adult continuing education classes. In addition to this program, I took numerous workshops related to human resources topics. Many of these were offered locally by a national program. Searching on Google will aid you in finding what workshops are currently available. Another suggestion is to confer with your state library association. The state library associations may have middle management sections that would include individuals who handle the human resources functions within their library.

The other difficult task will be balancing your work if you are to continue with other librarian responsibilities as well. Good time management skills will help you with this. It is important to keep these duties separate, and it is advisable to have two different physical spaces for these activities, if at all possible. The most difficult aspect of managing time may be the role of ombudsman, in which you must listen to individuals who have human resources–related issues. It is not easy to identify when a crisis will occur or someone needs to talk. This can easily engulf you. You may want to set specific office hours indicating that individuals will need to schedule a time to meet with you for this type of session. Having to make an appointment will make individuals consider whether it is really that important.

In the chapters that follow, you will learn some of the human resources professional roles, issues, concerns, legal ramifications and laws surrounding the human element, and how to deal with many of these concerns and issues as a library human resources professional.

REFERENCES

American Library Association (ALA). April 2007. *The State of America's Libraries: A Report from the American Library Association*. Chicago: ALA. Available: www.ala.org (accessed April 23, 2007).

Bliss, Elizabeth. 2006. "Staffing in the Small Public Library: An Overview." *Rural Libraries* 26, no. 1: 7–28.

"Changing Roles of Academic and Research Libraries." 2006. An essay derived from a roundtable on technology and change in academic libraries convened by the Association of College and Research Libraries (ACRL) on November 2–3, 2006. Chicago: ALA. Available: www.ala.org/ACRL (accessed March 21, 2007).

Chute, A., E. Kroe, P. Garner, M. Polcari, and C. J. Ramsey. 2002. *Public Libraries in the United States: Fiscal Year 2000* (NCES 2002-344): US Department of Education, National Center for Education Statistics, Washington, DC. Available: http://nces.ed.gov/pubs2002/2002344 (accessed March 14, 2007).

DiMattia, Susan. 2000. "Special Librarians Embrace Transformation in Baltimore." *American Libraries* 37, no. 7: 24–25.

Everhart, Nancy. 2000. "Looking For a Few Good Librarians." *School Library Journal* 46, no. 9: 58–61.

Farley, Y. S. 2002. "Strategies for Improving Library Salaries." *American Libraries* 33, no. 1: 56–59.

Fisher, Heather. 2000. "Children's Librarians: What Are They?" *Orana* 36, no. 1: 9–13.

George, Jennifer M. and Gareth R. Jones. 2002. *Essentials of Managing Organizational Behavior*. Upper Saddle River, NJ: Prentice-Hall.

Jin, Xudong. 2006. "Human Touch of Library Management in the United States: Personal Experiences of Creating and Developing a Harmonious Environment." *CLIEJ* no. 22.

King Research. 1983. *Library Human Resources: A Study of Supply and Demand*. Chicago, IL: American Library Association.

Losinski, P. 2005. "Trends and Tips for Paraprofessionals in Public Libraries." *Library Mosaics* 16, no. 3: 16–17.

Lynch, Mary Jo. 2003. "Public Library Staff: How Much Is Enough?" *American Libraries* 34, no. 5: 58–59.

Matarazzo, James M. 2000. "Library Human Resources: The Y2K Plus 10 Challenge." *The Journal of Academic Librarianship* 26, no. 4: 223–224.

Meisinger, Susan. 2006. "Good Things Come in Threes—for HR." *HRMagazine* 51, no. 7: 10.

Moorman, John A., ed. 2006. *Running a Small Library*. New York: Neal-Schuman Publishers.

Overman, Stephenie. 1992. "Reaching for the 21st Century." *HRMagazine* 37, no. 4: 61–63.

Poole, Michael and Malcolm Warner, eds. 1998. *The IEBM Handbook of Human Resource Management*. Boston: International Thomson Business Press.

Raschke, Gregory K. 2003. "Hiring and Recruitment Practices in Academic Libraries: Problems and Solutions." *Libraries and the Academy* 3, no. 1: 53–67.

Schachter, Debbie. 2006. "An Essential Function for Special Librarians." *Information Outlook* 10, no. 10: 8–9.

Stueart, Robert D. and John Taylor Eastlick. 1981. *Library Management*, 2nd ed. Littleton, CO: Libraries Unlimited.

Tabs, E. D. 2004. *The Status of Public and Private School Library Media Centers in the United States: 1999–2000*. (NCES 2004-313): US Department of Education, National Center for Education Statistics, Washington, DC. Available: http://nces.ed.gov/pubs2005/2004313 (accessed April 24, 2007).

US Bureau of the Census. 1983. *1980 Census of Population*. Washington, DC: The Bureau of the Census.

US Bureau of the Census.1984. "Earnings by Occupation and Education," in *1980 Census Population*, vol. 2. (54). Washington, DC: The Bureau of the Census.

US Bureau of Labor Statistics. 1975. *Library Manpower: A Study of Demand and Supply*. Washington DC: The Bureau of Labor Statistics.

Ward, Patricia Layzell. 2000. "Trends in Library Management." *Library Review* 49, no. 9: 436–441.

White, Herbert S. 1989. "The 'Quiet Revolution': A Profession at the Crossroads." *Special Libraries* 80, no. 1: 24–31.

2 LAWS AFFECTING THE MANAGEMENT OF LIBRARY PERSONNEL

One of the major functions of any human resources department or human resources manager is ensuring compliance with all of the relevant personnel-related laws and regulations. Federal and state law, regulations, and court decisions affect the way you carry out your responsibilities. Noncompliance can be costly to organizations and can have an adverse impact on the organization's image (Kohl, et al., 2004). In this chapter, we will identify the various laws and regulations affecting the management of library personnel and how organizations can ensure that they are in compliance. Instead of dreading what might happen if you violate one of these laws, with knowledge you can be better prepared so that the violation does not occur.

The sheer number of these regulations can be a daunting task. Both federal laws and state laws place requirements on employers which provide protection for the employees. Although we will mainly be covering the major federal laws, be sure to check on the specific laws that apply in your state.*

DISCRIMINATION

In 2002, there were more than 84,000 charges of discrimination filed with the Equal Employment Opportunity Commission (EEOC) (Smith and Mazen, 2004). These charges resulted in approximately $258 million dollars in settlement costs to organizations. This may sound like a great number of claims and dollars lost to discrimination charges and might cause you to wonder how you can ever be prepared to make sure this does not happen at your organization. The best way to prevent discrimination lawsuits is to understand the basics of the laws regarding discrimination and always seek counsel when you have questions. Establish a work environment where discrimination, harassment, and retaliation of any kind are

---

* Disclaimer: The information regarding the various federal and state employment laws in this chapter should not be considered legal advice. Readers should consult with a legal professional for guidelines that apply to their organizations.

not tolerated. Training all of your administrators, department heads, and supervisors regarding employment laws and compliance procedures is equally important. Finally, make sure that you have policies and procedures in place regarding these laws and post notices advising employees of their rights under the laws enforced by the EEOC.

MANAGEMENT IN ACTION

A new Senior Circulation Manager by the name of Nancy was hired at an academic library in the Northeast. All new support staff hires serve a six-month probationary period in this library. This position was supervisor over three other circulation assistants and two part-time shelvers. The incident described here occurred in the second month of the individual's probationary period.

Nancy was heard yelling and cursing at one of the part-time shelvers by another of the circulation assistants, Gloria. The part-time shelver, Janet, had dissolved into tears and was going to give her notice. Gloria brought Janet to the human resources professional, Elaine. Elaine listened to what had happened and documented it. Janet was offered a position in the Acquisitions Department far removed from Nancy. She accepted the new position and was transferred that day.

Elaine then met with the Head of Circulation, Dorothy, and the two decided to ask Nancy for her version of what had taken place with Janet. Nancy was asked to join the two in the Head of Circulation's office. Dorothy calmly told Nancy that they were aware that an incident had occurred and asked if she would relay what had happened. Shortly into the explanation, Nancy began yelling and raising her voice. Neither Dorothy nor Elaine had said anything yet. Nancy was clearly upset but evidently had yelled at Janet. When Dorothy tried to calm Nancy down, she became even more irrational and began yelling and verbally abusing her supervisor. The meeting was documented and after much discussion with the Campus Human Resources Administration, it was determined that this was not an appropriate match for the library and that the Nancy would be dismissed since she was still in the probationary period. In the discussion with Campus Human Resources, it was discovered that this individual had had several disciplinary actions filed against her from other departments on the campus where she had previously worked. These had not been sent to the hiring department prior to her hire.

As a result of the dismissal, the individual filed a complaint with the Affirmative Action Office and the Equal Employment Opportunity Commission (EEOC). She was a minority and claimed that she was terminated due to racial discrimination. Following procedure, both agencies met with

Elaine, Dorothy, Gloria, and Janet. All documentation was shared with both of the agencies as well. A hearing with the EEOC was scheduled and the library HR professional was asked to attend. The end result of the investigation was in favor of the library and the complaint was dismissed. The individual would not be able to apply for any other position on the campus as a result of this disciplinary action.

WHAT ARE THE PRIMARY FEDERAL ANTIDISCRIMINATION LAWS?

Many antidiscrimination laws are related to the hiring procedures of an organization:

- Title VII of the Civil Rights Act of 1964, prohibiting employment discrimination based on race, color, religion, gender, or national origin
- Age Discrimination in Employment Act of 1967, outlawing discrimination against workers age 40 and older
- Americans with Disabilities Act of 1990, protecting qualified individuals with disabilities
- Equal Pay Act of 1963, mandating that men and women who perform substantially equal work for the same employer under similar working conditions receive substantially equal pay

TITLE VII OF THE CIVIL RIGHTS ACT OF 1964

This law applies to all private employers, state and local government, and educational institutions that employ at least 15 workers. The laws prohibit employment discrimination on the basis of color, race, gender, religion, or national origin. Organizations will be held responsible for actions that have a disproportionate impact on one or more of the protected categories unless they can demonstrate that the basis for the action is job related and serves a legitimate business purpose (Smith and Mazen, 2004). This law affects all federally assisted programs, which could include libraries.

WHAT DO THEY MEAN BY DISCRIMINATION?

Title VII makes it illegal in hiring practices to discriminate against candidates of a particular race or color. You cannot refuse to hire someone because he or she is Asian or deny someone career development opportunities because he or she is Caucasian. The law also prohibits discrimination based on characteristics such as skin color, hair texture, or certain facial features.

You cannot consider an individual's religion or religious practices in hiring decisions. In addition, you must accommodate employee's religious practices when requested unless doing this would cause an undue hardship for the organization. The tricky part of this is that there is no set definition of what "undue hardship" means. The standards for demonstrating "undue hardship" vary from state to state.

National origin discrimination is discriminating against an individual because of the place where they are from. It would also be discriminatory to favor an individual more because of their country of origin. Accents, language requirements, and citizenship requirements also fall under this area. You cannot discriminate just because an individual speaks with an accent. In order for an accent to be a factor in a human resources decision, the accent must interfere with communication skills and effective communication skills must be a requirement for the job. Similarly, you can only require employees to be fluent in English if fluency is a real and reasonable requirement for the position for which they are applying. Title VII does not specifically outlaw discrimination based on citizenship, but it does prohibit using citizenship as a pretext for discrimination based on national origin. If you choose to adopt a rule of excluding noncitizens, it must be consistent for all individuals within the organization.

Gender discrimination is making hiring decisions based on a person's sex, sexual harassment, and pregnancy discrimination. We will discuss sexual harassment laws in more detail later in the chapter.

WHAT ARE THE REPORTING REQUIREMENTS FOR TITLE VII?

"If you are a private employer with 100 or more employees, or a federal contractor with at least fifty workers, you are required to file an EEO-1 employer information report with the EEOC by September 30 of each year" (Smith and Mazen, 2004, 152). Reporting procedures are found in The Code of Federal Regulations, Title 29, Volume 4, Part 1602, Section 1602.7 – Requirement for filing of report. See the actual code requirements in Figure 2.1.

This report provides a breakdown of the organization's workforce by gender, racial/ethnic classification, and job categories. This information is usually based on employment figures from any pay period from July through September and includes both full and part-time employees.

---

§ 1602.7 Requirement for filing of report.

On or before September 30 of each year, every employer that is subject to Title VII of the Civil Rights Act of 1964, as amended, and that has 100 or more employees shall file with the Commission or its delegate executed copies of Standard Form 100, as revised (otherwise known as "Employer Information Report EEO–1") in conformity with the directions set forth in the form and accompanying instructions. Notwithstanding the provisions of § 1602.14, every such employer shall retain at all times at each reporting unit, or at company or divisional headquarters, a copy of the most recent report filed for each such unit and shall make the same available if requested by an officer, agent, or employee of the Commission under the authority of section 710 of Title VII. Appropriate copies of Standard Form 100 in blank will be supplied to every employer known to the Commission to be subject to the reporting requirements, but it is the responsibility of all such employers to obtain necessary supplies of the form from the Commission or its delegate prior to the filing date.
[37 FR 9219, May 6, 1972, as amended at 56 FR35755, July 26, 1991]

Figure 2.1. Subpart B: Employer Information Report

If you have collected any data from hired employees that identify the individual's race or ethnicity, you must use this data for your report. If you do not have any such data, you will have to review your employees and make a best guess as to the employee's race and ethnicity. It is not recommended that you approach your employees directly and ask these questions.

AGE DISCRIMINATION EMPLOYMENT ACT OF 1967 (ADEA)

The ADEA applies to all employers with 20 or more employees, including state and local governments. This law protects individuals age 40 and older from discrimination in employment on the basis of age. It also prohibits employers from arbitrarily discriminating against these individuals with regard to discharge, pay, promotions, fringe benefits, and other employment decisions. The law is designed to promote fair treatment of older persons and is enforced by the EEOC. With individuals living longer, productive lives, the laws surrounding age will become of greater importance.

In 2003, the EEOC received 19,124 charges of age discrimination. EEOC resolved 17,352 age discrimination charges and recovered $48.9 million in monetary benefits for those who had made charges ("Age Discrimination in Employment Act," 2005).

The Older Workers Benefit Protection Act of 1990 (OWBPA) amended the ADEA to specifically prohibit employers from denying benefits to older employees. While it is well known that providing certain benefits to older workers is greater than the costs of providing those same benefits to younger workers, it is still discrimination to deny these benefits to older employees.

An employer may ask an employee to waive his/her rights or claims under the ADEA either in the settlement of an ADEA claim or in connection with an exit incentive program or other employment termination program. However, the OWBPA amendment sets out specific minimum standards that must be met in order for a waiver to be considered valid. The ADEA waiver must be in writing and be understandable, specifically refer to ADEA rights or claims, not waive rights or claims that may arise in the future; be in exchange for valuable compensation or other benefits; advise the individual in writing to consult with an attorney before signing the waiver; and provide the individual at least 21 days to consider the agreement and at least seven days to revoke the agreement after signing it (Smith and Mazen, 2004).

If an employer requests an ADEA waiver in connection with an exit incentive program or other employment termination program, the minimum requirements for a valid waiver are more extensive. If you consider requesting an employee to agree to an ADEA waiver, you should consult with an attorney to ensure that the waiver is appropriate in the situation and complies with the law.

CAN OUR ORGANIZATION ADOPT A MANDATORY RETIREMENT POLICY?

The answer is no. It is illegal to require an employee to voluntarily retire at a particular age unless age is a bona fide occupational qualification for performing the job.

The ADEA applies even when all the employees are over 40. For example, replacing a 55-year-old employee with a 45-year-old employee can still be found to be discriminatory even though both employees technically fall under the protection of the ADEA (Ossi, 2005). The best rule is to simply treat older workers the same as younger workers. Avoid making hiring decisions or judging employees' abilities based solely on age.

THE AMERICANS WITH DISABILITIES ACT OF 1990 (ADA)

The ADA covers employers with 15 or more employees. The law prohibits employers from making employment decisions that discriminate against qualified individuals with disabilities. It also prohibits discrimination against people with disabilities in public services, transportation, public accommodations, and telecommunications, and requires that reasonable accommodations be offered. This law is enforced by the EEOC and the Department of Justice. Also, employers cannot refuse to hire a person with a disabled spouse because of concern related to medical costs or fear of the loss of time by the employee to care for the disabled individual.

HOW IS A PERSON WITH A DISABILITY DEFINED?

A person with a disability is an individual who has a physical or mental impairment that substantially limits one or more major life activities; or has a record of such impairment; or is regarded as having such impairment. Some examples of disabling conditions include physical impairments (hearing, visual, motor, speech), mental or psychological impairments (retardation, learning disabilities, mental illness) and other hidden disabilities (diabetes, cancer, epilepsy). An individual with a disability may be protected under the ADA because they have an actual disability covered under the Act or because they experience discrimination based on the employer's perception that they are disabled, whether, in fact, they are disabled or not.

The ADA does **not** cover temporary impairments such as broken limbs, sprains, appendicitis, influenza, etc. The Act also does not cover current illegal users of drugs or alcohol, kleptomania, pyromania, sexual orientation, personality traits, or conditions that are correctable (e.g., with eye glasses or medications).

The ADA does not require that you hire a qualified applicant over other applicants or promote a qualified worker over other workers just because the individual has a disability. The law only prohibits discrimination on the basis of the disability.

WHO IS A QUALIFIED INDIVIDUAL WITH A DISABILITY?

An individual with a disability is qualified under the ADA if they meet the level of skill, education, experience, and other standards for a position as required for all and can perform all the "essential functions" of the position with or without a "reasonable" accommodation.

The "essential job functions" are those functions or tasks that are fundamental to performance of the job and are determined prior to any employment action such as recruiting, advertising, hiring, promoting, or firing. An individual must be able to perform all of the essential job functions of the position regardless of disability. However, if an individual is unable to perform a function and has a qualified disability, he or she may be able to perform the function with a "reasonable accommodation."

A "reasonable accommodation" is any change or adjustment that permits a qualified person with a disability to participate in the employment process, perform the essential job functions, gain access to goods or services, or enjoy other privileges of employment in a manner substantially equal to others. Examples of reasonable accommodations include: making existing facilities accessible; installing assistive equipment or devices; job restructuring; modifying work schedules and policies; reassignment to a vacant, equivalent position; modifying exams, training materials, or providing materials in alternate formats; providing qualified readers and/or interpreters; and leave (Abernathy, 2005).

Worth Repeating: A Very Reasonable Accommodation

"A small employer had an employee with a learning disability that caused him to make errors transcribing numbers. The company contacted its state department of labor for assistance and was referred to a low-cost, state-funded training program to help the employee work with his disability" (Smith and Mazen, 2004, 157).

THE EQUAL PAY ACT OF 1963 (EPA)

The EPA applies to virtually all employers. Under this law, employers must pay equal wages to men and women who perform jobs requiring substantially equal skill, effort, and responsibility under the same working conditions in the same organization.

WHAT DOES THIS MEAN?

When comparing the skill sets of two employees, it is important to look at the skills that are necessary for the job, not the total skills possessed by each of the individuals. For example, if a man and a woman are both general reference librarians with an accredited Master's degree in Library Science and ten years of library experience, you cannot use the fact that the man has a Ph.D. in History to justify his higher pay rate, because this graduate degree is not related to the job requirements.

The term "effort" pertains to the amount of physical or mental exertion that it requires to do the job. If you have two clerical employees, but one is required to lift heavy boxes of books and the other's main responsibility is to cover the circulation desk with minimal lifting, you are permitted to pay the first clerical more than the second.

"Responsibility" refers to the amount of accountability essential for the position. If only one of two desk clericals is permitted to handle cash, the increased responsibility justifies a higher wage payment. If the difference in responsibility is minor, say, for example, that one is designated to answer the telephone, higher pay is not justifiable.

"Working conditions" consists of both physical surroundings and hazards. An example of this would be a hospital where one nurse works in a children's ward and another nurse works with the violent patients. The increased risk incurred by the nurse working with the violent patients could merit a pay differential.

The term "establishment" refers to the "distinct physical place of business." You can generally pay diverse wages to employees doing the same job in different states. Employees in different states do not occur often in the library world.

You may pay employees varying wages if wages are based on factors other than sex, such as seniority or merit, but it is the organization's responsibility to prove that they are using valid rather than discriminatory criteria. Review your salary structure periodically to make sure that you are not unintentionally violating the EPA (Smith and Mazen, 2004). If you find that you need to make adjustments for salary equity, the appropriate action would be to raise the wages of the lower paid employee and not lower the wages of the higher paid employee.

MANAGEMENT IN ACTION

Not long ago, one of our support staff members in a specialized department was offered a position at another organization. This individual was highly specialized and had skills that would be very difficult to find easily in another person. The library countered the offer and the individual accepted our counter offer. As a result, the new salary was much higher than the other individual in the department with similar skills. In an effort to maintain salary equity between the two positions, Campus Human Resources Administration asked us to raise the other salary to match. The Library did so and salary equity was maintained between these two highly specialized individuals.

This covers most of the laws related to recruitment and selection practices but there are several other laws that must be considered as part of the laws that affect personnel management. These include sexual harassment, the Family and Medical Leave Act, the Occupational Safety and Health Act of 1979, the Immigration Reform and Control Act of 1986, the Fair Labor Standards Act of 1938, and worker's compensation. We will now review these laws and the regulations surrounding each of these.

SEXUAL HARASSMENT

Sexual harassment is defined as unwelcome sexual advances or requests for sexual favors or other verbal or physical conduct of a sexual nature. There are two forms of sexual harassment: quid pro quo and hostile environment. Sexual harassment protection applies to all individuals regardless of their gender or sexual orientation.

Quid Pro Quo involves a supervisory or authority relationship. One example could include a supervisor who demands sex in exchange for a promotion or a raise in pay. A second example would be an employee who receives a poor evaluation after refusing their supervisor's sexual advances.

"Hostile environment" situations are those where sexual conduct is not a perquisite for an employment decision, but the working environment is so pervaded by discrimination, insult, or abuse that it becomes unpleasant or threatening for employees to do their job. Often a hostile environment claim is ambiguous and complex. Hostile environment claims make up the majority of sexual harassment complaints (Smith and Mazen, 2004).

For conduct to be considered illegal sexual harassment, it must be unwelcome, severe, and pervasive. Unwelcome behavior is that which the complaining individual did not solicit and found offensive or undesirable. One problematic situation occurs when a sexual relationship is initially consensual, but later one of the employees wants to end the relationship, and the other persists in sexual conduct. Behavior that continues past the point where it is consensual for both is considered sexual harassment.

WHAT STEPS CAN OUR ORGANIZATION TAKE TO PREVENT AND CORRECT HARASSMENT?

The most important thing to do is to have a written policy prohibiting workplace harassment. This should include a statement that the organization will not tolerate harassment, whether sexual or based on religion, race, national origin, age, or disability. You should have a clear procedure for reporting complaints and conducting investigations. The policy should also include a statement that although the organization will protect the confidentiality of all parties to a complaint to the extent possible, it may have to share certain information with those with a need to know.

Your complaint procedure should designate more than one individual to whom the employee can report harassment, preferably one male and one female, so that complaining employees can select individuals with whom they feel comfortable. Some states require employers to conduct mandatory sexual harassment training for managers and supervisors. Check your state regulations to see what applies to your organization.

It is extremely important to conduct a comprehensive investigation of all employee complaints. During the investigation, take steps to keep the complaining and the accused individuals apart. Reasonable steps may include assigning one or both employees to different work areas to minimize the opportunity for contact or placing the accused on paid leave pending the results of the investigation.

If, as a result of the investigation, you find that harassment has occurred, you must take appropriate action to end the harassment and keep it from happening again. The discipline given to the accused should correspond with the seriousness of the offense. The US Supreme Court mandates that a supervisor with knowledge of sexual harassment must act promptly to eliminate it. The supervisor and/or organization must ensure that staff are fully aware of sexual harassment policies and procedures and that individuals have full opportunity to seek redress for sexual harassment (Abernathy, 2005).

Begin work toward eliminating harassment or inappropriate behavior in an organization before it starts by training employees to recognize and report harassment and to handle complaints if they do occur. If you are aware that employees are using the organization's e-mail system to distribute questionable jokes, remind the staff that this is inappropriate.

IF AN EMPLOYEE DOES NOT COMPLAIN, CAN THE ORGANIZATION STILL BE HELD LIABLE FOR HARASSMENT?

Yes, if the failure to complain was reasonable under the circumstances. Legitimate reasons can include fear of retaliation or the knowledge that the organization has not acted to investigate and deal with harassment complaints in the past.

It is the employer's responsibility to prove that the failure to complain of harassment was unreasonable. If you create a workplace environment where an employee feels comfortable filing a complaint and knows that the organization will handle the complaint seriously without retaliation, it will be harder for an individual to justify failure to report a problem.

FAMILY AND MEDICAL LEAVE ACT OF 1993

The Family and Medical Leave Act (FMLA) guarantees employees 12 weeks of unpaid leave of absence per year and requires employers to protect the employee's job and continue health benefits coverage during the periods of leave. Eligible employees are those with tenure of at least a year and 1,250 hours of work. Organizations with at least 50 employees are subject to the FMLA law. The law recognizes that workers may experience health and/or family situations that necessitate a leave of absence. It was designed to help employees achieve a balance between their work lives, their health, and personal considerations (Baum, 2006).

Some states have laws similar to the FMLA and some provide more generous benefits than the federal law, which is administrated by the US Department of Labor. If you are in a state with leave regulations that differ from those of the federal FMLA, you are required to give your employees the benefit of whichever law offers the most generous protection to your employees. This law has become increasingly important in the workplace environment. There is a great deal of literature related to different aspects of FMLA and this attention will increase as new situations arise.

Employers must post notices informing workers of their FMLA rights in prominent places in the work environment. If you have an employee handbook or collective bargaining agreements, these should have sections describing employee rights and employer policies under the law. When employees return from FMLA leave, they are entitled to reinstatement to the same position or one of equivalent stature with no loss of benefits (Hesse and Ehrens, 2006).

A "health care provider" is any person authorized to provide health care services, including medical doctors, podiatrists, dentists, psychologists, optometrists, chiropractors, nurse practitioners and midwives, clinical social workers, Christian Science practitioners, and any HCP recognized by the organization's health plan.

WHEN CAN AN ELIGIBLE EMPLOYEE TAKE FMLA LEAVE?

The FMLA leave is restricted to certain defined conditions, including birth, adoption, or foster care of a child; a serious health condition of an employee; or a serious health care condition of a family member.

Birth, Adoption, or Foster Care of a Child

Employees who become parents through birth, adoption, or foster care placement may take a leave of absence within one year after the arrival of their child. In certain situations, the expectant parents can begin the leave before the child arrives. The leave is available to both men and women, but if the husband and wife work for the same employer, their leave may be limited to a combined 12 weeks.

Serious Health Condition of the Employee

The health condition must render the employee unable to do his/her job. The law is quite specific and complicated regarding the types of health conditions that qualify for the FMLA leave, but generally these conditions include inpatient care; a period of more than three days where the employee is unable to function normally and is under the care of a doctor; pregnancy or prenatal problems; or other material health issues. Chronic conditions such as diabetes, epilepsy, and asthma and permanent or long-term conditions such as Alzheimer's or a terminal disease may also be considered valid conditions for FMLA. Conditions which require multiple treatments such as chemotherapy, dialysis, or mental heath consultations may also be considered FMLA eligible.

Serious Health Condition of a Family Member

If a family member has a serious health condition, the employee may take leave to care for this individual. "Family member" under the law is limited to parents, children, or spouses. Other family members and domestic partners are not included (Martin, 2006).

HOW SHOULD EMPLOYEES REQUEST FMLA LEAVE?

Employees should give at least 30 days' notice in advance for leave that is foreseeable such as the birth or adoption of a child. For a condition that is unforeseeable such as an emergency personal or family health issue, notice should be given as soon as possible. The notice should specify the reasons for the leave and the anticipated duration of the leave.

CAN AN ORGANIZATION REQUEST CONFIRMATION OF A SERIOUS HEALTH CONDITION?

When the leave is for a personal or family member health condition, an organization may request that the employee provide medical certification to confirm the condition. The employee is allowed up to 15 days to comply with this request. If the employee fails to provide the medical certification within the timeframe, you may delay the process until you receive the information. You have the right to require that the employee obtain a second opinion from an independent physician at the organization's expense. The employee may only take the amount of time off that is necessary under the circumstances for which the leave is requested. An organization may not request details of the health condition, but if the employee grants permission, you may have your health insurance carrier contact the medical provider to obtain confirmation that the claimed condition exists.

DOES THE ORGANIZATION HAVE TO PROVIDE EMPLOYEES ANYTHING IN WRITING WHEN THEY REQUEST AN FMLA LEAVE?

The organization must provide the employee with a timely written notice specifying employee rights and obligations under the law, preferably within two business days (Smith and Mazen, 2004). If you do not provide this notice in a timely manner, you may not be able to deny the leave, even if the employee was not eligible.

The notice must specify the following:

- Whether, and how much of, the time off will count toward the FMLA entitlement
- Requirements for submitting medical certification and the consequence of failure to do so
- The employee's right to substitute paid leave, such as vacation time and sick days. As an employer, you may require that available paid leave be used first, provided you notify the individual of this requirement
- Whether you require a medical certification of fitness to return to duty upon the employee's return from a personal medical leave
- The employee's right to return to his/her previous position or an equivalent position upon return from leave
- Whether the employee is a "key employee" under the FMLA. Key employees are those salaried employees in the top 10 percent of the organization's pay range. The law takes into account that these individuals may be so important to the organization that their extended absences would cause the organization substantial harm. You do not have to guarantee restoration of position to these employees as long as you notify them of their key employee status when they request the leave. You must still give the key employee a reasonable opportunity to return to work from the FMLA leave
- Requirements for making any contribution for health care premiums and consequences for failure to pay on time. You may only require co-payments at the same level the employee was required to make prior to the leave
- Whether employees have the obligation to repay the employer if they do not return to work. This notification applies if your organization is paying any portion of employee health care premiums during the leave.

Group health benefit premiums can be recovered under limited circumstances according to FMLA regulations (Jackson et al., 2006). Generally, an employee must return to work for 30 calendar days to avoid having to reimburse the employer for its contributions during unpaid leave. An employer cannot recover premium costs when an employee is on paid leave, the employee does not return because of a recurrence of the health condition or an onset of another serious health condition, the individual begins retirement within 30 days of taking FMLA leave, or the employee cannot return because he/she is needed to take care of a family member with a serious health condition. The elimination of an employee's position during the FMLA leave is a circumstance beyond the employee's control and again would not require the employee to repay the premium costs (Jackson et al., 2006).

An employer may request certification that the employee's presence is needed for the purpose of taking care of the family member, and the employee would have up to 30 days from the date of the request to provide the employer with the certification. If the employee does not provide the certification, the employer can require the employee to pay 100 per cent of the health premium costs that were paid by the organization.

CAN AN EMPLOYER INQUIRE ABOUT EMPLOYEE STATUS DURING THE LEAVE?

It is acceptable to maintain contact with employees during their leaves, but you cannot contact medical providers or other third parties. You may, with advance notice, require employees to contact your periodically to report on their status, as long as you require all employees on FMLA to do so. Requesting that only certain workers report in may be considered discriminatory. You may also, with notice, require subsequent medical certifications, but not more frequently than every 30 days.

WHAT IS AN INTERMITTENT LEAVE? WHO IS ELIGIBLE FOR THAT AND HOW DOES IT DIFFER FROM THE NORMAL 12-WEEK LEAVE?

Chronic conditions seem to present the greatest number of requests for intermittent leave. A World at Work survey in 2004 found that 18 percent of FMLA leave granted in 2004 was for chronic conditions ("Intermittent Leave: The FMLA's Biggest Trouble Spot," 2005). Employees requesting intermittent leave are still eligible for 12 weeks of unpaid leave; however, the leave can be taken in the shortest increment that their payroll system uses to track other types of absences. For some organizations, this could be in increments as small as six minutes. There are some organizations seeking changes to FMLA that would set the minimums ranging from four hours to half a day ("Intermittent Leave," 2005).

There are safeguards that employers can take to curb suspected abuse of intermittent leave. Employers can ask for medical recertification. Review absence patterns and other conduct for possible fraud and abuse. Keep an ear to the grapevine in case the employee says things to coworkers that are inconsistent with the stated reasons for taking the FMLA leave.

MUST ORGANIZATIONS GIVE THE INDIVIDUALS THEIR JOBS BACK AFTER THEY RETURN FROM LEAVE?

By law, you are required to hold the individual's position open, or provide an equivalent position upon his/her return. An equivalent position is considered one that is virtually identical to the previous one in pay, benefits, working conditions, and status. When a position is highly specialized, it may be harder to prove that a new position is equivalent. Although it may be expensive and inconvenient to hold a job open, if you are not sure that you can provide an alternate position that is truly equivalent, you may have no other choice.

CAN YOU FIRE AN EMPLOYEE ON FMLA LEAVE?

You can terminate an employee on FMLA leave only under proper circumstances. If you conduct a layoff during the leave period and you have valid reasons for eliminating the position, you may do so and you will not be obligated to offer an equivalent job. Your obligations to the employee will end on the date of the layoff except that you will be required to offer the same termination benefits offered to other laid-off employees. In this situation, be sure to document the legitimate reasons for eliminating the position in the event of future legal challenges.

MANAGEMENT IN ACTION

A clerical employee in a public library filed for FMLA for minor back surgery. Shortly after she returned to her position, she began having carpal tunnel syndrome problems and then filed for an Intermittent FMLA for care and treatments for the carpal tunnel problem. She was granted this FMLA as she had not used up the total 12 weeks allowed for FMLA in one year. The problem persisted and the individual quickly ran out of FMLA and sick time to cover her treatments. She opted for voluntary resignation rather than disciplinary procedures that would have occurred had she not been able to perform her duties. The voluntary resignation would then allow her to reapply for a position on the campus once her health had improved. The individual regained her health but did not return to the library.

OCCUPATIONAL SAFETY AND HEALTH ACT OF 1979

The Occupational Safety and Health Act (OSHA) was established to ensure certain national standards and guidelines to promote safe and healthful workplaces. The Act is administered by the Occupational Safety and Health Administration, which sets workplace safety and health standards and conducts inspections to ensure that employers are complying with those standards.

Statistics indicate that since the formation of this agency, workplace fatalities have decreased by 50 percent and work-related illnesses and injuries are down 40 percent (Smith and Mazen, 2004). However, incidents and deaths are still occurring. The Bureau of Labor Statistics reports that in 2001, 5.7 million workers suffered job-related illnesses or injuries and almost 6,000 employees died on the job (www.bls.gov, 2004). OSHA standards are divided into four major categories: general industry, construction, maritime, and agriculture. Libraries fall into the general industry category.

WHAT RESPONSIBILITIES DOES MY ORGANIZATION HAVE IN RELATION TO THE OSHA REQUIREMENTS?

All employers are required to maintain a safe workplace, free of hazards that are likely to cause death or serious physical harm. Employers must post notices informing employees of their workplace safety rights in plain view. Libraries probably fall into the category of low-risk industry and may not have regularly scheduled inspections. However, any company may be subject to OSHA inspection if it has report of an accident involving a worker's death or the hospitalization of three or more employees. You might also be subject to an inspection if OSHA receives a complaint from an employee or other party. Under the law, OSHA is permitted to keep the identity of any complaining employee confidential and you are not permitted to retaliate against any employee for filing a compliant or participating in an OHSA investigation.

OSHA inspectors usually notify an organization prior to the inspection. Organizations do have the right to request that the investigators obtain an inspection warrant before allowing them to enter the premises. You may accompany the inspector on the facility tour, but the inspector is permitted to speak to individual employees only.

WHAT HAPPENS IF A VIOLATION IS FOUND DURING THE INSPECTION?

OSHA will issue a citation to your organization that details the violations, notifies you of the proposed penalties, and informs you of your rights to appeal the charges. You may then determine whether to pay the penalties, correct the violations, enter into settlement negotiations with OSHA to reduce the penalties, or file a "notice of contest" indicating your intent to contest the findings before the Occupational Safety and Health Review Commission. This is an independent agency unrelated to OSHA or the Department of Labor.

Penalties will vary depending on the seriousness of the violation and whether your organization has been in violation before or not. If your organization knew or should have known that it was committing a serious violation or if you were aware that there was a hazardous condition and no steps have been taken to remedy it, this is considered a "willful violation." This carries a minimum penalty of $5,000 to a maximum of $7,000. If this willful violation resulted in the death of an employee, a more substantial fine could be imposed and those responsible could face possible imprisonment.

There have been recent efforts by OSHA to establish an ergonomics standard that would greatly affect the library workplace. President Clinton signed off on it, but it was retracted by President Bush. This particular standard covered reports of musculoskeletal disorders, or MSDs, which include tendonitis, back injuries, carpal tunnel syndrome, and work-related illness from typing eight hours a day or running a checkout counter (Flynn, et al., 2001). This standard would have enormous impact and libraries should keep a watch on it should it finally pass.

IMMIGRATION REFORM AND CONTROL ACT OF 1986

While businesses are encouraged to have diversity in their workforce, they must ensure that those they hire have a right to legally work in the United States. The Immigration Reform and Control Act (IRCA) sets out rules that employers must follow to make sure that employees are eligible to work in the United States, whether they are US citizens or aliens authorized to work here. With the increased immigration of foreign individuals into the United States, it is imperative that organizations comply with the immigration regulations. This is especially difficult in academic settings with many international students seeking employment on the campus.

HOW DOES AN ORGANIZATION COMPLY WITH THE IRCA RULES?

Employers must complete and retain a Form I-9, Employment Eligibility Verification, for all employees hired after November 6, 1986. These forms can be obtained from the Bureau of Citizenship and Immigration Services.

A new hire cannot begin work until the I-9 form has been completed and verified. Employers are responsible for ensuring that the form is completed in full but they should be completed by only applicants that you actually hire. Since the form contains information about citizenship and national origin information, you could risk a discrimination lawsuit if you do not hire the applicant.

The employee must present original documents from a list of documents considered acceptable by the government, e.g., birth certificate or driver's license. The employee is required to present this documentation within three business days after beginning work. If they are unable to provide the documentation, they must present a receipt for application for the chosen documentation within the same three-day time frame and the actual documents within 90 days after beginning employment.

Retain the Form I-9 for three years after the date the employee begins work or for one year after the termination date, whichever occurs later. The Form I-9 must be made available for inspection by government immigration officials upon at least three days' prior notice. For privacy reasons, do not keep the form in the employee's human resources file.

WHAT HAPPENS IF AN EMPLOYEE'S WORK AUTHORIZATION EXPIRES?

The employer is responsible for tracking I-9s and updating them and/or recertifying an employee's eligibility for work. It is wise to remind employees to renew their work authorizations at least 90 days before the expiration date. If you rehire an individual within three years of the date of completion of the original I-9 form, you may update the I-9 instead of preparing a new one. If the employee's work authorization documented in the original form has expired, ask for proof of an extension and then record that information on the form. It is wise to stay on top of these employees and make sure that they stay in compliance with this law.

FAIR LABOR STANDARDS ACT OF 1938 (FLSA)

This Act has commonly been referred to as the "Wage and Hour Law." It was designed to protect employees and address economic conditions during the Great Depression. It is enforced by the Wage & Hour Division of the US Department of Labor.

The FLSA regulates child labor, minimum wage, employee exemption status, overtime pay, and record-keeping requirements. The Act restricts the hours and conditions of employment for minors. As a general rule, minors are not allowed to perform tasks that may be detrimental to their health, or physical or mental safety.

Under the age of 14, minors are prohibited from most non-farm work. Certain jobs are permitted such as employment by parents or as actors or newspaper carriers. Between the ages of 14 and 15, minors are not permitted to work during school hours and they can work no more than three hours a day or 18 hours a week. Between the ages of 16 and 17, they are prohibited from working hazardous jobs but there are no other restrictions. Many minor workers are in public libraries, which may hire teenagers to work as pages shelving materials and so on.

FSLA also defines employees by two categories for overtime pay, exempt or nonexempt. The functions of the position and the percentage of time spent performing those functions determine exemption status. The law recognizes five classifications of exempt employees (executives, outside salespeople, professionals, administrative, and computer related) and each class has a multi-part test that a position's functions must pass for the position to be considered exempt.

Exempt employees receive their full salaries for each workweek regardless of the number of hours worked. However, you cannot avoid your overtime obligations by merely classifying employees as exempt and paying them salaries. The FLSA sets out strict guidelines for determining whether a person qualifies for an exemption.

In August 2004, new regulations went into effect that define which employees are exempt from minimum wage and overtime requirements under the classifications of executive, administrative, professional, and computer related. The salary levels for exempt employees were raised considerably and other test measures changed for classification of exempt employees (Addington, 2004). Under these new regulations, some administrative exempt employees are not overtime eligible and must be paid for any hours worked over the 40-hours-a-week limit. The fact sheets on exempt classification can be found at: www.dol.gov/esa/regs/compliance/whd/fairpay/fact_exemption.htm

As a result of this new regulation, our library as well as the entire Indiana University campus reviewed all of the positions that might fall into the new classifications. Several positions were identified and were classified as PAO, which meant that they were professional assistants eligible for overtime pay. These positions must carefully monitor their hours and be paid overtime for any amount over the 40-hour work week. Out of approximately 17 positions, four were found to fit within this category of PAO.

HOW CAN OUR ORGANIZATION AVOID MISTAKES IN CLASSIFYING POSITIONS?

Review your current wage and hour practices of all employees. Look at the job description and how the job is actually performed very closely. A position is not automatically exempt because it has a managerial-sounding title or because the employee has a professional degree that is not applicable to the job. The actual duties and the percentage of time performing those duties determine the position's status. With limited exceptions, you cannot take deductions from an exempt employee's pay because of sickness, partial-day absences, or jury service.

Basic FLSA overtime provisions require that all non-exempt employees (full-time, part-time, hourly, and now some exempt overtime eligible) must be paid 1½ times their regular rate for hours worked in excess of 40 in any given week. This includes shift premiums. Overtime is paid for time worked, not time compensated. Therefore, no overtime must be paid on sick pay, holiday pay, vacation pay, or similar compensation for days not worked.

WHAT HAPPENS IF AN EMPLOYEE WORKS OVERTIME WITHOUT AUTHORIZATION?

An organization is obligated to pay nonexempt employees for time worked whether or not the work was authorized, even if the work was voluntary. Even if you have a policy stating that supervisors must approve all overtime, if your employees were working with or without permission, they are entitled to pay. If employees continue to work beyond the normal workweek and you have addressed this with them, the problem becomes one of performance and you would address it from that standpoint. Organization sponsored meetings and training sessions also count as hours worked for overtime purposes. Some organizations have a stated policy that any overtime compensation will be in compensatory time rather than cash at a rate of 1½ hours off for every hour worked beyond the 40-hour work week.

Make sure that you know your local and state regulations regarding the payment of overtime or setting work hours or break times as well as the federal regulations. There is no federal requirement to pay overtime for hours worked on Saturday, Sunday, or holidays, but some state or local governments require employers to pay premiums to those who work on those days. In some locations, you must pay overtime to nonexempt employees if they work more than eight hours in one workday regardless of the number of hours they work in a week.

The Wage & Hour Division of the Department of Labor has broad power to enforce the FLSA. They will investigate claims brought to their attention directly or claims made through unions or lawyers. Most of these investigations are triggered by a complaint from a disgruntled current or former employee. Audits are very time consuming and penalties for violation can be significant. It is best to be prepared in understanding and complying with the laws.

WORKERS COMPENSATION

Workers compensation is a state-governed benefits scheme that requires employers to pay medical bills and partial lost wages that result from work-related injuries and illnesses. Twenty states have their own workers compensation funds, to which some states mandate employer contributions (Smith and Mazen, 2004). The cost of the workers compensation insurance is usually based on the risk level of the organization and the claims history of the employer. Keep in touch with your employees when they are out of work because of work-related injuries or illnesses. Regular contact will maintain their connection with the workplace, show that you care, and speed their return to work.

Workers compensation costs have increased sharply because of the increased medical costs and rising claims connected with stress-related illnesses, repetitive motion injuries, and back problems. Library work activities include many hours spent working on a computer, which can lead to carpal tunnel syndrome and some back-related injuries. Work with your workers compensation carrier or state fund to identify potential hazards in your workplace. Then take action and provide training to reduce these risks. Many organizations consider worker's compensation among their benefits. We will discuss other benefits in a later chapter.

STAYING CURRENT

Kohl, Mayfield, and Mayfield present a set of useful Web sites offering a wealth of information for managers with HR responsibilities (2004). It is important that all of those dealing with HR responsibilities stay current on legal issues at the local, state, and federal levels.

Maintaining compliance with all of these laws and regulations may seem like a daunting task especially to the librarian who has little or no experience in these areas. Agencies responsible for these regulations are eager to assist you and will send you brochures and posters to help guide you through this process. There are also workshops to help you learn the various aspects of employment regulations. Knowledge of appropriate action is important to your organization as well as to you as the human resources professional.

REFERENCES

Abernathy, Robert. 2005. *Smooth Legal Sailing!: Americans with Disabilities Act.* (Workshop, IUPUI University Library, Indianapolis, IN).
Abernathy, Robert. 2005. *Smooth Legal Sailing!: Sexual Harassment.* (Workshop, IUPUI University Library, Indianapolis, IN).

Addington, Mark A. 2004. "Overtime Regs: What They Mean for You." *Lodging Hospitality* 60, no. 14: 30.

"Age Discrimination in Employment Act: Equal Employment Opportunity Commission Interpretation." March 2005. *Supreme Court Debates* 8, no. 3: 67–96.

Baum II, Charles L. July 2006. "The Effects of Government-Mandated Family Leave on Employer Family Leave Policies." *Contemporary Economic Policy* 24, no. 3: 432–445.

Bouton, David. 2005. *Smooth Legal Sailing!: FLSA.* (workshop, IUPUI University Library, Indianapolis, IN).

Code of Federal Regulations. Title 29, Volume 4. Chapter XIV—Equal Employment Opportunity Commission, Part 1602, Section 1602.7

Flynn, Gillian, Matthew T. Miklave, A. J. Trafimow, D. Diane Hatch, and James E. Hall. 2001. "Legal Insight: HR Within the Law." *Workforce* 80, no. 3: 76–81.

Hesse, Katherine A. and Doris R.M. Ehrens. 2006. "Family Medical Leave." *Benefits Quarterly: Third Quarter 2006* 22, no. 3: 57–58.

"Intermittent leave: The FMLA's Biggest Trouble Spot." (December) 2005. *HRFOCUS* 82, no. 12: 10–13.

Jackson, Saundra, Diane Lacy, Liz Petersen, Liz and John Sweeney. 2006. "Health Premiums, Raises, Warnings, Contrarians." *HRMagazine* 51, no. 6: 53–56.

Kohl, John, Milton Mayfield, and Jacqueline Mayfield. 2004. "Human Resource Regulation and Legal Issues: Web Sites for Instructional and Training Development." *Journal of Education for Business* 79, no. 6: 339–343.

Martin, Theresa. 2005. *Smooth Sailing!: Family Medical Leave Act.* (workshop, IUPUI University Library, Indianapolis, IN).

Ossi, Gregory J. 2005. "Age Discrimination Protection Is Not Limited to Seniors." *Coal Age* 110, no. 12: 39.

Smith, Shawn and Rebecca Mazin. 2004. *The HR Answer Book.* New York: AMACOM. Available: www.bls.gov (accessed January 22, 2007).

US Department of Labor. "US Department of Labor in the 21st Century." Available: www.dol.gov/esa/regs/compliance/whd/fiarpay/fact_exemption.htm (accessed January 22, 2007).

RECRUITMENT AND SELECTION OF LIBRARY STAFF

The success of the organization depends on the successful hiring and retaining of qualified employees. This is as true in libraries as it is in the corporate world. We are constantly reminded of the graying of the library profession, the shrinking of library schools, and the decreasing numbers who are entering the profession. By the year 2010, some 80,000 librarians will reach the age of 65 and are expected to retire from the profession (Perry, 2004). Libraries also face stiff competition from more alluring fields of computer and technological work. In a survey conducted by RewardsPlus of America, 52 percent of employers cited recruitment and retention as the number one employment issue they face today (Langan, 2000). Issues in library recruitment have remained relatively stable over the last two decades. These issues include requirements for entry into the profession, patterns of supply and demand in the library workforce, compensation, and the need to attract minorities to librarianship (Harralson, 2001).

In this chapter, we will look at recruitment issues including search committees, job descriptions, interviewing and interviewing techniques, adding diversity to the workforce, selection of a candidate, and evaluation of applicants.

WHAT DOES THE POSITION LOOK LIKE AND WHO DOES IT REPORT TO?

The first step in any search is to identify the position that you want to fill. Is this a new position or a replacement for a vacancy? Do you really need the position or are you filling it because it is vacant? When did you last look at the position description? Does it meet expectations for today's work environment or does it need revising? How does this position interact with others in the organization and what impact does the position have on the efficiency and success of the organization?

The position definition has been called the "blueprint for recruitment" (Meneses and Kleiner, 2002) and an accurate description is necessary to find the right fit for the organization. Many human resources professionals believe that long job descriptions are unappealing to top performers in today's environment (Langan, 2000). Keep the position description simple and brief but make sure that it covers all of the tasks and responsibilities needed to accomplish the job efficiently.

HOW DO YOU WRITE A JOB DESCRIPTION?

The job description answers two questions: what is the job, and what mental and physical abilities and preparation does the job require (education and experience)? You might begin by answering the following questions:

- What are the principal job duties including specific and significant details of these tasks?
- Who gives the assignments and who checks to see if they are accomplished?
- How accurate must the work be and what are the consequences of an error?
- What duties are performed only periodically or occasionally?
- What is the degree of responsibility?
- Does this position supervise others and, if so, is the position responsible for hiring, discipline, and termination for these individuals?
- How closely is the employee supervised—what decisions can he/she make independently?
- Is there anything particularly strenuous or difficult about the job, e.g., noise, interruptions, excessive heat or cold, standing for long periods of time, or other physical conditions regarding the position?
- With whom does this employee come into contact on a regular basis?
- What happens to his/her work when it is finished? Where does it go next or what is it used for?

The job description should include explicit outcomes of the performance. Setting parameters for each task will not only provide the groundwork for the performance evaluation but also will provide clear direction to the employee. An example of a job description for a copy cataloger or cataloging assistant is shown in Figure 3-1.

Librarian positions are often written in a much broader sense but still need to be clear, concise and brief. An example of a job description for a reference librarian is shown in Figure 3-2.

A good rule of thumb is that most jobs have no more than three major functions and very few have more than five. Narrative or essay-style writing leads to lengthy dissertations that invite confusion, misunderstanding, and inconsistency. Wordiness can be avoided by omitting the subject (the employee) and starting all sentences with action verbs.

Often when an organization is creating a job description, a particular individual might come to mind. Then, instead of creating a position that fits the needs of the organization, the position is designed to meet the attributes of that particular individual. This is the wrong approach both because the equal employment opportunity practice goes by the wayside, and because if that individual does not accept the position or leaves it, you may have position requirements that no one else can meet.

Primary responsibilities: Ensure the accuracy of machine-readable records by assigning, verifying, and creating correct codes, tags, call numbers, subject headings, and literary/artistic headings for both bibliographic and authority control records input; resolve problems related to obsolete, conflicting, or incorrect data resulting from database migrations; create original series and name authorities for a wide variety of records; create original series for staff as requested. Catalog [name of library] Library print, media and metadata bibliographic records. Create original records in the OCLC database by deriving existing bibliographic records. Edit, enhance, and correct a variety of bibliographic records by locking/replacing data in the OCLC database. Independently assign call numbers and subject headings for records. Create templates, macros, shortcuts, and files as needed to expedite and streamline workflow. Use technology and the Internet to assist in interpreting and analyzing data to increase task efficiency and overall productivity. Create and delete added volumes/copies and MARC holdings; transfer and merge bibliographic or/and authority records. Create statistical reports as needed. Work with team colleagues, Acquisitions and Public Services areas and frequently make recommendations so that materials flow smoothly and rapidly through the system to the shelves; update and delete holdings for XXX Library in the OCLC database. Answer staff questions regarding established cataloging policies and procedures, especially queries related to media, art/series concerns, and assist in training staff and students; discharge lost and missing items using the SIRSI circulation module.

---

1. Job Responsibility: Copy Cataloging (print monographs). Tasks include editing of bib record, creation of call/copy records, verifying/creating call number and subject headings, OCLC work, creating and attaching labels:

   • Generally a high level of performance: Performs all tasks with few errors.
   • Generally a medium level of performance: Takes care of tasks with some errors.
   • Generally a low level of performance: Does not take care of tasks, has frequent errors.

---

2. Job Responsibility: Database Maintenance. Tasks include fixing typos, correcting tags, recon, resolving call numbers, migration cleanup, withdrawals and transfers.

   • Generally a high level of performance: High level of accuracy; will include a few errors.
   • Generally a medium level of performance: Includes some errors, but attempt is made to perform tasks accurately and to correct errors.
   • Generally a low level of performance: Does not perform maintenance tasks.

Figure 3-1. Cataloging Assistant

Responsibilities as a Primary Reference Librarian:
- Provide brief consultation reference, quick answers, assistance in using reference sources in many formats (CD-ROM, print sources, Internet) in person, over the telephone, and by electronic means to all users of [name of library] Library.
- Participate as an active team member by providing input in the development and management of the reference collections.
- Share reference expertise with fellow team members informally, while providing reference services, and formally in training workshops.
- Work with team to set objectives, plan team strategies, address issues, and solve problems for continuous improvement of the Reference Team functions.
- Develop skill sets and resource contacts to accomplish Reference Team related responsibilities.

Figure 3-2. Responsibilities as a Primary Reference Librarian

The job description will also determine if a position is exempt or nonexempt. Classification and rank of these positions will be determined by the essential job functions of the position, education requirements, experience requirements, and other measures. This is especially true of nonlibrarian, paraprofessional or support positions.

Nonexempt positions in libraries might include reference assistants, copy catalogers, clerical staff, and book shelvers. Nonexempt positions are highly structured and most subject to federal and state labor regulations. More information on nonexempt employees is provided in the section on the FLSA in Chapter 2.

WHAT ARE ESSENTIAL JOB FUNCTIONS?

Essential job functions are the major elements, tasks, or activities that are necessary to perform the job. If attendance is an important factor, it should be a required essential job function. Some functions may seem obvious to you but it is important to clarify should someone challenge you that "it was not in the job description." Essential job functions for the copy cataloging assistant position might include editing of bibliographic records, creation of call/copy records, verifying/creating call numbers and subject headings, OCLC work, and creating and attaching labels.

You need not indicate every aspect of the job in the essential job functions, but if it is significant, it should be listed. Some organizations have begun using a different format for writing job descriptions which includes a process for evaluation of the position.

Organization Name
Behavioral Performance Standards
Provides performance standards for job responsibilities
for:

Staff Member: _____ Date: ___/___/___

Department: _____ Job Title: _____

Review period: From ___/___/___ To ___/___/___

Identify primary job responsibilities

➢ Summary of job duties. (Include key customers served.)

Identify each job responsibility and performance standards

List primary job responsibilities, identifying high, medium, and low levels of performance. Use the list of performance standards below as a reference when completing this form.

➢ **Quantity**   How much or how many must be done
➢ **Quality**   How well the job responsibility must be done
➢ **Timeliness** How fast or by what deadline the job responsibility must be done
➢ **Expense**   Under what cost constraints the job responsibility must be done
➢ **Other**   Customer satisfaction; independent initiative required; other relevant, verifiable measures

1	2	3	4	5	6	7
Very Poor	Poor	Below Average	Average	Good	Very Good	Excellent

1 Job Responsibility:

Generally a **high level of performance**: rating 6 or 7

Generally a **medium level of performance**: rating 3, 4, or 5

Generally a **low level of performance**: rating 1 or 2

2. Job Responsibility:

Generally a **high level of performance**: rating 6 or 7

Generally a **medium level of performance**: rating 3, 4, or 5

Generally a **low level of performance**: rating 1 or 2

3. Job Responsibility:

Generally a **high level of performance**: rating 6 or 7

Generally a **medium level of performance**: rating 3, 4, or 5

Generally a **low level of performance**: rating 1 or 2

4. Job Responsibility:

Generally a **high level of performance**: rating 6 or 7

Generally a **medium level of performance**: rating 3, 4, or 5

Generally a **low level of performance**: rating 1 or 2

Additional Comments for Supervisor and Staff Member _____

_____

_____

_____

_____

Staff Member's Signature _____ Date _____

Supervisor's Signature _____

Figure 3-3. Sample Job Description

If possible, have several individuals review the position description to make sure that all necessary skills and education and experience requirements have been included. The supervisor of the position should definitely review the description before recruitment begins.

Essential job functions usually include mental and physical aspects of the job as well. Mental skills might include problem solving, multitasking, working with interruptions, or handling difficult patrons. Physical aspects would be sitting for long periods of time, lifting books on and off book trucks or shelves, or computer data entry.

HOW DO I BEGIN THE RECRUITMENT PROCESS?

Today's work environment requires a different approach to recruitment. Rebecca Martin, in an article about recruitment for library leaders, suggests that we need to begin seeking individuals who are creative, risk takers, innovators, and who see change as an opportunity rather than a threat (Martin, 1997). I would suggest that we consider these types of individuals for all library positions, not just those at the top. We need staff at all levels who can challenge the organization with new ideas and procedures that will move the organization forward. Employees usually have an investment in the organization and can provide good ideas for improvement and efficiency. They are attuned with what is working and what is not working. If they are allowed input, they will be empowered to make sure their suggestions or recommendations succeed and see that their ideas and recommendations are valued by the organization.

A systematic recruitment process can prevent wasted time, effort, and money and helps ensure that positions are filled successfully. It has been suggested that organizational success depends on a well-implemented systematic selection process for effective hiring (Meneses and Kleiner, 2002). Things to consider while planning include:

- Where will the position be advertised?
- When is the closing date?
- Who will receive the applications? A central office?
- Who will review the applications? Human resources personnel, search and screen committees, supervisor, or director?
- Who will determine which applicants to interview?
- Who will set the criteria for evaluation?

- How many candidates will be interviewed?
- Do you have a timetable for when the process is to be completed?

WHERE SHOULD I ADVERTISE?

In today's competitive market, recruitment does not begin with advertising but with the environment of the organization itself (Marcus, 2006; Smith and Mazin, 2004). Is your organization a good place to work? Do you offer opportunities for growth, both personal and professional? Are you up-to-date technically? These things must be in order before you begin advertising. Use your Web site as a major recruiting tool. Your site should reflect your organization as exciting and one that anyone would want to work for. Available positions should be easy to access and contain clear instructions for applying. If job listings are embedded under several layers, the difficulty of finding them could send the wrong message.

Advertisements should contain the job description, required qualifications, a statement about salary, included benefits, and instructions concerning deadlines and required application materials. Be clear about whether your organization wants letters of reference or names, addresses, and phone numbers of references sent with the application and resume. You may also request e-mail addresses for references as this will expedite the process.

If you are hiring a support staff position, you may want to consider using job or career fairs in the community or, if there is a college, university or trade school in the area, posting on their job boards. According to a study done by MRI Cyberstats, "more than 8-of-10 college graduates used the Web in 1999 to search for jobs and 66 percent e-mailed their resumes to employers" ("To Become Critical for F/S," 2001). Another great resource for hiring is networking and referrals. The "network" is usually familiar with the type of work conducted in your organization and will know what type of employee you typically hire. Those providing referrals can identify an individual that they can recommend without reservation to the hiring organization. Some organizations even set up an employee referral program with incentives or rewards if a hire is made from their recommendation. This approach can be used at all levels.

Recruitment of librarians is often done through professional organizations or publications. *Library Journal*, *C&RL News*, and Association of College and Research Libraries (ACRL) publications are examples of trade sources that post ads and most of these publications now list their job ads online. The *Chronicle of Higher Education* is a primary publication for ads from academic libraries. Another popular way of advertising is through electronic listservs, especially specialized listservs on reference, instruction, etc.

There is generally no cost to the organization for this "word-of-mouth" advertising and it can produce immediate results.

Where you advertise may be determined by the budget allocated to your recruitment process. Advertising in well-known publications, such as *The Chronicle*, can be unaffordable for smaller libraries. These libraries may benefit from using listservs. Networking through professional organizations is another cheaper type of advertising for smaller libraries.

For major leadership positions such as dean or director of a library, you might engage the services of a recruitment firm or "headhunter." Consider this choice carefully. Once you sign an exclusive agreement, you must pay a fee even if you hire a person you located through another source. The fee for a retained search can be as much as one-third of the position's annual compensation (Smith and Mazin, 2004). This type of recruitment may involve an up-front fee and expense charges with the balance payable after a hire is made. Do not let the search firm talk you into a candidate if that individual does not meet your requirements or expectations.

WHO IS RESPONSIBLE FOR COLLECTING THE APPLICATIONS AND PROCESSING?

It is advisable to have a central location to receive applications, such as the administration office or the human resources department. If applications are to be received electronically, a secure shared drive should be established for those personnel who will need to process the applications. One individual could be designated to receive them through e-mail and dump them into the shared file. It is important that date received be included, perhaps in the file name. A checklist, listing such items as job requirements, education requirements, references, and so on, needs to be constructed and attached to each application. These items are crucial to any search and might be requested by affirmative action or personnel offices.

WHO WILL REVIEW THE APPLICATIONS?

Once you have a preliminary file of potential candidates, it is wise to have one individual to review all of them against the checklist to see if the applicant has the minimum requirements for the position. This first check may eliminate individuals who do not meet the minimum requirements and save time in the long run. Each applicant should be notified of receipt of their application. This would be the appropriate time to let those who do not meet the minimum requirements know that they will not be considered. It is important to treat all of the applicants fairly and not leave them waiting a long time before they know whether they are seriously being considered for the position or not (Meneses and Kleiner, 2002). Responsiveness is also important to the image of the organization as a potential workplace. Once the applications have been checked, the candidates are now ready to be reviewed by the search committee or those who will be involved in the interviewing process.

WHAT IS THE SEARCH COMMITTEE'S ROLE? WHO SHOULD BE ON IT?

The search committee or screening committee is usually comprised of a small number of people who might interact with the position. The committee usually includes the supervisor of the position as well as peers. The chair is often the supervisor. There is no specific size recommended, but keeping it small reduces delays due to scheduling conflicts and so on (Raschke, 2003). It is the committee's role to review all of the qualified applicants, evaluate and rate them according to the criteria and requirements, review references, interview the applicants, and make recommendations for hire. The actual job offer and appointment will be conducted by the human resources manager, administrator, director, or dean of the library. Apprising committee members of equal employment opportunities and affirmative action issues is encouraged.

Before reviewing the applications, the committee should devise a scheme or system of criteria. This should probably include a rating scale so that the committee can differentiate between the various applicants. The committee should carefully screen all candidates one at a time. See sample rating forms in Figure 3-4.

Each applicant should be reviewed completely. Read the application form or resume for a clear understanding of the applicant's work history, training, and education. Consider the work environment, length of time employed, and the individual's role in the organization. Consider all data provided in the letter and application that supports the applicant's ability to do the job.

Once the initial screening has been completed, the committee should meet and determine which individuals they would like to interview. A larger number of applicants can be considered if you are using telephone interviews

---

SAMPLE A

CANDIDATE _____ POSITION _____

INTERVIEWER _____ DEPARTMENT _____ DATE _____

Instructions: This is a weighted interview evaluation form. Assign a percentage weight based on the importance of the job's dimensions. Total weights must equal 100 percent. Upon completion of the interview, assign a rating for each dimension. Multiply weight times rating to determine point total. Sum the point total to determine the grand total and final ranking. Complete comments in the section provided. Mail completed evaluations to Personnel, Address XXX

DIMENSON	%WEIGHT(W)	RATING®	(WxR)Point Total
INTERPERSONAL SKILLS	_____%	10 20 30 40 50 60 70 80 90 100 Poor Outstanding Are the candidate's thoughts clearly expressed? Is there a sense of confidence and ease? Is the personality open and optimistic?	_____
TECHNICAL ABILITY	_____%	10 20 30 40 50 60 70 80 90 100 Poor Outstanding How does the candidate's technical expertise and education compare with the position requirements? How much additional training will be needed? How readily willthe candidate be able to acquire new skills?	_____
WORK EXPERIENCE	_____%	10 20 30 40 50 60 70 80 90 100 Poor Outstanding How does this person's work experience compare with position requirements? What levels of job-related experience have been achieved? Has this person demonstrated competence to be successful in this position?	_____
MOTIVATION COMMITMENT	_____%	10 20 30 40 50 60 70 80 90 100 Poor Outstanding Does this person display a positive attitude? Is there real interest in and enthusiasm for work involved? Is there a history of goal setting and achievement?	_____
FLEXIBILITY/ GROUP SKILLS	_____%	10 20 30 40 50 60 70 80 90 100 Poor Outstanding Does this individual appear to adjust to change? Is this the type of person who could integrate comfortably within the work group?	_____

Figure 3-4. Sample Rating Forms for Candidates

SAMPLE B

INTERVIEW RATING SHEET

POSITION: _____   CANDIDATE: _____

DATE: _____   INTERVIEWER: _____

The Performance Skills to be evaluated include:

	Very strong evidence skill not present	Strong evidence skill not present	Some evidence skills is present	Strong evidence skill is present	Very strong evidence skills is present	Insufficient evidence for or against skill
(1)	1	2	3	4	5	Skill Unmeasured
(2)	1	2	3	4	5	Skill Unmeasured
(3)	1	2	3	4	5	Skill Unmeasured
(4)	1	2	3	4	5	Skill Unmeasured
(5)	1	2	3	4	5	Skill Unmeasured
(6)	1	2	3	4	5	Skill Unmeasured

The Technical/Job Skills to be evaluated include:

	Very strong evidence skill not present	Strong evidence skill not present	Some evidence skills is present	Strong evidence skill is present	Very strong evidence skills is present	Insufficient evidence for or against skill
(1)	1	2	3	4	5	Skill Unmeasured
(2)	1	2	3	4	5	Skill Unmeasured
(3)	1	2	3	4	5	Skill Unmeasured
(4)		2	3	4	5	Skill Unmeasured
(5)	1	2	3	4	5	Skill Unmeasured
(6)	1	2	3	4	5	Skill Unmeasured

RECOMMENDATION   _____   _____

                                              Hire   Not Hire

REASON FOR RECOMMENDATION: _____
_____

Figure 3-4. Sample Rating Forms for Candidates *(Continued)*

first to narrow the selection of candidates to be brought in for an in-person interview. Telephone interviewing is a good way to get to know the "person behind the resume without investing the time and effort of a formal interview" (Herring, 1986). This preliminary interview helps determine if the candidate warrants further consideration and can aid in determining whether or not the candidate will "fit in" with the organization's culture.

Many larger organizations require the department to submit a request for interview before the interview process begins. This allows human resources time to ensure that all equal employment obligations have been met before allowing the interview to take place.

HOW DO YOU HANDLE INTERNAL CANDIDATES?

While it is great to offer employees the opportunity to advance, there may be backlash if internal candidates are turned down. Choosing one internal candidate risks alienating those not chosen, and if the successful candidate is someone who is a personal friend of any member of the search and screen committee, you risk the perception of bias as well. On the other hand, choosing an external candidate may damage morale among current employees, especially if the organization has an objective of hiring and promoting from within.

Unsuccessful internal applicants may react negatively for many reasons. They may be embarrassed about not being chosen and about revealing their desire to leave their current position. They may fear that their supervisor will hold it against them because they sought another position. Most importantly, they may feel cheated by the process and become disengaged from the organization. If the hiring process lacks employee buy-in, unsuccessful candidates may feel that they were passed over for reasons unrelated to the job. Employees may question the fairness of the process in light of their years of service and loyalty to the library.

One way to avoid negative backlash when hiring or promoting from within is to incorporate principles of procedural fairness. Research indicates that most people can accept losing if they lose fair and square, but problems surface when the decision process appears to be less than objective. If you ensure that procedures are fair, most people can accept unfavorable outcomes and remain productive and useful members of the organization.

Use selection methods directly related to the position description. Avoid subjective methods such as an unstructured interview or stereotypes (for example, the reputation of the applicant's alma mater). Inform the applicants about how the hiring process works and what standards they must meet. Communicating this information early on will most likely cause applicants who are not fully committed to lose interest and withdraw their application, thereby saving valuable time.

Provide feedback to unsuccessful applicants. Feedback is vital to maintaining relationships within the organization. After a decision has been made and an offer accepted, it is time to let the others know. Provide feedback in a constructive way. Show respect to all applicants for their time and willingness to apply for the position. Being disrespectful can have a profound and detrimental effect on attitudes and relationships for years to come.

HOW MANY CANDIDATES SHOULD BE FORMALLY INTERVIEWED? WHO SHOULD MEET WITH THEM?

There is no magic number. For equal employment opportunity reasons, many human resource departments require at least three, if at all possible.

With a staff position, the hiring department and/or search committee are usually the only ones who meet with the applicants. They might be introduced to other library staff members on a facility tour but they rarely are asked to do a presentation or full staff discussion. Final candidates might also be asked to meet with the administrator.

Librarian applicants are often brought in for a full-day to one-and-a-half-day site visit. This may include interviews with the selection committee, the supervisor of the position, and groups of prospective colleagues. Some organizations include an "open session" in which all members of the library staff are invited to meet and ask questions. If a presentation is conducted by the candidate, this might be the appropriate session for the "all staff" group. In the case of academic libraries, an additional meeting with the HR representative and/or the Promotion and Tenure representative might be included. The interviewing process usually invites all who have met with the candidate to provide comments on the applicant to the search committee or administrator (Lehner, 1997). In these cases, it is best to provide an evaluation form for the interviewers to complete and send to the committee. This standardizes responses and makes rating scales consistent.

When hiring for the head of a library, you may choose to use a more formal procedure in which the applicants demonstrate their abilities through a formal presentation. This would be open to anyone who would interact with the library. For public libraries, this might include the library board and the general public, if it is a fairly large organization. In academic libraries, this might include other units on the campus who frequently use the library services.

Following the site visits, the search committee will complete its deliberations and present its recommendation to the administrator, director, or dean of the library. This will conclude their responsibility as a search committee. All notes, paperwork, and memos related to the search should be kept for a minimum of three years in case the procedures are questioned by a nonselected applicant who feels discrimination has occurred.

HOW SHOULD THE INTERVIEW PROCESS BE CONDUCTED?

There has been much discussion on whether to use a structured or unstructured interviewing process (Harralson, 2001; Lehner, 1997; Fietzer, 1993). The unstructured interview is usually open-ended, using questions that have not been preconceived before the interview session. Depending on the interviewer, the candidates may not be asked the same questions. In a structured interview, the same set of questions will be used for each applicant and the same group will be meeting with the candidate and asking these questions. Recruitment in academic libraries is usually structured. Determining how you will rank the responses is also part of the structured interview process. Because of the various laws surrounding interviewing processing, the structured interview process seems more reliable in keeping participants on task. Nonetheless, the interview process will always be subject to personal bias which is one of the reasons that personnel psychologists continue to debate the validity of the process (Kennedy, 1994).

The basic steps in preparing for the interview are:

- Carefully select members for the search committee that represent a cross section of the organization and include members who will interact directly with the position.
- Develop a scripted list of questions, developed with input from the entire committee.
- If possible, have them reviewed by the organization's lawyer or human resources personnel to make sure that they are lawful questions.
- Take detailed notes during the interview to help you accurately recall a candidate later.
- Be sure to allow the candidate an opportunity to ask questions.

- Have an evaluation or rating scale that will be used for all candidates.

WHAT HAPPENS ON THE DAY OF THE INTERVIEW?

Prepare for the interview session ahead of time. Schedule a private place for the interview. Make sure the physical setting is comfortable and encourages conversation. Be on time and offer coffee or water to the candidate prior to the interview.

The interview process might include a facility tour. Consider this a walk-around interview. The candidate will meet other employees, and this is a good way to observe how the candidate interacts with others (Pergander, 2006).

During the interview, it is best to begin with less intense questions. Maintain eye contact with the applicant and use humor when appropriate. Establishing a comfortable rapport allows the candidate to feel more relaxed and could lead to more honest information (Shiparski, 1996). It is usually best to have the candidate meet separately with the supervisor and/or manager from the committee.

Always end by thanking candidates for their interest and time. If possible, let them know the timeline for making a decision.

WHAT ARE UNLAWFUL QUESTIONS?

Unlawful questions are those questions which would be in violation of the equal employment opportunity laws. Inquiries concerning a candidate's race, sex, marital status, disability are examples of unlawful questions. Do not assume that applicants with an accent are not US citizens. Do not ask an applicant about their financial affairs or credit status. If the applicant is a female, it is also unlawful to ask about family arrangements, such as care for children.

Keep questions structured to the job and attributes that might be necessary to fulfill the job requirements.

Worth Repeating: Careful What You Ask!

Although it is good to set the candidate at ease using small talk, it is illegal to ask questions such as: Are you married or do you have children? This could end up in a lawsuit.

WHAT KINDS OF QUESTIONS SHOULD YOU ASK?

Appropriate questions will depend on the nature of the job and the job description. There are various types of interview questions including traditional, behavioral, holistic, power interviewing questions, and pressure interviewing questions (Falcone, 1992). Following are examples of each of these types of questions:

Traditional Interview Questions

- What is the greatest strength that you will bring to our organization?
- If there were one weakness you could identify, which, if strengthened, could make you an even stronger contributor to our organization, what would it be?
- Where do you see yourself in five years?

Behavioral Interview Questions

Behavioral questions usually follow up on the answers a candidate has given to a traditional type of interview question.

- Give me an example of the last time that you could have delegated work to a subordinate but carried out the whole task to its completion yourself. What triggered your decision to go above and beyond? How did your supervisor and subordinates react?
- What type of mentoring style do you have? Give me an example of how you have nurtured or fostered a colleague or subordinate's personal development on the job.

Holistic Interview Questions

Holistic questions attempt to measure a candidate's understanding of where and how they will fit into your organization. These questions allow the candidate to express their philosophy about work.

- What aspect of your current position do you consider most critical and why?

- What areas of your skills do you want to improve upon in the next year?
- Describe how your job relates to the overall goals of your department, team, or organization.

Power Interview Questions

Power questions focus strictly on a candidate's patterns of achievement in previous positions. They are asked to measure the individual's awareness of his accomplishments.

- In retrospect, why is [name of company where applicant has worked] a better place for your having worked there?
- Every company relies on key employees to make effective decisions on a day-to-day basis. Tell me one decision that you made that stands out in your mind which had a particularly strong impact on the organization.

Pressure Interview Questions

Pressure questions measure an applicant's ability under fire and determine how they land. Examples are:

- Tell me about your last performance appraisal. In which area were you most disappointed?
- Tell me about the last time you felt angry with your boss. What caused your anger and how did you approach solving the problem with your supervisor?
- I assume that you researched our organization before coming for this interview. Tell me what you learned and share with me what potential problems you see us facing.

All of these styles and types can be incorporated into a standard interviewing process but you have to determine what works the best for your organization. The question, "What makes you stand out among your peers?" remains one of the most telling questions for identifying an individual's level of self-esteem and achievement awareness (Falcone, 1992). Statistics indicate that only two people out of ten can clearly articulate the answer to this question. Achievement-oriented questions need to be linked to the candidates' performance record. This is not always easy to determine through the interview. Candidates' perception of themselves can provide insight into their work ethics and philosophy about work, service, and personal values.

HOW DO YOU ENCOURAGE AND/OR MANAGE DIVERSITY IN THE RECRUITMENT PROCESS?

By definition, diversity means having distinct or unlike elements. In the workplace, that translates to people who vary widely by age, ethnic background, gender, religion, and physical abilities. Forward-thinking companies recognize diversity as an important business issue. Eighty percent of the people in the world are not white and 50 percent are not male (Wollenhaupt, 2007). Companies today are beginning to realize the need to attract and retain a diverse work force that reflects the marketplace and society.

Diversity has long been a goal of the library profession. In 1997, the American Library Association began the Spectrum Initiative as part of an effort to address the need for a diverse workforce (Perry, 2004). The Spectrum Initiative awarded scholarships to attract minorities into the profession. This program alone cannot solve the diversity issues that the profession is facing. The numbers of minorities entering into library schools and education is still a relatively low number. Minority enrollment at the Louisiana State University library school has increased in past years, but this is a historically black campus along with Baton Rouge and Shreveport (Perry, 2004). There is a strong mentoring commitment in this program, which is attributed to some of the recruitment success. In a recent study conducted at IUPUI among African-American and Hispanic students, mentoring was also voiced as key to students considering this field of study (Stanley, 2007). With fewer numbers of available minority students, recruitment for diversity becomes even harder. Our profession remains invisible to potential minority applicants. We have not reached out to potential recruits early enough in the education process.

If organizations are serious about diversity, they will have to be creative in their efforts to attract these candidates to their organizations. One study suggests that the most effective way to manage diversity is to have one individual responsible for tackling the diversity issue in an organization (Kalev, Dobbin, and Kelly, 2006). This individual should be given the authority, resources, support of, and access to top management to ensure the effective implementation of diversity initiatives.

Organizations will need to seek recruitment among associations connected with various minority groups, e.g., Black Caucus of ALA (BCALA), the American Indian Library Association, the Asian/Pacific-American Library Association, and the Chinese-American Library Association.

Organizations might also consider internships as a possible means of increasing diversity. This has been done in several libraries successfully. Another possible avenue is to "grow your own." Look among your current staff and see if there are workers who would be excellent future librarians.

Develop a program to sponsor individuals who enter the program and attain their professional degree by providing tuition reimbursement or practical experience opportunities.

When you have an applicant pool, you will not know if you have a diverse group. You must still select by choosing the best fit for the organization. However, when you have several equally qualified individuals who match the fit for the organization, it is strongly suggested that if you are trying to diversify your organization, give great consideration to the minority applicant.

HOW DO YOU SELECT A CANDIDATE AND WHAT HAPPENS NEXT?

Now it is time to think about which candidate stands out above and beyond the other applicants. Review the evaluation and comments of everyone who was involved in the interviewing process. Is there a consensus regarding the applicant? Often, the organization will require a second interview with the top candidates. This is usually conducted with the search committee and the supervisor or hiring manager. A second interview is recommended when two applicants are equally qualified to perform the job (Meneses and Kleiner, 2002).

You should also review the references for the final candidates. Many researchers contend that the written references are not always valid and recommend that phone reference interviews also be conducted. Individuals committing themselves in writing, may be more cautious because they know that the applicant has the right to view the letter. Phone references tend to open up more and be more honest in their reflections of the candidate. Always contact more than one reference. Have the applicant submit at least three references.

Some applicants may not have an extensive work experience. In this scenario, checking with former or current teachers might be a valid source of information. Try to ask questions that would relate to the job performance. An example might be, "Can you describe the applicant's presentation skills?" This might be a key element if you are searching for a librarian who will be responsible for instruction sessions and will be conducting presentations in front of a class or group. Questions centered around the group work would be relevant to working in library teams or library group projects.

In selecting the ideal candidate, evaluate the candidate realistically. Do not compromise on standards. You should continue the recruiting process until you find what you are looking for in a candidate (Stanton, 1977).

Once you have made a decision, make a verbal and a written offer. Contact the candidate by phone and make an offer. During this conversation, allow the applicant to ask questions to clarify any doubt he/she may have. Provide the candidate with a timeframe in which he/she would start working and when to let you know. Send a letter of offer that specifies the nature of the job, the benefits to the candidate, and the expectations of the organization. If your organization requires a background check before a final offer can be issued, let the candidate know that the hire is contingent upon completion of this background check.

Once the decision has been made, the offer given and accepted, it is time to notify the other candidates that a decision has been reached. Some suggest that it is unwise to reveal why an applicant was not chosen but to simply state that after a review of all qualified applicants, a decision was made and offer was accepted. This practice alleviates the concern of lawsuits.

Sometimes, the candidates decide not to take the job because another job offer fits their needs better or because with the job offer in hand, they can negotiate a higher salary with their current employer. Be prepared for this and turn to your second candidate of choice or continue recruiting.

WHY SHOULD I DO A BACKGROUND CHECK?

Many employers do employee screening in an effort to avoid fallout from a bad hire. Wal-Mart had an incident in which a Wal-Mart employee was accused of sexually assaulting a young girl on the job. The accused employee was a previously convicted, registered sex offender. At the time, Wal-Mart did not conduct background checks on their new hires. As a result of this suit, Wal-Mart now requires a criminal background check on all new hires (Keller, 2004). There are various state regulations on background checks and employers should verify with authorities what information will be released and how it can be used in employment practices.

Employers should consider an applicant's criminal history as a part of the applicant's total qualifications. If the applicant seems better qualified than other applicants and has a more extensive criminal history, the employer should carefully decide whether the criminal history outweighs the applicant's other qualifications (Martucci and Coverdale, 2004). The law requires that the extent of the preemployment background check be appropriate in relation to the job (Smith and Mazin, 2004). Be sure to check with counsel before acting.

There will be costs regarding the background checks. This procedure is usually done by an outside agency. On some academic campuses, the campus police unit can do a simplified check on student employees. Employers will need to determine if the expenditure for background checks is worthwhile.

SHOULD I HIRE STUDENT EMPLOYEES? WHAT PROCEDURES SHOULD I FOLLOW WITH THEM?

Student employees supply many types of libraries with an important labor force. Hiring student employees can be beneficial to both the student and to the library. The students have an opportunity to gain job skills, earn money, and learn about balancing a schedule involving work, school, and social activities. Libraries have the opportunity to provide a positive, often first work experience to the student. Librarians and support staff can serve as role models for these students, answer student questions, and help them learn more about the working environment of the library. Student employees often gain a respect for and a better understanding of the work of libraries and learn to view the library as a vital and relevant part of their future. They may also become future library professionals.

In public libraries, students are usually at the high school or college level and are primarily hired to do book shelving, shifting of materials, searching for and processing patron reserve materials, and straightening and maintaining the public area. In school libraries, students may be elementary or high school age depending on the school level of the library. Activities will be similar depending on the needs of the library. In academic libraries, student employees are usually members of the campus environment. On campuses with a library school program, students in the program are hired as graduate assistants and may provide service at the reference desk and assist in simple library instruction classes. Using graduate library students provides the student with first-hand experience in library activities and provides some relief to librarians.

Finding and hiring the right student employees is paramount to the success of using student employees. In the school library, the school librarian normally selects students who have shown interest and ability in using the library. They are normally hand picked and work out fairly well. For public and academic libraries, hiring the right student is more difficult. Often, students apply at a library under the assumption that this will be an easy job. In academic libraries, the students may anticipate being able to study while on the job. Having a detailed process including job descriptions, application information, hiring procedures, evaluation reviews, schedules, and payroll information will make the whole operation much smoother.

This provides a more professional approach to hiring and, due to the more formalized hiring procedure, the library secures more qualified student workers.

Recruitment of a sufficient number of applicants is the first step. Organizations need to actively recruit student employees by advertising open positions through job fairs at high schools or college campuses, placement in local newspapers, or any other place where potential employees might congregate. Another successful recruitment practice is word of mouth through current or former student workers. These individuals can advocate the positive work experience.

Create a job description that conveys what the work entails, what skills are needed, and the work schedule. Explain any special qualities that may be needed to fill the position, i.e., reading knowledge of a certain foreign language. Since students may not have prior work experience, ask not only about the applicant's prior work experience but also any volunteer experience. Activities such as scout experience may be useful. Outside activities such as sports or music commitments will need to be considered as they could present problems in the work schedule. Academic achievement is also good to review.

As with any job search, one should carefully review all of the applicants and determine which students best fill the requirements of the position. When interviewing prospective student employees, it is wise to have more than one staff member participate to get several perspectives.

Ask open-ended questions so that the students can respond with more than a yes or no answer. Encourage the students to ask questions. Often, their questions will reveal in greater depth the knowledge and interests of the student. Give the students information about the library, its goals, and a taste of the library culture. If there is a dress code, be sure to address this so that problems will not arise later. Check references as you would in any other hire. Final decisions on who to hire should be based on the applicant's qualifications, background, and experience.

The challenge with student employees is to bring them into the organization and help them understand how their jobs fit into the library operations. The student employee who understands the total picture becomes the ideal student employee. Most new student employees do not really understand how a library functions. A formal orientation to the library, including a tour of the entire facility, is important. This orientation welcomes the student to the organization, allows the student the opportunity to meet all of the employees, and shows how his or her job contributes to the organization's success.

Training is another key issue in hiring student employees. An effective training program should identify what needs to be learned first so that it can be built upon later. The training process begins with a well written job description that clarifies performance measures so that the student will know what is expected. Because of their part-time employment status, student employees have only a partial commitment to the organization. Students are usually expected to begin immediately and the training is conducted in a relatively short period of time. A large number of people may need to be trained at the same time, especially during the beginning of a semester in the academic library. All new employees deserve a quality orientation and training. One common pitfall is that student employees are usually supervised by other individuals who may have duties other than just supervising the student employees. The supervisor of these employees must be given appropriate time to select, orient, and train the students. Andrew Melnyk believes that "an average student aide needs at least two months of work training before he/she starts performing quite efficiently" (Melnyk, 1976).

One mistake in training is trying to teach the student everything that could possibly happen. Over the first few weeks, the supervisor should spend time in each work period reviewing the student employee's work and adding additional information that will aid the student in his/her work. Some libraries use checklists to identify areas that the student will need to learn. A review or evaluation of the employee three to four weeks after hiring is helpful. This can serve a twofold purpose: the student will get feedback on how he/she is doing, and it is an opportunity to let the student employee know how much his/her comments and feedback are appreciated.

ARE VOLUNTEERS A GOOD USE OF MANPOWER IN LIBRARIES?

Volunteers serve an important role in many libraries. While most of these volunteers are individuals who love libraries and want to become more involved, they are not all retirees and philanthropists. In the case of student volunteers, they might become the librarians of the future. Volunteering can improve a student's self image and give him or her a work record upon which to base a resume and references. Volunteer experience also fosters a philosophy of giving back to the community.

Though volunteers serve without pay, they still need the same respect and value as a paid staff member. It is essential to determine if the volunteer's needs match the library's stated needs or goals. Volunteers are commonly recruited to do behind-the-scenes library work such as mending books or processing materials, but a few are trained to perform customer service functions.

Volunteer programs are not free; it costs to nurture and train these workers. Before establishing a volunteer program, staffers should design tasks and job descriptions that identify special projects or supplementary tasks. A volunteer coordinator should be chosen to facilitate planning and oversee all volunteer activities. Ideally, this individual should be someone who is currently on staff or knows the library and the community well. If the library is large enough and the program warrants it, the volunteer coordinator could be released from regular duties at least half-time. If the program grows, this individual might be able to take this on as a full-time role.

There are drawbacks to the use of volunteers. Some librarians do not want to have volunteers because they do not like spending the time to recruit and train them. Other librarians are uncomfortable with delegating or sharing tasks and authority. Sometimes, librarians are concerned that the presence of unpaid staff somehow devalues professional work (Linke and Breitenbach, 2000).

Ideally, a volunteer program can provide an incredible supplement to professional staff. However, the success of the program relies on a high-quality training program, professional management of these workers, recognition of customer services as a top priority, acceptance by the paid staff of the volunteers as partners, challenging work assignments for the volunteers, and support by the administration and staff. The parameters of responsibility and authority must be clear so that expectations will be realistic. Specific procedures for evaluation and correcting unproductive behavior must also be put in place so that everyone will be treated fairly and equitably. Volunteers should know that their work will be documented and their performances appraised in confidence. The volunteer program will only be as successful as the management of the program. Organizations have to put time, talent, and dollars into volunteers. Volunteers can repay you a thousand times over in actual work, in resources saved, and in community support.

A good recruitment and hiring process will make a lasting impression on your new employee, whether student, paraprofessional, or librarian. Now that the process is completed, make sure that you do not neglect your new employee. We will discuss orientation, training, and retention in further chapters.

REFERENCES

Falcone, P. 1992. "Power Interview Skills Will Find 'The Best' Quickly." *HR News* 69, no. 11: 14.

Fietzer, W. 1993. "World Enough, and Time: Using Search and Screen Committees to Select Personnel in Academic Libraries." *Journal of Academic Librarianship* 19, no. 3: 149–153.

Harralson, D. M. 2001. "Recruitment in Academic Libraries: Library Literature in the 90s." *College & Undergraduate Libraries* 8, no. 1: 37–68.

Herring, J. J. 1986. "Establishing an Integrating Employment Recruiting System." *Personnel* 63: 47–52.

Kalev, A., F. Dobbin, and E. Kelly. 2006. "Best Practices or Best Guesses? Assessing the Efficacy of Corporate Affirmative Action and Diversity Policies." *American Sociological Review* 71, no. 4: 589–617.

Keller, S. 2004. "Employee Screening: A Real-World Cost/Benefit Analysis." *Risk Management* 51, no. 11: 28–32.

Kennedy, R. B. 1994. "The Employment Interview." *Journal of Employment Counseling* 31, no. 3: 110–114.

Langan, S. 2000. "Finding the Needle in the Haystack: The Challenge of Recruiting and Retaining Sharp Employees." *Public Personnel Management* 29, no. 4: 461–464.

Lehner, J. A. 1997. "Reconsidering the Personnel Selection Practices of Academic Libraries." *Journal of Academic Librarianship* 23, no. 3: 199–204.

Linke, Lynn and Anya K. Breitenbach. 2000. "The Librarian's Understudy." *American Libraries* 31, no. 6: 78.

Marcus, B. W. 2006. "How to Recruit in a Competitive World." *New Jersey Law Journal* 184, no. 4: Index 245, April 24, 2006.

Martin, R. A. 1997. "Recruiting a Library Leader for the 21st Century." *Journal of Library Administration* 24, no. 3: 47–58.

Martucci, W. C. and B. N. Coverdale. 2004. "Effective Use of Background Checks by Employers." *Employment Relations Today* 31, no. 2: 99–110.

Melnyk, Andrew. 1976. "Student Aides in Our Libraries." *Illinois Libraries* 58 (Fall): 142.

Meneses, A. and B. H. Kleiner. 2002. "How to Hire Employees Effectively." *Management Research News* 25, no. 5: 39–48.

Pergander, M. 2006. "Mastering the Group Interview." *American Libraries* 37, no. 2: 44, (February).

Perry, E. B. 2004. "Let Recruitment Begin with Me." *American Libraries* 35, no. 5: 36–38.

Raschke, G. K. 2003. "Hiring and Recruitment Practices in Academic Libraries: Problems and Solutions." *Libraries and the Academy* 3, no. 1: 53–67.

Shiparski, L. 1996. "Successful Interview Strategies." *Nursing Management* 27, no. 7: 32F–32H.

Smith, Shawn and Rebecca Mazin. 2004. *The HR Answer Book*. New York: AMACON.

Stanton, E. S. 1977. *Successful Personnel Recruiting and Selection*. New York: AMACON.

Stanley, Mary J. 2007. "Where Is the Diversity: Focus Groups on How Students View the Face of Librarianship." *Library Administration & Management* 21, no. 2: 29–35.

"To Become Critical for F/S: Job-Seekers Turning to Web as Online Recruiting Grows." *FoodService Director* 14, no. 4: April 15, 2001.

Wollenhaupt, G. 2007. "Diversity Strengthens Companies and Employees." *The Indianapolis Star*, Supplement, G2, January 15.

4 TRAINING, RETENTION, AND PROFESSIONAL DEVELOPMENT

In the ideal world, the new recruit would possess all of the skills and background needed to perform flawlessly in the position. However, the world changes and continuous learning is necessary. Chapter 4 will focus on orientation, professional development, training, building leadership skills, motivation, recognition, and rewards that will enable the good employee to become even better—and help the organization retain good employees.

NOW THAT THE NEW HIRE IS ON BOARD, WHAT DO I DO?

Once a candidate has signed on the offer, maintain contact with him/her. If the candidate is moving from a distance, you might send suggestions of residential areas to consider or other information. Keeping in contact with the individual between the hire and the starting date shows that the organization cares about this new individual. Some even suggest that you might want to consider offering to help them unload their belongings when the moving van arrives (Weingart, Kochran, and Hedrich, 1998). This may not be feasible for some libraries, but it certainly suggests that the individual is coming into a warm, supportive environment.

WHAT SHOULD I DO BEFORE THE NEW EMPLOYEE ARRIVES?

Make sure that you have the new employee's workstation area or office sufficiently supplied and ready. Make sure that the computer workstation is working. Provide basic office supplies. Have the area clean and presentable. If the individual needs to complete paperwork, make sure that is done first.

On the individual's start date, it is important that the supervisor be there to greet and welcome him or her. The employee should be given instructions on how to logon/logoff the computer, the protocol for answering and making calls on the telephone, and what e-mail system the organization is using and how to connect. This is a good opportunity to go over with the employee task expectations and policies on time off and how this is recorded. The supervisor should discuss the expected working schedule for the new employee, break and lunch periods, and other daily routines. One orientation procedure that is often neglected is emergency and disaster procedures (Weingart, Kochran, and Hedrich, 1998). This procedure should be discussed with the employee, as one never knows when a disaster will occur. The new employee will also want to know about when pay distribution occurs.

Take the new employee on a tour of the facilities and introduce him/her to other staff members. Some organizations offer a small breakfast gathering to introduce the new employee to coworkers. This sets a good tone and allows the new employee to relax and adjust to the new environment. It is important to show where the break room and lavatory facilities are located as well as copy machines and where to go for supplies. This may all seem like common sense, but it does not hurt to have a checklist. Little things like keys can often get overlooked unless you have them written down.

Figure 4-1 is a sample checklist taken from the IUPUI (Indiana University Purdue University Indianapolis) Human Resources Administration.

SHOULD I HAVE A FORMAL ORIENTATION PROGRAM?

Whether or not to have a formal orientation program is entirely up to the organization. In much of the literature, a formal orientation program is critical to the retention and motivation of employees (Ragsdale and Mueller, 2005; Ballard and Blessing, 2006; Weingart, Kochran, and Hedrich, 1998). A well-planned, formal orientation can reduce turnover, shorten the period of adjustment, and lay the groundwork for a successful career for the new employee.

North Carolina State Libraries (NCSU) has built a strong employee orientation program that emphasizes early social interaction (Ballard and Blessing, 2006). Much of their program is based on Maslow's hierarchy of needs and Herzberg's theory of motivation factors related to job satisfaction. Their orientation program has three components: 1) orientation sessions that focus on library culture and values, 2) checklists that ensure

Departmental Orientation Checklist

Items covered:
- ❑ Institution History
- ❑ Distribution of Employee Handbook
- ❑ Safety Orientation
- ❑ Paid Time Off
- ❑ Institutional Policies
- ❑ ADA and Special Accommodations
- ❑ Benefits Package
- ❑ Employee Services and Perks

PRE-ARRIVAL SET-UP	NEW EMPLOYEE PACKET	EQUIPMENT & ETCETERA
***Supervisor Ensures Availability the Entire First Day**	***Review Contents with Staff Member**	***Schedule Time to Discuss Training and/or Other Topics**
ADMINISTRATIVE PAPERWORK ❑ Hire Documents ❑ Computer User Agreement (pdf) ❑ Direct Deposit ❑ I-9 Form ❑ State and Federal Withholding Forms ❑ Personal Profile Form (ED) (pdf)	❑ Welcome Letter from Department Head ❑ Copy of Job Description ❑ Department's Mission and Value Statements ❑ Department and Institution Organization Chart	**TELEPHONE** ❑ Pass Code & Authorizations ❑ Long Distance Information ❑ Quick Reference Card ❑ Voice Mail ❑ Administrative Options ❑ Department/Campus Phone Numbers ❑ City Phone Books
PREPARE WORK AREA ❑ Name Plate for Desk ❑ In-box and Mailbox ❑ Scissors ❑ Clean Trash Can ❑ Notebooks ❑ Calendar ❑ Pens/Pencils/Highlighter ❑ Tape Dispenser ❑ Stapler ❑ Post-its ❑ Order Business Cards ❑ Keys for office, building	❑ Map of Building and Department ❑ ADA Accommodation Resources ❑ Department Policies ❑ Time Reporting Procedures ❑ Time Off Procedures ❑ Overtime Procedures ❑ Dress Requirements	**TECHNOLOGY** ❑ Passwords ❑ Workstation ❑ Electronic Mail ❑ Printer Path ❑ Other Resources ❑ Pagers ❑ Cell Phones ❑ Laptops ❑ Copier ❑ Fax Machines ❑ Websites
COMMUNICATE TO DEPARTMENT ❑ Schedule Department Tour ❑ Assign Mentor (if applicable) ❑ Announce Arrival via Publication or Electronic Mail ❑ Schedule lunch for day one ❑ Schedule necessary training	❑ Emergency Procedures ❑ Departmental Standards ❑ Performance Expectations ❑ Building Access Procedures ❑ Parking Procedures ❑ Police and Security	**ETCETERA** ❑ Department Identification ❑ Post Office ❑ Mail procedures ❑ Break Rooms ❑ Credit Unions and ATMs ❑ Eating Establishments ❑ Bookstores or other close shopping areas

Figure 4-1. Sample Checklist for Orientation (Source: Reprinted with permission from IUPUI [Indiana University Purdue University Indianapolis] HRA)

all topics, supplies, etc., are in place for the new employee as well as policies and procedure information, and 3) one-on-one sessions with individuals who are important and who will interact with the new employee. NCSU schedules orientations in each month that more than three new employees join the staff. The sessions combine activities with discussion to involve the new employee immediately. Diversity, safety, and technology are covered. The overall tone is light but professional. Support staff and librarians are oriented at the same time which helps establish a spirit of collaboration.

The checklist allows for consistency in the treatment of new employees. The list is made available online, and supporting policies, Web sites, and other resources can be linked to the list.

The one-on-one sessions include appropriate personnel representatives and key faculty and staff so that new employees can learn about the organization's expectations related to internal and external communications, fiscal responsibility, and accountability. NCSU is working on an assessment of this formal orientation program to determine whether staff members believe that the orientation experience has affected their inclination to work in the organization and/or their overall job satisfaction (Ballard and Blessing, 2006).

The Disney Corporation has all new employees attend an orientation called "Traditions" on the first day of work (Outlaw, 1998). During this program, they learn about the history, culture, and management style of the company and how the different parts of the organization relate to each other. The theory behind this is that the more time and effort invested in the new employee, the less time you spend later correcting problems.

HOW LONG SHOULD ORIENTATION BE?

Orientation should last long enough for the new employee to feel comfortable in the job, understand the culture and values of the organization, and become a successful member of the organization. This may take a few hours, a few days, or weeks. Following up afterwards ensures that the employee has reached an understanding of expectations. Each time you meet with new employees, provide feedback on how they are doing and discuss areas that might need to be addressed. Allow time for the employee to ask questions and provide input on how he or she is doing. This will give both of you a good idea of accomplishments and tasks that might need more instruction. Too often new employees are left to their own devices after orientation.

WHAT IF MY ORGANIZATION IS SMALL AND I NEED ALL OF MY EMPLOYEES TO DO THEIR JOBS DURING NORMAL WORK HOURS? HOW CAN I IMPLEMENT AN ORIENTATION PROGRAM?

Orientation in small organizations could be scheduled for off-peak hours when other workers can assist in the orientation. The orientation could also be scheduled outside normal work hours. The important thing to remember is that you need to do whatever is necessary to orient your new employee and ensure his or her success.

WHAT SHOULD BE INCLUDED IN THE ORIENTATION?

The orientation should be tailored to fit your organization. Think about the goals or outcomes you want from the orientation. Topics useful for any organization include the culture and values of the organization, the work environment, team and personal responsibilities, diversity, customer service principles, benefit and compensation packages, dress and decorum, safety and security practices, and organization policies and procedures. Remember to include stretch breaks, which provide a needed break and also allow movement that stimulates thinking.

Allow employees the opportunity to interact with as many other employees in the organization as possible, especially informally. This will help the new employee relax and feel a part of the new community.

SHOULD I USE MENTORS? DO THEY REALLY HELP?

The term "mentoring" has varying meanings. A mentor has been defined as someone senior in the field who serves as a role model and works to achieve another's career advancement. Another definition describes a mentor as "anyone who enhances, enriches, and encourages the professional development of another member of the profession" (Kaplowitz, 1992: 219).

Some form of mentoring exists in all organizations. A colleague may offer to help a new employee or a manager might offer support to a new subordinate. The more formal type of mentoring requires planning and training of the mentors.

There are pros and cons to mentoring which should be viewed seriously before starting such a program. Evidence to support the theory that mentoring helps the new employee to be successful is not available (Tonidandel, Avery and Phillips, 2007). Some studies suggest mentoring impacts the career and psychosocial development of the one who is mentored. Much of the research indicates that one of the success factors in the mentoring process is the mentor. In a study done at the IUPUI University Library with minority students and minority librarians, mentoring was referred to as an important factor for both students and librarians (Stanley, 2001).

HOW DO YOU SELECT MENTORS?

Most mentoring programs ask for volunteers. Often, individuals are reluctant to volunteer for such a program. One researcher suggests developing a selection of potential mentors by asking staffers to nominate potential mentors (Miller, 2006). Pairing of mentor and mentee is a critical element in mentoring success. Carefully match the mentor and mentee since this individual might have great impact, good or bad, on the new employee. If the mentor was not a willing participant in the program, this could have adverse effect on the mentoring. One of the worst scenarios that could happen would be to pair a new employee with a senior librarian who has lost enthusiasm or is negative about the organization, setting a negative tone for the new employee.

Desired Mentor Attributes	**Desired Mentee Attributes**
• Good communication skills • Knowledge of the organization and its political structure • Wide range of professional skills and resources • Willingness to share these skills with others • Time and effort to invest in developing an effective professional relationship • Previous experience in developing others and genuine interest in helping them advance	• Desire to work towards a professional goal • Ability to accept help from others • Good listening skills and a desire to learn new things • Eagerness to cooperate and have a positive attitude • Ability to ask for advice and actually use it • Ability to handle setbacks and willingness to work hard juggling multitasking

Figure 4-2. Attributes of Mentors and Mentees

Training of the mentors is also critical for setting a clear understanding of their role. Training could include effective listening skills, coaching, goal setting, conflict negotiations, and giving and receiving feedback. Training also says to the participants that the organization values this process. Training will bring consistency into what the new employee learns from the mentor since you will be establishing protocols. A training agenda for library mentors might look something like the one shown in Figure 4-3.

Part 1: Understanding the Novice Librarian	Part 2: Building the Effective Library Mentor
Discussion of Issues the New Librarian Might Face: • How the organization works, its history and political structure • What is expected of librarians in terms of professional development • What is expected of librarians by their peers	*Qualities of an Effective Mentor* • Defining highly effective librarian behavior • Building a relationship of trust and open communication • Initiating candid discussions on sensitive topics • Being an advocate for the novice librarian • Providing information about the library and the organization *Library Mentoring Strategies* • Building a common vocabulary • Learning active listening and questioning skills • Coaching and goal setting • Strategies for giving and receiving feedback • Handling conflict and negotiation skills

Figure 4-3. Sample Training Agenda for Mentors

WHAT HAPPENS IN THE MENTORING PROCESS?

The mentoring process usually includes building and establishing personal relationships, providing information and support about the organization and how things operate, facilitating change, handling challenging tasks, modeling the role of the librarian according to the organizational expectations, and helping the individual plan for the future (Golian and Galbraith, 1996). The process may benefit both the mentor and the mentee. Benefits to the mentor will be discussed later. Benefits to the mentee include a support system, an opportunity for professional growth and knowledge, and an understanding of the culture and values of the new organization. Hopefully, through this mentor relationship, the new employee will determine that the organization is one where they want to stay and develop their potential.

PROFESSIONAL DEVELOPMENT, TRAINING, RECOGNITION, MOTIVATION, AND REWARDS

Professional development, training, recognition, motivation, and rewards all help in retention. In our changing times, growing costs and shrinking budgets inevitably lead to fewer staff. Yet the volume of work is increasing and the technology is becoming more sophisticated as are the information needs of our users. Libraries must ensure that their remaining staff have the necessary skills and knowledge to meet these challenges.

Training and developing your employees to their highest potential will benefit not only your employee but also your organization. Providing training and professional development opportunities is a first step in letting the staff know they are valued. Recognition can be a motivational tool and a reward in itself. A formal staff training and development program is a cost-effective way of ensuring staff efficiency and providing more interesting and rewarding careers (DeBruijn and Friesen, 1996).

WHAT KIND OF TRAINING SHOULD BE PROVIDED FOR EMPLOYEES?

A training-needs survey is probably the best place to begin. The survey shown in Figure 4-4 was designed and administered by the Staff Training and Development Committee at the University of British Columbia Library in August 1991. Even simple informal surveys through e-mail or round-table discussions, can lead to the discovery of training needs.

For a new employee, determine what core skills training is needed. Each individual's needs will be slightly different depending on his or her background. The bulk of this type of training will occur within the operating unit where the staff member works. Some skills such as word processing and e-mail are best taught by experts in a more formal setting rather than one-to-one (De Bruijn and Friesen, 1996). Online or electronic programs allow individuals to learn these skills at their own pace and schedule.

A survey of Library staff to determine what training programs the Library should offer. Please fill in the form and return it to [Human Resources Office] by [date].

	Useful in current job	Useful for career development	Not relevant
1. Online catalog database training			
Introduction to system	_____	_____	_____
Tips and tricks for searching	_____	_____	_____
Advanced searching	_____	_____	_____
Specific files (i.e., Headings, Bibliography)	_____	_____	_____
Please list the file(s) you would like to learn more about _____			
2. Human Resources Department Workshops			
Management skills	_____	_____	_____
Personnel appraisal	_____	_____	_____
Time management	_____	_____	_____
"Training the trainer" skills	_____	_____	_____
3. Personal Skills	_____	_____	_____
Supervisory skills			
Stress management	_____	_____	_____
Written communication	_____	_____	_____
Public speaking	_____	_____	_____
Conducting meetings	_____	_____	_____
Creative thinking	_____	_____	_____
Interviewer/interviewee skills	_____	_____	_____
Counseling skills	_____	_____	_____
Budgeting skills	_____	_____	_____
Grant proposal writing	_____	_____	_____
Assertiveness			
Coping with change in the	_____	_____	_____
Workplace	_____	_____	_____
Other	_____	_____	_____
4. Technological Skills			
Introduction to microcomputers	_____	_____	_____
Hard disk managementprocessing	_____	_____	_____
Personal file management	_____	_____	_____
Spreadsheet	_____	_____	_____
Statistical software	_____	_____	_____
Online searching of remote databases	_____	_____	_____
Desktop publishing	_____	_____	_____
Communication software	_____	_____	_____
Internet systems	_____	_____	_____
Database management systems	_____	_____	_____
Keyboarding skills	_____	_____	_____
Office equipment operation	_____	_____	_____
AV equipment operation	_____	_____	_____
Preservation of materials	_____	_____	_____
Other	_____	_____	_____

Figure 4-4. Sample Training Needs Survey

	Useful in current job	Useful for career development	Not relevant
5. People Skills			
Communication with people from different cultures	_____	_____	_____
Serving and working with people with disabilities	_____	_____	_____
Working with problem patrons	_____	_____	_____
Teaching skills	_____	_____	_____
Telephone skills	_____	_____	_____
Conflict resolutions in the workplace	_____	_____	_____
6. General Interest			
First aid	_____	_____	_____
CPR	_____	_____	_____
Rescue skills	_____	_____	_____
Copyright	_____	_____	_____
Information malpractice	_____	_____	_____
Disaster procedures	_____	_____	_____
Library ethics	_____	_____	_____
Research methods	_____	_____	_____
Evaluating library services	_____	_____	_____

Please indicate which position you currently hold:

Librarian _____   Clerical _____   Technical _____   Administrative _____

How long have you worked at XXX Library _____ ?

What area do you work in the Library?

Reference _____   Circulation _____   Acquisitions _____   Cataloging _____

Special Collections or Archives _____   Interlibrary Services _____   Technology _____

Administration _____   Other (please specify) _____

Thank you for completing this survey to assess training needs for the XXX Library.

Figure 4-4. Sample Training Needs Survey *(Continued)*

HOW CAN I AFFORD A TRAINING PROGRAM? TRAINING PROGRAMS ARE EXPENSIVE.

The costs of training programs are as diverse as the types of training available. You have to determine what you are willing to spend to make your staff efficient and up-to-date. Many larger organizations have a HR staff that provides training as part of the organization package. Smaller organizations may have to look outside the organization for their training. State library associations often have members with training expertise.

These individuals are usually willing to provide training for smaller organizations at a lower cost than a professional training organization. Check with local colleges and universities as well. They often are willing to provide training as part of their research activities. And always look within your own staff for potential trainers. Some individuals just seem to have a knack for teaching others and this might provide a development opportunity for them as well.

WHAT IF MEMBERS OF THE STAFF ARE RESISTANT TO TRAINING?

Not all staff, including managers, are eager to spend time in training (Holt, 1999). Training represents something changing and many do not adapt well to change. Some managers gripe about the time taken away from work for training. This type of attitude sends a message to employees that training is not really valued and resistance to training becomes even greater. You must work on changing this attitude and find ways to show the value of the training to these managers.

Staff members often expect training on new technology. Providing training for soft skills, such as communication, time management, or stress management, is more difficult (Smith and Mazen, 2004). Many employees feel that they already know these skills and see this training as a waste of time. How do you convince them that this is worthwhile and important?

Frame the training as an opportunity for staff development and let them know how they will benefit from the training. Encourage all levels of staff to participate. When the director or dean participates with the clerical or support staff, it demonstrates commitment by the organization to the process.

Provide plenty of notice regarding the training so that the staff may plan their schedules accordingly. Organizations may require attendance at training as part of performance expectations. Remind staff members if there are any preprogram assignments, to arrive on time, and to turn off any communication devices that might interfere with the program.

When the IUPUI University Library moved to a team-based organization, they established "organizational week" (Stanley, 2001) three times a year (at the end of the fall and spring semesters and during the summer). The purpose of these "organizational weeks" at first was to orient and develop the staff in team thinking. Professional trainers were brought to the library to do workshops on team building, time management, and stress management, to name a few. As time progressed, the May week became one of goal setting for the next academic year and the summer week was reduced to one day with an outside speaker discussing current trends in the library. The week in January remained set aside for professional development. Attendance at these "organizational weeks" is mandatory and staff is requested not to schedule other activities during this time period.

The Birkman Method, a questionnaire-based motivational assessment tool, was also introduced to the staff during one of the organizational weeks. The Birkman Method is used for hiring and selection, environmental team-building, sales training, determination of career paths, mid-career guidance, mentor relationship building, identification of leadership skills and styles, and training needs assessment. The questionnaire generates a report that provides employees with their most productive behavior as well as their sources of motivation. The Birkman Method was first introduced only to the senior managers. Each senior manager received an intense two-hour consultation with the Birkman consultant and then one full day was spent with the managers as a group. The individuals shared reports with one another and discussed how each individual's strengths contributed to the group's efforts. The process also served as a trust-building exercise because it was very revealing; individuals had to feel secure sharing their personal profiles. Later, the method was presented to all of the 14 team leaders and eventually the rest of the organization was "Birkmanized." Currently, as new employees start, they are offered the opportunity to complete the questionnaire. It is strictly voluntary, but it is a great opportunity to collectively gather organizational strengths in one swoop. Reports for the whole organization can generate this information readily.

Training provides staff with tools that will help them do their jobs better. Training also shows that the organization values its employees. Training often results in the empowerment of the staff in new initiatives. As they build confidence and expertise, they are more willing to use their new knowledge and take on new opportunities. As one author put it, "Not to train is to disrespect staff" (Holt, 1999: 91).

WHAT OTHER TYPES OF PROFESSIONAL AND/OR PERSONAL DEVELOPMENT SHOULD BE PROVIDED?

Professional development usually includes continued education and participation in professional organizations. Successful leaders know the value of retaining good employees and fostering their development. In order to accomplish this, organizations must provide both time and money for employees' development, as well as holding the employee accountable for what they accomplish. This demonstrates commitment on the organization's part and stresses the value of an engaged employee who strives to become better prepared. Professional and personal development should be offered to all staff members, whether librarians or support staff.

In many academic libraries, professional development for librarians is a requirement. Librarians who are on tenure track must be involved in professional development through leadership in professional organizations and associations, through publication, or through expanding their educational degrees, in order to achieve tenure and/or be promoted to the next rank. The achievement must also be documented. The ACRL Statement on Professional Development, approved on July 8, 2000, states, "Professional development is an important manifestation of the academic librarian's commitment to personal excellence" (ACRL Professional Development Committee, 2000). Librarians commit themselves to lifelong learning and personal growth when they take on this "manifestation" as their way of professional life. Public libraries, special libraries, and school libraries, are also committed to professional development as evidenced by the abundance of professional associations tied to these libraries and the programs that they offer.

Development might include a career ladder program as libraries will need new leaders when current ones retire or leave. While a professional development program will not retain every employee, opportunities for acquiring new skills, career development, and sharing with colleagues will go a long way in keeping good employees (Marks, 2001).

SHOULD WE INCLUDE DEVELOPMENT FOR THE SUPPORT STAFF?

Library assistants now perform tasks that used to be the domain of librarians, such as copy cataloging, reference, instruction, collection development, and book selection. We often neglect these employees in both research and the recognition they should receive for their work. Providing support for personal growth and professional development might lead to a decision to become a librarian and will definitely add value to the organization as a whole.

In a study done among academic libraries on the status and working conditions of library paraprofessionals, Oberg found that 96 percent of member libraries of the ACRL provided release time to support staff to attend local, state, and regional meetings (Oberg, 1992). Taking this a step further, the Western New York Library Assistants conducted a survey to better understand the training needs of library assistants and what barriers they faced (Buchanan, 2005). The survey included academic libraries, school media libraries, special libraries, and public libraries. The survey indicated that approximately 23 percent of library assistants of Western New York are current members of a library professional organization and an additional 33.1 percent indicated an interest in joining one (Buchanan, 2005). In addition, 26.6 percent of the survey respondents have joined a library-related listserv. Nearly all of the respondents indicated they would attend professional development training, workshops, or conferences if their employer would provide both release time and funding. Release time was slightly more important than funding. On the downside, while library assistants have significant interest in training, many felt they were not fully trained nor given the time to learn necessary technical skills. I am confident that this is not limited to this group of library assistants.

If you are a smaller organization and cannot affording funding for support staff to attend professional events, you should make every effort to allow release time for them to do so. It is an investment in your future as well as theirs.

Without a strong professional growth program, it will be more difficult to attract and retain the talent you need to accomplish your organizational mission and goals. Developing your staff to excel will allow your organization to find ways to grow and be a leader regardless of the changes the future may bring.

HOW DOES A LIBRARY DEVELOP LEADERSHIP SKILLS IN THEIR EMPLOYEES?

While great emphasis has been placed on skills training, little is being done to develop the next generation of leaders, who will replace the leaders retiring in the next five years. Leadership training as a topic for research was almost nonexistent until the late 1980s and 1990s. Even in library schools, leadership training is not a focus but more of a management skill sandwiched between communication and interpersonal skills (Mason and Wetherbee, 2004).

Many companies are developing their own comprehensive in-house leadership training programs to ensure a homegrown supply of leaders (Bisoux, 2005). This philosophy has been used in Chesterfield County, Virginia's firefighters organization for the last 20 years (Avsec, 2006). This organization has developed and implemented leadership training programs beginning with the entry-level firefighter training program and extending all the way to the fire chief. They begin by introducing staff to the concept of leadership roles as crew leaders. The crew leaders are given specific tasks and expectations for their crew's performance and are held accountable for the successful completion of the jobs assigned to the crews. Those who wish to advance to officer levels must engage in further leadership programs. As part of their program, individuals are required to read three leadership books. Among the titles are *The Seven Habits of Highly Effective People,* by Stephen Covey; *Who Moved My Cheese?* by Spencer Johnson, MD; and *The Leadership Secrets of Attila the Hun* by Wess Roberts (Avsec, 2006). Each of these convey a different perspective on leadership and the students must complete a written assignment related to each book as well as group discussion about the assignment. The students are also required to keep a journal to encourage the art of reflection, another leadership skill. It would behoove us to look inward at our staff for leaders of the future as this company has done.

Leadership training programs are emerging as a tool for retention (Berta, 2006). It is important that employees demonstrate leadership whether they manage someone or not. Leadership is especially important as organizations are flattened and advancement for librarians is more difficult. The special projects these librarians are involved in will require some leadership ability. Any staff member may be called upon to lead a particular library project.

WHAT ARE LEADERSHIP SKILLS?

According to one research study, "the exact nature of leadership skills remains elusive" (Mason and Wetherbee, 2004: 188). There has been much discussion over what constitutes a leadership skill; however, here are a few that seem to be mentioned over and over again: honesty, inspiration, competence, respect, vision, risk taking, communication, and collaboration. Many of these are considered "soft skills" which make training even more difficult. Training for these skills varies as much as the skills themselves.

Two highly recommended library leadership programs are the one-week ACRL/Harvard Leadership Institute program and the two-week Frye Leadership Institute program (Gjelten and Fishel, 2006). Both of these assume a certain level of experience with leading an organization or a department in the higher education environment. These institutes are both very limited to a certain type of librarian, the academic librarian. Both are also very limited in the number of participants and require time away from the job.

The first formal leadership development for librarians may have been the Senior Fellow Program, developed in 1982 (Mason and Wetherbee, 2004). The Association for Research Libraries (ARL) has been offering leadership activities and skills-building programs for librarians for more than 25 years through its Office of Leadership and Management. Again, these have been mostly attended by academic librarians. Most library programs are residential programs or workshops, often lasting multiple days or a week. Selected participants spend time in a retreat or remote setting. The programs usually focus on the bonding of the individuals into groups and many of the exercises are intended to encourage long-term relationships. Sometimes, mentors are included in the programs.

In Indiana, a program called Academy for Leaders in Indianapolis Libraries and Media Centers was developed (Champlin, Gall, and Lewis, 2004). The program was a partnership between the libraries of Indianapolis and the Indianapolis Foundation. The purpose of the academy was to empower educator-librarians to provide leadership in and for learning environments, which in turn would increase the level of information literacy among the library users. The participants committed to over two weeks during the course of a year. The academy required participants to apply for a Library Fund Small Grant to fund a field project, which also gave them experience in grant writing. Each academy project is contracted with input from the participant's director or manager and must be approved before implemented. Participants also learn the principles of collaboration with other libraries and non-profit organizations.

For smaller libraries who cannot afford to send individuals to retreats, workshops are one alternative. Workshops usually offer one or two days of training with no overnight activities. They usually focus on a particular leadership skill or attribute. Mentoring is less likely to be offered. Some local development programs may offer excellent workshop leadership training. State library associations also usually offer leadership development workshops either at the annual program or throughout the year.

HOW EFFECTIVE HAS LEADERSHIP TRAINING BEEN FOR LIBRARIANS?

The jury is still out on this question. There is not much assessment of training programs out there. Most of the commentary comes from self reporting by the participants or comments from evaluation forms. These sources indicate a positive experience for individuals and acknowledgment that they have learned skills that they can use (Mason and Wetherbee, 2004).

The graying of the profession and the ensuing retirement of today's leaders make it imperative that we brace for the future. Many organizations are becoming team based. Each of these teams will need a strong leader. These team leaders will need to know how to lead a team toward organizational goals and missions. The military is a good example: they push hands-on leadership all the way down to the lowest level because in battle they will be faced with different situations and will have to think and reason for themselves (Monroe, 2005).

Another reason to provide leadership training is to increase motivation. If the employees are allowed to enrich their skills and use these new skills, the environment will be intrinsically rewarding (Deeprose, 2007).

HOW DO YOU INCREASE JOB SATISFACTION AND MOTIVATION?

"Job satisfaction is the degree to which people like their jobs" according to one author (Spector, 1997). Not all people like their jobs. Some are working only to make a living. Another definition of job satisfaction and one most used in research is by Locke: "... a pleasurable or positive emotional state resulting from the appraisal of one's job or job experiences" (Locke, 1976: 1304).

In a study looking at job attributes, employees ranked interesting work as the most important job attribute and monetary rewards ranked fifth (Kovach, 1995). Individuals want to be challenged in their work and have varying things to do to make their work more satisfying. Other studies have shown that dissatisfied employees are more likely to leave the organization or have absenteeism problems than those employees who are satisfied. These studies also indicate a correlation between job dissatisfaction and other negative behaviors such as lateness, grievances, substance abuse, and early retirement (Hackett and Guion, 1985; Kohler and Mathieu, 1993).

In a workshop, I was given this list of ten ways to motivate an employee (see Figure 4-5). This was developed by a professional trainer who had conducted research to find out what really motivated employees. As you can see, appreciation topped the list for employees and good wages or

What Employees Really Wanted	What Supervisors Thought They Wanted
Appreciation	Good Wages
Feeling "In" On Things	Job Security
Understanding Attitude	Promotion Opportunities
Job Security	Good Working Conditions
Good Wages	Interesting Work
Interesting Work	Management Loyalty
Promotion Opportunities	Tactful Discipline
Management Loyalty	Appreciation
Good Working Conditions	Understanding Attitude
Tactful Discipline	Feeling "In" On Things

Figure 4-5. Ten Ways to Motivate an Employee

"pay" actually ranked fifth. Time after time, employees tell me that what they really want is to be appreciated. Additional pay is always nice but what is really important to them is the recognition of their contributions.

CAN A MANAGER MAKE SURE THAT ALL EMPLOYEES ARE MOTIVATED AND SATISFIED?

I doubt that anyone would insist that it is the employer's responsibility to make sure all their employees are happy. That would be an insurmountable task. Everyone is motivated by different things. For example, for the employee who likes a challenge, it would be best to direct varying assignments to this individual and allow opportunities for growth. For the individual who just wants to do her job and punch out at five o'clock, the supervisor should allow this as long as the employee is keeping up with quality and quantity expectations, pitches in when needed, and meets the changing demands of the job. If a manager takes the extra step to discover what each employee's internal motivators are and tries to tie them to the work, motivation will increase.

Dialogue with your employees is an important way to discover what they like or do not like about their jobs. During the hiring process, pose questions to the applicants that will help you find out what motivates or inspires them or what they consider accomplishments. Discussions with employees should be ongoing and can stimulate other ideas on what is working and what should be changed.

The success of this is also dependent upon the employee. If someone fails to do what he or she is supposed to be doing or has a negative attitude toward work, that person should be dismissed (Lloyd, 2006).

WHAT ARE SOME WAYS THAT THE ORGANIZATION CAN INFLUENCE EMPLOYEES?

Share as much information as you can with your employees. One of the most common complaints from employees is lack of communication from the top. Employees want to be involved and know what is in store for them, good or bad. Too often, employers share information with a small circle of individuals, assuming that this information is passed on. Disgruntled employees often indicate that they never know what is happening and feel left out of the conversation. Employees like to be asked questions and listened to and can often offer suggestions. The HR professional can encourage discussion up and down the ladder.

Acknowledgment and respect are inexpensive ways of rewarding and motivating your employees (Wilson, 2006). Employees want to feel good about themselves and their work and want to relate their work to the larger picture of the organization. Recognition is a form of reinforcement and feedback. Lack of recognition has been given as the number one reason why people leave their jobs (Sigel, 1992). HR professionals should know a lot about praising individuals, but managers may not share the same knowledge. Some supervisors are better at giving praise than others and some do it in a mechanical way that is not sincere. This is one thing that every supervisor should continue to practice: acknowledging individuals for what they have accomplished. HR professionals should encourage recognition of contributions by individuals. One simple and easy recognition is acknowledgment of an individual's anniversary date with the organization.

In recognition of a team's success, acknowledge the successes of all team members. This will help in building a high performing team. Providing team recognition even in small ways can bolster team spirit and group morale.

How does one affirm a team's collective effort and its different individual's contributions, especially when each individual effort is not the same? You want to acknowledge performance in a way that neither undermines those who contributed the most to the team's work nor reinforces the behavior of those team members who added little or nothing to the team. One way to circumvent the dilemma is to be sure the team leader recognizes the achievements of individual members during group sessions. To turn a group into a high performing team, leaders must use recognition and rewards to reinforce the team's overall objectives. As tangible results are attained, the team members are likely to feel better about themselves and, in turn, are likely to become more productive.

Leaders must also learn to couple individual performance with group output. Teams generally have developed mutually agreed upon and challenging goals. Strategies for achieving these goals are clear and each member understands his or her role in realizing the goal. Policies, rules, and team process enable members to do their jobs easily. Individual and team accomplishments are recognized by the team leader as well as by other team members by celebrating milestones, accomplishments, and events. Members feel important within the team and experience a sense of personal accomplishment in relation to their contributions.

Starbuck's Warm Regards recognition program was developed to highlight outstanding achievement embodying the principles, mission, and goals of the company (Arthur, 2001). Specific awards include "The MUG"

(Moves of Uncommon Greatness); "BRAVO" which recognizes employee achievements; and "The Spirit of Starbucks," honoring passion and action. Employees who receive public recognition for their achievements feel valued and appreciated and are less likely to leave.

Each generation may have different motivators. One author suggests that younger workers are motivated by challenges and interest (Strebler, 2006). On the other hand, she says that older workers were motivated more by involvement in the decision-making practices and opportunities to develop. Both suggest that employees want and need to be engaged to be motivated by their work.

Below are some ideas for recognizing or rewarding your employees at little or no cost. Small gestures mean a lot and will go a long way in providing a warm and inviting environment.

- Have a staff luncheon or celebration to recognize the end of a library project
- Mention individual's accomplishments in staff meetings or internal communications
- Provide learning or additional learning opportunities
- Celebrate employee anniversaries at staff meetings
- If appropriate, have an annual all-day, all-staff planning and problem-solving session away from the office; it helps to recognize the contributions of each staff person
- Have "treats" to eat when not expected
- Verbally, praise an employee every day
- Make it a point to smile and say hello to coworkers
- Have a staff suggestion box and reward employees who make good suggestions
- Tell staff what they did right—be specific
- Greet employees by name when you pass their office space or pass them in the library
- Make a photo collage about a successful project that show the people who worked on it, its stages of development, and its completion and presentation
- Give a person a candle with a note saying, "No one holds a candle to you"

Figure 4-6. Reward and Recognition Ideas

WHAT OTHER TACTICS CAN BE USED TO RETAIN GOOD EMPLOYEES?

In today's whirlwind environment, you will never be able to keep all of your good employees. However, attractive compensation and benefits, a supportive work environment, opportunities for career development and advancement, and flexibility to balance work/life demands all help (Messmer, 2006; Meisinger, 2006).

Flexible work hours and time off to pursue a goal such as having a baby or taking classes at a local university are important perks to today's employees (Spinelli, 2006). In the *2005 Emerging Workforce Study*, 60 percent of workers rated time and flexibility as important in retention (Anonymous, 2006). Other organizations have permitted employees to volunteer for their favorite charity during company time (Abbasi and Hollman, 2000).

Some organizations have added "a fun day" to the organization schedule. This might be as simple as a catered theme lunch like Mexican food for Cinco de Mayo or something as silly as a Crazy Hat Day. This type of excursion from the routine adds value for the employee, making the organization a fun place to work.

As you work with your employees, you will learn what stimulates or motivates them. Most employees simply want to be valued and recognized for their contributions to the library and its goals. There will always be some disgruntled or unhappy employees. It is best to focus on the positive side and continue acknowledging individuals for what they have done well. It is not always about money, although salary and other benefits play a role in the satisfaction and retention of employees. We will cover the aspects of compensation and benefit packages in the next chapter.

REFERENCES

Abbasi, Sami M. and Kenneth W. Hollman. 2000. "Turnover: The Real Bottom Line." *Public Personnel Management* 29, no. 3: 333–343.

ACRL Professional Development Committee. 2000. "ACRL Statement on Professional Development." *C&RL News* 61, no. 10: 933.

Anonymous. 2006. "Employers Work to Retain Staff, Despite Rise in Job Seeking." *HR Focus* 83, no. 1: 8.

Arthur, Diane. 2001. *The Employee Recruitment and Retention Handbook*. New York: AMACOM.

Avsec, Robert. 2006. "Grow Your Own Leaders." *Fire Chief* 50, no. 8: 38–41.

Ballard, Angela and Laura Blessing. 2006. "Organizational Socialization Through Employee Orientations at North Carolina." *College & Research Libraries* 67, no. 3: 240–248.

Berta, Dina. 2006. "Leadership Development Bolsters Employee Retention." *Nation's Restaurant News* 40, no. 37: 18.

Bisoux, Tricia. 2005. "What Makes Leaders Great?" *BizEd* 4, no. 6: 40–45.

Buchanan, Robert A. 2005. "Library Assistant Training: Perceptions, Incentives, and Barriers." *Journal of Academic Librarianship* 31, no. 5: 421–431.

Champlin, Connie, Carole Gall, and David W. Lewis. 2004. "The Indianapolis Foundation Library Partners." *Indiana Libraries* 23, no. 1: 11–15.

De Bruijn, Erik and Margaret Friesen. 1996. "Investing in Human Resources: Staff Training and Development at the University of British Columbia Library." *Library Administration and Organization* 14: 63–94.

Deeprose, Donna. 2007. *How to Recognize and Reward Employees*, 2nd Ed. New York: AMACOM.

Gjelten, Dan and Teresa Fishel. 2006. "Developing Leaders and Transforming Libraries: Leader Institutes for Librarians." *C&RL News* 67, no. 7: 409–412.

Golian, Linda M. and Michael W. Galbraith. 1996. "Effective Monitoring Programs for Professional Library Development." *Advances in Library Administration and Organization* 14: 95–124.

Hackett, R. D. and R. M. Guion. 1985. "A Re-Evaluation of the Absenteeism-Job Satisfaction Relationship." *Organizational Behavior and Human Decision Processes* 35: 340–381.

Hicks, Sheila, Mary Peters, and Marilyn Smith. 2006. "Orientation Redesign." *T&D* 60, no. 7: 43–45.

Holt, Glen E. 1999. "Training, a Library Imperative." *Journal of Library Administration* 29, no. 1: 79–93.

Kaplowitz, J. 1992. "Mentoring library school students: A survey of participants in the UCLA/GSLIS Mentor Program." *Special Libraries* 83 no. 4: 219–233.

Kohler, S. S. and J. E. Mathieu. 1993. "An Examination of the Relationship between Affective Reactions, Work Perceptions, Individual Resource Characteristics, and Multiple Absence Criteria." *Journal of Organizational Behavior* 14: 515–530.

Kovach, K. A. 1995. "Employee Motivation: Addressing a Crucial Factor in Your Organization's Performance." *Employment Relations Today* 22: 93–107.

Lloyd, Joan. 2006. "Just Whose Job Is It to Motivate Employees?" *The Receivables Report* 21, no. 8: 9–11.

Locke, E. A. 1976. "The Nature and Causes of Job Satisfaction," in M.D. Dunnette (ed.), *Handbook of Industrial and Organizational Psychology*. Chicago: Rand McNally, 1297–1349.

Marks, Jim. 2001. "Neglect Development of Your Staff at Your Own Risk." *National Underwriter/Life & Health Financial Services* 105, no. 19: 36–38.

Mason, Florence M. and Louella V. Wetherbee. 2004. "Learning to Lead: An Analysis of Current Training Programs for Library Leadership." *Library Trends* 55, no. 1: 187–217.

Meisinger, Susan. 2006. "Workforce Retention: A Growing Concern." *HRMagazine* 51, no. 4: 12.

Messmer, Max. 2006. "Four Keys to Improved Staff Retention." *Strategic Finance* 88, no. 4: 13–14.

Miller, Marcus. 2006. "Developing an Effective Mentoring Program." *CMA Management* 80, no. 1: 14–15.

Monroe, John S. 2005. "5 Keys to Better Leadership." *Federal Computer Week* 19, no. 40: 24–30.

Oberg, Larry R. 1992. "The Emergence of the Paraprofessional in Academic Libraries: Perceptions and Realities." *College & Research Libraries* 53: 99–112.

Outlaw, Wayne. 1998. *Smart Staffing: How to Hire, Reward, and Keep Top Employees for Your Growing Company*. Chicago: Upstart Publishing.

Ragsdale, Mary Alice and John Mueller. 2005. "Plan, Do Study, Act Model to Improve an Orientation Program." *Journal of Nursing Care Quality* 20, no. 3: 268–272.

Sigel, Randy. 1992. "Seven Steps to Keep Top Performers." *Public Relations Journal* 48, no. 2: 12.

Smith, Shawn and Mazin, Rebecca. 2004. *The HR Answer Book*. New York: AMACOM.

Spector, Paul. E. 1997. *Job Satisfaction: Application, Assessment, Causes and Consequences*. Thousand Oaks, CA: Sage Publications.

Spinelli, Lisa. 2006. "Accentuate the Positive." *Accounting Technology* 20 (Fall Supplement): 6.

Stanley, Mary J. 2001. "Taking Time for the Organization: How IUPUI University Library Is Building Teams." *C&RL News* 62, no. 9: 900–908.

Strebler, Marie. 2006. "Why Motivation Holds the Key to an Engaged Age-Diverse Workforce." *People Management* 12, no. 23: 48.

Tonidandel, Scott, Derek R. Avery, and McKensy G. Phillips. 2007. "Maximizing Returns on Mentoring: Factors Affecting Subsequent Protégé Performance." *Journal of Organizational Behavior* 28: 89–110.

Weingart, Sandra J., Carol Kochran, and Anne Hedrich. 1998. "Effective Orientation for New Employees." *Library Administration & Management* 12, no. 3: 156–158.

Wilson, Jennifer. 2006. "Motivating Your Team by Putting 'The Six' into Action." *Accounting Today* 20, no. 21: 22–28.

5 COMPENSATION AND BENEFITS

Compensation and benefits can be the most complicated aspects of human resources but are perhaps the most dynamic. The benefits package can play an important role in the recruitment process. In this chapter, various aspects of benefits packaging to meet the individual needs of employees will be discussed. We will also discuss the role of unions and collective bargaining, types of salary systems, and other compensation issues.

WHAT IS COMPENSATION?

For the purposes of this book, compensation refers to money and money-related extras. In addition to base pay, compensation could include signing bonuses, merit increases, variable pay, and long-term compensation. Base pay is the foundation for total compensation because it establishes the standard of living. *Benefits* refer to just about everything else, including healthcare, pension plans, and other perks—tuition reimbursement, alternate work schedules, and so on. The subject of compensation could fill an entire book. In this chapter, we will focus on basic information on compensation and how it affects the organization's budget and planning. For a complete coverage of library compensation, refer to David A. Baldwin's *Librarian Compensation Handbook: A Guide for Administrators, Librarians, and Staff*.

Compensation policies and practices affect all library employees. Employee compensation remains a major cost in all libraries and it is not unusual that salaries and benefits demand the greatest portion of a library's budget. Compensation and benefits are also key issues in recruitment and retention.

HOW DOES ONE ESTABLISH A SALARY OR COMPENSATION SYSTEM?

The salary system is usually based on a classification scheme with a range for each category of employee. Criteria such as education, experience, and skill base are used to establish where each employee would fit within a range. One basic system is to use the categories Senior Professional/Academic, Other Professional/Academic, Paraprofessional, Other Crafts, Office/Administrative/Secretarial and Unskilled (Dansker and Pomerantz, 1989).

This system is somewhat dated. In today's world, one could use a classification set up on a point system structure as indicated in *The Library Compensation Handbook* by David A. Baldwin (2003). Baldwin describes a point system using a set of factors that are present in varying degrees in most jobs. In the sample he presents, the basic evaluation plan has four points: knowledge, initiative, complexity, and supervision. For example:

Knowledge

Level 1 = Elementary knowledge: simple arithmetic, reading and punctuation	*—10 points*
Level 2 = English grammar, typing laboratory and clerical procedures, departmental systems	*—20 points*
Level 3 = Library-wide systems, applied technologies	*—30 points*
Level 4 = Non-professional skills	*—40 points*
Level 5 = Professional skills	*—50 points*
Level 6 = Advanced professional skills	*—60 points*

A value system would be set for each of the four factors and then positions would be compensated based on the point values for the position. Each position would have a basic level for each point factor. The position distribution might look similar to this:

Circulation Aide: Counter worker charges and discharges books

Knowledge	Level 3	30 points
Initiative	Level 1	20 points
Complexity	Level 1	10 points
Supervision		0 points
Total		60 points

Cataloger: Original cataloguing without revision

Knowledge	Level 5	50 points
Initiative	Level 3	30 points
Complexity	Level 2	20 points
Supervision	Level 1	10 points
Total		110 points

Branch Library Director: Library has 14 staff

Knowledge	Level 6	60 points
Initiative	Level 6	60 points
Complexity	Level 5	30 points
Supervision	Level 3	30 points
Total		200 points

Once point values have been determined for all library titles, one can construct a salary structure. Baldwin cautions the use of this evaluation system as he feels that people are marketable but positions do not usually carry that same weight. Using this system can also be problematic if individuals are aware of the point system set up. Individuals then try to change positions' activities in order to achieve the highest value for their position.

Other systems might use a more simplistic form of classification such as:

- Senior librarian—Librarians with a master's degree and five or more years of library experience.

- Beginning librarian—Librarians with a master's degree and no library experience (at the professional level). The beginning librarian may have had some experience while going through school or working as a nonprofessional.

- Support staff—All employees working in a non-MLS position. Examples could include assistants, copy catalogers, associates, and clerks.
  - Assistant—Any position requiring at least 1–2 years of previous library experience and some college education.
  - Technician—Any position requiring at least an Associate's degree or 2 or more years of previous library and/or computer experience. May include more sophisticated or responsible positions.
  - Clerk/Aide—Entry level position requiring a high school diploma and/or previous library experience. Examples might include circulation desk clerks or processing clerks, etc.
  - Other—High level position of responsibility or expertise requiring a bachelor's or specialized degree and/or specified relevant experience. Examples might include video or audiovisual specialists, computer specialists, etc.

In academic libraries, the librarian categories are generally broken out by Librarian (full rank), Associate Librarian, Assistant Librarian, and Affiliate Librarian. The Affiliate Librarian would be a librarian just completing the master's degree with no professional library experience.

Establishing a range system groups jobs of similar values into grades with each range having a pay scale dependent upon the job tasks and responsibilities. You should determine a minimum, midpoint, and maximum for each grade. The minimum and maximum are usually about 15–20 percent lower/higher than the midpoint (Smith and Mazin, 2004). People with little or no experience usually start at the minimum of the pay range. Determining a range in each classification allows the organization flexibility in recognizing differences in individual performance and job expectations.

In smaller libraries, the director may be the one who establishes the ranges for each position. The library board serves as the personnel committee and the director recommends the salary schedule to them annually. In many cases, the board agrees on a cost of living increase across the board. Typically, the director would recommend adjustment to the ranges every several years. This type of arrangement does not recognize employees who go above and beyond and also awards an increase to some who may not deserve it.

The human resources administration of a larger organization may already have the clerical and technical positions set up under a classification scheme, but you will probably have the option of setting compensation ranges for professional librarians.

Even if you already have a system in place, it is worth reviewing on a regular basis to determine if you are competitive with the job market and compliant with any changes in the wage rules. Your salary structure will depend on your budget, federal and state wage laws, and your location. A good rule of thumb is to check the ALA salary statistics, which are updated frequently, to see what salaries libraries nationwide are offering (www.ala.org).

DO I NEED JOB DESCRIPTIONS FOR ALL POSITIONS IN ORDER TO ESTABLISH COMPENSATION?

While job descriptions are not mandatory in establishing your salary system, they are helpful. Do not put them aside once they are written. They should be reviewed annually to ensure that they are relevant to what the employee is doing and the organization's goals.

HOW DOES LIBRARY COMPENSATION COMPARE TO OTHER PROFESSIONS?

The literature indicates that libraries are far behind in addressing the low pay status of library employees. One article indicated that librarians are underpaid relative to the educational requirements needed for their positions and the complexity of the work that they do (Long, 2004). According to this author, the Department of Labor has classified the work of librarians as comparable to the work of systems analysts, but the salary for a beginning systems analyst is $61,000, while a beginning librarian is usually paid around $34,000. Likewise, other library employees tend to be paid lower in comparison to their nonlibrary counterparts. The issue of increasing salaries for librarians and other library employees was a major agenda item for the ALA Midwinter Meeting in 2003. The ALA established the Better Salaries and Pay Equity Task Force to address this issue. They also published a toolkit on this area in 2003 (Singer and Goodrich, 2006). In the most recent salary survey from ALA with information from more than 1,000 public and academic libraries, there was an increase of about 4.6 percent from 2005 to 2006 ("Survey Reports Increased Salaries," 2007). Leslie Burger, director of the Princeton Public Library and a member of the ALA's Task Force on Better Salaries and Pay Equity, feels that "the bottom line is that you can't raise salaries if you don't raise library budgets" ("Pushing for Higher Library Salaries," 2003).

Sadly, librarians do not serve as good advocates for their own cause. The profession as a whole is often described as selfless and dedicated workers who work tirelessly in spite of low financial compensation. One librarian retired to save the library money and then came back and volunteered her services (Baugher and Freedman, 2004). Behavior such as this promulgates the stereotype of the librarian who will serve the patrons regardless of low compensation. This does not help the fight for better pay and does an injustice to our profession.

HOW CAN THE LIBRARY HUMAN RESOURCES PROFESSIONAL ADVOCATE FOR HIGHER SALARIES?

The issue of low pay in libraries is almost as old as the profession itself. Geography also influences salaries. According to one researcher, public libraries in the Southeast offer the lowest salaries (Farley, 2002). In addition, men in the library profession have earned more than women. Librarians as a group earn less than male-dominated professions.

The library human resources professional should make sure that the individuals who must face the library boards and make budget proposals are armed with the evidence and information they need to advocate for higher salaries for their staff. The ALA is the first place to check for the most recent salary surveys. The Bureau of Labor Statistics collects data for all professions and these figures will also provide evidence that the library staff needs higher salaries to match the market.

Encourage library employees to become more visible in the community they serve so that people understand what the library does, what librarians do, and what other individuals who work in libraries do. Many community libraries are at the bottom of the pile in terms of public support. We need to raise the value of the library and the community's willingness to fund library services. If the community is aware of the need for higher salaries, they can affect the board's decisions.

Often, the head of the library sees the need for a larger budget for additional resources and equipment but neglects the human factor. The HR professional should make sure that the staff and their salaries are included in budget requests. As library professionals, we want the best and the brightest in the profession, and so we must make sure that we have the means to pay individuals to do that kind of work.

HOW DO COLLECTIVE BARGAINING AND UNIONS TIE INTO COMPENSATION?

When people think of unions and unionization, they usually picture picket strikes and manufacturing, but some unions are linked with nonprofit organizations. Usually poor employee-management relations provoke employees to seek the aid of unions (Pynes, 1997). Literature related to unions and libraries indicates that reasons for joining unions was to collectively bargain in shaping goals and services for the staff. One writer stresses that if you look at the court decisions, the reality is that the unions are limited to negotiating about wages, hours, and other terms and conditions of work (Ballard, 1982). Cameron Johnson, a library union steward at Everett Public Library in Washington State, argues that the main benefit of unions is to empower the workforce by giving employees a voice in making work policies (McLean, 2005). Often, librarians are part of a larger union and make up a small part of the union's voice such as school librarians who are part of a teacher's union. In these cases, the librarians' issues may be lost in the shuffle of the teachers' issues (Banas and Heylman, 1990). The question of whether to unionize or not remains a puzzle that is not easily put together.

In a 2005 salary survey conducted by the ALA, public and academic libraries were asked, "Which of your library's employees are covered by a collective bargaining agreement?" (Office of Research Statistics, 2005). The survey indicated that in the responding libraries, 13 percent of the librarians, 8 percent of the other professional group, and 17 percent of the support staff were covered by such an agreement (Office of Research Statistics, 2005). The report goes on to indicate that in 1309 libraries out of 2040 libraries responding to the survey, none of the staff were covered by collective bargaining agreements. Only 113 libraries had collective bargaining agreements for all staff. In 146 of the responding libraries, all of the support staff and other professionals were covered. In 33 of the responding libraries, only the support staff were covered. There was only one instance where the support staff and other professionals were covered but the librarians were not covered.

However, these statistics do not indicate whether unions are a good way for librarians and other library staff to be heard. Let us examine situations in libraries where unions were involved in the collective bargaining process. The first scenario occurred in the late 1980s when unions had started to appear in libraries.

In 1989, the University of Cincinnati had two union contracts covering library workers. The American Association of University Professors (AAUP) represented the faculty and librarians. The other union, Service Employees International Union (SEIU), represented the library clericals. The clerical staff had been paid on average $5 to $6 per hour in wages and had a comprehensive health care package at no cost to UC employees. This health care plan was to be replaced with one that would cost the employees from $63 to $176 monthly and would be an HMO owned and operated by UC with its own medical center doctors. In addition, the staff would lose their annual 15 days of sick leave.

Ohio State mediators and a fact-finding team were called in to break an impasse. When the management and union efforts failed, 80–90 percent of the UC clericals staged a one-day mini-strike. A second mini-strike occurred and finally a new contract was reached guaranteeing a 5.5 percent wage increase, plus $200 lump sum; shift differentials; a choice of four health care plans; six months childcare leave (pre-FMLA); grievance procedures; tuition remission; language forbidding the public humiliation of employees by management; and the retention of the 15 sick days. This is a clear example of how collective bargaining and negotiation in libraries can work (Harger and Rosenzweig, 1990).

The story of UC's AAUP negotiation is not as dramatic and did not include a strike by the library professionals. However, wage gains of 5 percent and a "cafeteria style" health care plan requiring employee contributions were contracted. In addition, more language was achieved in the area of "faculty governance"—input into university decision-making processes by faculty and librarians (Harger and Rosenzweig, 1990).

More recently, workers at Providence Public Library (RI) voted 53–59 to unionize ("Providence Public Library Staff Votes...," 2005). This decision was reached following more than a year of staff layoffs, cuts in operating hours, and public dissatisfaction with the library board. The professional librarians voted to enter a joint union with nonprofessional staff rather than form their own union. It will be interesting to follow this library and see if the new union helps the library staff in gaining higher salaries and a voice in the library's operations.

There is no simple answer as to whether a union should exist in a library organization. Many libraries depend on professional associations to rally for their rights. The ALA's Allied Professional Association (ALA-APA) is a nonprofit organization established apart from ALA to promote the mutual professional interests of librarians and other library workers. APA advocates for improving salaries and status of library workers by supporting national comparable-worth and pay-equity initiatives. The APA is not union affiliated and cannot negotiate contracts, but it does share with unions a desire to improve the pay and status of workers. It also provides certification of individuals in specializations beyond the initial professional degree and other activities designed to improve salaries and status of librarians and other workers. For additional information, check www.ala-apa.org.

WHAT ARE EMPLOYEE BENEFITS?

Employee benefits are all benefits and services, other than wages, provided to employees by the employer, including legally required social insurance programs, health and life insurance coverage, retirement plans, payment for time not worked, and any other program the organization may offer to employees. It may also include tuition reimbursement or tuition assistance for library employees and/or spouse and dependents. While most libraries are non-profit, often receiving state or federal funding, and are included in the retirement packages offered by their funding sources, health and life insurance plans often remain under the jurisdiction of the library. Directors or library human resources professionals must search among the vendors for the most competitive packages and present their choices to the library board for review and approval.

You will need to establish a benefits policy or philosophy (see Figure 5-1). What level of benefits can the organization afford for its employees? Will you require employees to pay for all or a portion of the benefit? How do your benefits stack up against the companies you

Employee Benefit Research Institute (EBRI)—Nonprofit committed to effective and responsible employee benefit plans. www.ebri.org

International Foundation of Employee Benefit Plans (IFEBP)—Offers Employee Benefits Infosource, a comprehensive online database of benefits information. 222.ifebp.org

National Committee for Quality Assurance (NCQA)—An independent nonprofit dedicated to evaluating the quality of managed care plans. www.ncqa.org

Figure 5-1. Benefits Resources

compete with for your employees? What kind of benefits are your employees most interested in? These are just a few questions that you probably want to answer before you decided on a benefit package for your organization.

ARE THERE MINIMUM BENEFITS AN ORGANIZATION MUST PROVIDE?

You are required by federal law to provide Social Security contributions, unemployment insurance, and workers compensation coverage. In some states, you may also be required to provide short-term disability or other benefits (Smith and Mazin, 2004). Social Security provides retirement, disability, death, survivor, and Medicare benefits for those over 65. An amendment in 1983 included a special section that provided for nonprofit employees 55 years and older to be considered fully insured for benefits after acquiring at least 20 quarters of coverage (Pynes, 1997). Another amendment in 1986 required all individuals hired by a state or local government to be covered by the Medicare segment of the program and subject to employer and employee payroll taxes.

All nongovernment employers are required to contribute a designated percentage of each employee's pay toward Social Security, up to a maximum amount determined by the federal government. An organization is obligated to make Social Security payments whether an employee is full- or part-time, temporary, or newly hired.

Unemployment insurance was established by the federal government to provide individuals who are out of work through no fault of their own with temporary cash assistance while they actively look for a new position. Each state administers its own program under the federal guidelines. The state determines its own waiting period for eligibility, level of benefits provided, and the length of time that benefits are paid. Employers are required to contribute a percentage of their payroll toward federal taxes under the Federal Unemployment Tax Act (FUTA) and toward state unemployment taxes. The contribution rate is based on the claims experience or the historical record of unemployment benefits charged (Pynes, 1997. Employee benefits are usually based on a percentage of the employee's previous earnings up to a state maximum. Employees who are terminated or laid off for a reason other than misconduct are typically entitled to unemployment benefits if they have worked for a minimum period established by the state. Workers who have been temporarily laid off or had a number of work hours reduced may also be eligible. Generally, employees who voluntarily resign cannot collect benefits. Be sure to check your state's guidelines related to unemployment insurance practices. Respond in a timely manner when contacted by the local unemployment office as you can incur fines for missed deadlines.

WHY SHOULD I WORRY ABOUT WORKERS COMPENSATION SINCE WE RARELY HAVE ANY ACCIDENTS?

Workers compensation is a state-governed benefit program that requires employers to pay medical bills and partial lost wages that result from work-related injuries and illnesses. There are rising medical costs and claims connected with stress-related illnesses, repetitive motion injuries from keyboard typing, and back problems (ergonomic stress from improper workstations). Library employees are among the 1.8 million workers in the US Bureau of Labor Statistics that typically suffer musculoskeletal disorders (repetitive stress injuries) (Turner, 2004). This was 26.2 percent of all workplace injuries in 2000 (Turner, 2004).

It is best to determine hazards in your work environment before injuries happen. Workers compensation carriers or state workers compensation offices can help determine hazards and offer training to reduce the risks. Turner suggests that in addition to identifying potential hazards, one should carefully review the work space, equipment, or furniture of each staff member, and reconfigure if necessary. As Director of the Libraries for the Santa Cruz City-County Library System, she involved all staff members in the process and staff suggested ways to make the environment safer. The library system has incorporated safe ergonomic practices and each work site has a person in charge of leading stretch exercises to alleviate stress-induced injuries. Three minutes of stretching is recommended for every two hours of work.

Programs and costs of administration vary from state to state, but all programs include the following:

- Employees receive wage loss, medical, and death benefits for accidental injury.
- Fault is not an issue; if the employee was somewhat or entirely at fault, the employee still has the right to receive workers' compensation benefits.

- In exchange for the assurance of benefits, the employee and the employee's dependent family members give up the right to sue the employer for damages for any injury covered by a workers' compensation law.
- The responsibility for administering the system usually resides with a state board or commission.
- Employers are generally required to insure their workers' compensation liability through private insurance, state insurance funds, or self insurance.

The Office of Workers' Compensation Programs (www.dol.gov/esa/owcp_org.htm) administers four major disability compensation programs which provide wage replacement benefits, medical treatment, vocational rehabilitation and other benefits to certain workers or their dependents who experience work-related injury or occupational disease. The Office is regulated under the US Department of Labor.

The Workers' Compensation Service Center (www.workerscompensation.com) Web site provides workers compensation news and information for employees, employers, insurers, and medical providers. The research center can aid in locating an insurance provider, getting information on your state's program, and finding professional help relating to workplace injuries and disabilities.

SHOULD WE OFFER LIFE INSURANCE?

Life insurance and disability insurance are economic security benefits that provide payments to employees and/or their families in the event that the employee dies or otherwise becomes unable to work. Life insurance is fairly inexpensive but offers employees and their families a great deal of security. If an employee dies, the group policy pays a flat dollar amount to the designated beneficiary. The amount of the payment can be tied to the employee's position, annual salary, or a multiple of the annual salary with a cap of maximum payout. Premiums are calculated based on the total dollar amount of coverage, the ages of your individual participants, or a rate determined from a census of the entire group. Most group plans require minimal or no prescreening to identify high risk medical conditions. If the plan chosen for your organization has prescreening requirements or limitations on benefit payouts, be sure to communicate this to your employees.

WHAT IF EMPLOYEES WANT ADDITIONAL LIFE INSURANCE?

Offering supplemental or optional life insurance allows employees a convenient way to purchase additional coverage at their own expense. Coverage is usually available in multiples of the employee's salary up to a maximum amount. Employees may also be able to purchase limited life insurance coverage for a spouse or child. Individuals wishing to purchase supplemental insurance coverage may be required to submit medical evidence of insurability, especially for the higher levels of coverage.

WHAT ARE THE DIFFERENT CHOICES IN DISABILITY PLANS?

There are two basic types of disability plans, short-term disability (STD) and long-term disability (LTD). These insurance programs pay covered employees a percentage of their earnings when they are unable to work because of an illness or injury.

Short-term disability plans pay a percentage of the employee's weekly earnings for a fixed period of up to 12 months, often limited to six months. Employees are usually required to satisfy a short waiting period before payments begin. The usual payment for these plans is 50 to 67 percent of an employee's earnings. Some states require a minimum STD benefit level. The policy should clearly define "disability," meet state requirements, and cover any disability that occurs as a result of pregnancy in the same way as other disabilities.

Long-term disability coverage is an extended coverage plan for more extreme situations. If an employee has STD coverage, the LTD coverage will not go into effect until the STD insurance has run out. If there is no STD, the waiting period before the LTD takes effect can range from three to 12 months. Benefits on average are set about 60 percent of the employee's base salary, with a plan maximum, either for a specified number of months or until the employee turns age 65 or 70. The terms and definitions for disability for a LTD plan are generally more rigid than the STD plan and may limit benefits to individuals who are unable to perform any type of work at all.

Rates for both types of plans are based on the claims experience of the organization. Many organizations share the plan cost by requiring an employee contribution. Employers can also help control costs by requiring employees to use accrued sick and vacation time before receiving disability benefits. Some organizations offer voluntary STD and LTD plans, through which the employee has the opportunity to purchase individual policies at group rates and through payroll deductions.

WHAT KINDS OF HEALTH INSURANCE PLANS ARE THERE TO CHOOSE FROM?

Health care coverage will probably be your largest employee benefit expenditure, costing on average from 10–15 percent of payroll (Smith and Mazin, 2004). However, health insurance plans can be a strong factor in recruitment and retention. Costs for health insurance will vary depending on the number of covered employees, whether they have single or family coverage, and the level of benefits chosen. Including a prescription plan, vision plan, and dental plan will all add to the costs. Often, employers offer a variety of plans so their employees can choose the right plan for them.

In today's world, employees pay a bigger portion of the health care premium and the employer subsidizes the cost, which allows for group rates. Some of the more popular plans are:

Indemnity Plans: Traditional plans. These plans have changed over the years. Employees send claims directly to the insurance companies. Insurers often limit reimbursements to a percentage of "usual and customary rates" to discourage high-fee providers.

Health Maintenance Organizations (HMOs): These plans offer a pre-determined set of benefits for a fixed cost to the employer. They usually emphasize preventive care. Generally there are minimal or no co-payments or deductibles. The HMO model is designed to cover a wide range of care and minimize out-of-pocket expenses by requiring participants to use specified providers for all medical services. Under most HMO systems, patients need a referral from the primary care physician before seeing a specialist, hospital stays must be pre-approved and limited to network hospitals, and prescriptions must be filled at designated pharmacies.

Managed Care: Each employee is assigned to a primary care physician who determines whether or not a specialist is needed. The specialist must be one of the providers in the plan. The employer contracts with selected providers for a comprehensive set of services. Often, going outside these providers will result in the individual paying the full cost of the services.

Preferred Provider Organizations (PPOs): PPOs are groups of hospitals and health care providers who contract with employers to provide health care at a discounted price. This model combines the HMO model with other features to provide more options for employers and employees. Participants can either seek care from doctors in the PPO network or choose their own out-of-network care providers. The costs for an out-of-network service will invoke much higher co-payments.

Point of Service Plans (POS): Employees who select POS plans, a variant of the PPO plan, want an unlimited choice of providers and hospitals. The employee is usually responsible for a deductible and a co-payment. POS plans are generally the most expensive health care plans.

Health Savings Account (HSA): The most recent trend in health care options is health savings accounts. In the HSA plan, a portion of the money goes to pay for a high-deductible plan and the remaining funds go into a personal health savings account. The funds are put into the account before taxation and stay there until used by the individual for health care needs. One can withdraw money tax-free at any time to pay for eligible out-of-pocket medical expenses. Any funds in the HSA not used for medical expenses during the year roll over into the next year. While account holders cannot pay over the amount of their deductible in one calendar year, there is no limit on the amount of funds they can accumulate (Kieke, 2006). If someone loses his or her job or retires early, the account and the money follow the employee. In 2006, a high-deductible policy is one that has a deductible of at least $2,100 for a family or $1,050 for an individual (Anderson, 2006). After age 65, one can use the money for any purpose without paying a penalty, although income taxes are owed on withdrawals for non-medical purposes.

In a 2006 health benefits study done by the Henry J. Kaiser Family Foundation, the average annual cost for all forms of coverage is $4,242 per single employee and $11,480 for a family of four (Bell, 2006). Families were paying 27 percent of the premiums as compared to 26 percent in 2005. Single workers were paying 16 percent of the premium, about the same as in 2005.

Which plans should employers offer? That will depend on the size of the organization, what the organization is willing to pay towards the premiums, and what the employees want in a health care package. Do your homework and make sure that you consider all possible options.

HOW CAN A SMALL LIBRARY AFFORD TO PROVIDE HEALTH INSURANCE?

A group health insurance plan can help an organization hire and retain the best workers. There are also special tax incentives for business that provide health insurance.

Smaller libraries often have a difficult time finding a carrier interested in covering a small group of employees. Some smaller libraries have united to procure a plan under a state-wide library association, which helps reduce the premium costs. Through this type of program, the library pays the cost of the single benefit premium of each employee participating. Employees may then choose to add family members at their own cost according to the parameters of the plan. The plan usually applies to employees working an average of 40 or more hours per week. The libraries must put their trust in negotiation by the statewide representative, but it does provide for a more reasonable plan for smaller libraries. The plans are reevaluated each year and revised to accommodate the best plan and coverage. This is probably one of the best solutions for smaller libraries if your statewide library association offers such a program.

Various programs have surfaced to combat the rising costs of health care insurance, which is especially burdensome for small organizations and businesses. One example is the HSA law, discussed above. A licensed health insurance agency, eHealth Insurance, will find, compare, and buy individual health insurance, family health insurance, small business health insurance, self-employed health insurance, and health savings accounts. By providing your zip code and some basic information, you can receive free quotes, compare plans side by side, and apply for coverage online. For further information, check www.ehealth insurance.com.

SHOULD WE OFFER DENTAL AND VISION COVERAGE?

Dental rates have remained fairly stable and insurance is usually available through most national insurance plans. Dental plans are traditionally focused on preventive care and have annual per-person limited reimbursements. Coverage for orthodontics is typically limited to employees or children and mandates the use of in-network providers to control the costs. Many employers position the dental plan as a benefit separate from the medical plan, allowing employees to choose whether they want coverage.

Vision care is offered through HMOs or PPOs, but is usually an optional benefit with the employees paying all or part of the costs. Many national retail eye care chains promote employer discount plans, which allow employers to offer discounts without providing an actual vision care plan.

IS THE ORGANIZATION RESPONSIBLE FOR INSURING EMPLOYEES AFTER THEY LEAVE?

If an organization has 20 or more employees, they are covered under the terms of the Consolidated Omnibus Budget Reconciliation Act of 1986 (COBRA). COBRA requires employees to offer laid-off, terminated employees, or retirees the opportunity to continue their health insurance coverage. This allows former employees, spouses, and dependents to purchase insurance coverage for a limited time after leaving the organization. It also applies to divorced, separated, or widowed spouses. New regulations determined that the termination of employment, death, divorce, or other qualifying event is the measuring date from which the COBRA date is determined ("When Does COBRA Coverage Begin...," 1999).

HOW DO THE NEW MEDICAL PRIVACY LAWS (HIPAA) AFFECT EMPLOYERS?

The year 1996 marked the implementation of the Health Insurance Portability and Accountability Act (HIPAA) giving patients broad protections over the privacy of their medical records. Under this Act, patients must give specific authorization before health plans, doctors, pharmacies, or other parties can release protected health information in most non-routine circumstances. These laws are very complex and relatively new, so the full measure of the law on employers is not clear. Make sure that you have safeguards for keeping employee health information private. Keep medical records confidential and separate from other employment records and limit access to the data to only those employees with a need to know.

WHAT TYPES OF RETIREMENT PLANS CAN WE PROVIDE?

There are basically two types of employer-sponsored retirement plans: defined benefit and defined contribution plans. Defined benefit plans are traditional pension plans. Employers make 100 percent of the contributions toward these plans and, upon retirement, employees receive a specific monthly benefit. The benefit may be a flat amount or it may be based on a formula including age, earnings, and years of service. The plan is funded through employer contributions and investment of plan assets. Defined benefit plans are common in the public sector and in large companies, especially those with long-standing union contracts (Smith and Mazin, 2004).

Defined contribution plans provide an individual account for each participant, and the value of the account is based largely on the amount contributed by the individual. Depending on the market, there will also be gains or losses. The 401(k) plan is the most well known of these types of plans. Similar to the 401(k) plan is the 403(b) plan. This plan is a defined-contribution retirement plan available only to employees of private organizations that are tax-exempt under IRC 501(c)(3) or educational organizations of a state, political subdivisions of a state, or an agency or instrumentality of a state, which would include most libraries.

HOW DO YOU SET UP A 403(B) OR 401(K) PLAN?

Employees can put an elective amount into a retirement savings account on a pretax basis, up to a maximum (usually about 15 percent of their annual earnings) set by the IRS each year. Employees who are age 50 or older may contribute at a higher level. Not all plans require employers to contribute, but most provide that employers either match or contribute a percentage of the employee contribution. All of these contributions are given to a third-party administrator who invests the funds as the employee directs. If employees withdraw their money before they reach the age of 59.5, they have to pay taxes on it, plus a 10 percent fine to the IRS. However, individuals can sometimes take loans against their accounts or can take a hardship withdrawal under specific situations defined by the IRS.

Since employees have the ability to make decisions about and watch their investments in these type of programs, they are very popular. When employees change jobs, they can roll over their funds to a new 401(k) or other qualified retirement plan. A qualified plan is one that meets all of the IRS requirements for favorable tax status. Employers also save money because they fund contributions with pretax dollars.

Vesting is automatic in most 403(b) plans while vesting periods of up to three years are more common in 401(k) plans (TIAA-CREF, 2007). Overall contribution limits are calculated differently. 403(b) funds accumulated to 1987 are not subject to mandatory federal minimum distribution rules. An individual can defer taking a distribution on this amount until age 75.

Your third-party administrator can be an insurance carrier, an investment company, or another administrator that meets the qualifications. These third-party administrators will have administrative service fees and the options of investment may differ. Be sure that you or your accountant or fiscal officer checks the varying services and fees to make sure that you are running a nondiscriminatory plan for your employees.

If you are an organization with 100 or fewer employees who each earned at least $5,000 in the previous year, you are eligible to adopt a Savings Incentive Match Plan for Employees of Small Businesses (SIMPLE). A SIMPLE plan allows both the employer and the employees to make pretax contributions under rules that are much less complicated than those for traditional 401(k) plans. Information about this type of retirement plan and other retirement plan options can be found at "Choosing a Retirement Plan: Retirement Plan Options" at www.irs.gove/retirement/article/O,id=109169,00html. Here you will find options for IRAs (Individual Retirement Accounts) and other types of plans.

WHAT HAPPENS WHEN EMPLOYEES LEAVE?

The answer to this will, of course, depend on the employee's reason for leaving. Any money that an employee contributes into a plan is always 100 percent fully vested (Smith and Mazin, 2004). Employers may allow only a specific percentage of employer contributions to vest each year so that the employee must work for the organization a certain number of years to be fully vested in the employer portion of the retirement account. These are under strict guidelines. In these cases, an employee who leaves the company will be entitled to take away the full employee contribution and the vested percentage of the employer contribution.

Organizations must complete a Form 5500 for each of their benefit plans at the end of each plan year. Retirement plans fall under the Employment Retirement Income Security Act (ERISA), which sets out detailed reporting and compliance rules to ensure benefit plans are properly administered.

WHAT OTHER BENEFITS ARE INCLUDED IN BENEFIT PACKAGES?

Often taken for granted, but included in benefit packages are days off with pay, including holidays, vacation days, and sick days.

Holidays: Public employers are required to give employees certain holidays off but private employers can devise their own holiday schedule. Some organizations opt for "floating" holidays that workers may use as desired. Floating holidays provide an easy way to accommodate diverse religious or cultural observances. In devising your holiday schedule, consider:

- Will you pay premiums to employees who work on designated holidays?
- What alternative day will you give employees when the holiday falls on a nonworking day?
- Are new hires eligible immediately for paid holidays or is there going to be a waiting period?
- Should part-time employees get full or prorated holiday benefits?

Vacation Days: Employers generally encourage or even require employees to take vacation time. Employees usually return from this time rested and recharged and ready to renew task responsibilities. Two key factors in determining a vacation policy are how much paid vacation time employees receive and how vacation days are earned.

If you decide that employees will earn 12 days a year, you might decide that workers will earn one day per month. Some organizations set a certain period of time that the employee must work before they can earn or use their vacation time. Organizations are permitted to use other restrictions on employee vacation time, such as requiring advance notice before taking time, limiting vacation time to be used for vacation only (and not in place of "sick" time), and implementing "blackout" dates during which, because of organizational demands, employees cannot take vacation time. You may also limit the number of unused or carryover days of vacation to the next year. Most problems occur when individuals leave and want to be paid for unused vacation time. Be very explicit in your policy on how these situations are handled.

According to a survey conducted by Harris Interactive and Ipsos Reid, US employees will leave an average of four vacation days unused in 2006, an increase of about one day compared to vacation days unused in 2005 (Expedia, 2006). The US continues to lag behind other Western countries in use of vacation time. Americans also receive the fewest vacation days per year (14 on average). Great Britain averages 24 vacation days per year and France is on top with 39 vacation days per year. To make matters worse, 38 percent of workers indicate that they put in extra hours and 19 percent say they have canceled or postponed vacations because of work demands (Expedia, 2006).

Another study indicated that 33 percent of US employees typically take work with them on vacation and 35 percent feel they need to maintain connection with the office either by cell phone or e-mail while on vacation (SHRM, 2006). Employers need to encourage employees to use their vacation time as it results in a more relaxed, productive worker in the long run.

Sick Days: Sick day amounts and considerations are similar to vacation time. Employers determine eligibility, accrual rate, and whether they can be carried over. Some employers allow employees to take sick time in partial-day increments to cover doctor's appointments and medical tests. Many employers are reluctant to give employees sick days because they believe that they will take the time off whether or not they are sick.

A growing number of organizations are moving away from separating sick days, vacation days, personal time, and floating holiday time and are instead using the concept of "paid time off." Under the PTO concept, the employee receives a specified number of paid days or hours to use as they wish as long as they provide sufficient notice for planned absences. PTO can discourage absenteeism. This system creates equity between those employees who traditionally use all of their sick time and those who rarely use it. It also simplifies recordkeeping and eliminates the need to track reasons for absences. Since PTO does not distinguish between vacation time and other types of leave, you may be required to pay employees for earned, unused PTO at the time of termination.

Flextime or Flexible Working Schedules: Another popular benefit for employees is the ability to work a flexible or alternate working schedule. Flextime allows for variance in the start and end times of workdays while still working a standard number of hours within a given workweek. This helps employees deal with family issues, commuting, and educational activities.

The downside of flexible scheduling is arranging team meetings or coordinating work assignments. In addition, if it is not made available to all employees, those not participating may be disgruntled. Organizations may grant flextime benefits selectively as long as discrimination does not occur and your criteria are reasonable in relation to your business.

Telecommuting: Increasingly popular, telecommuting allows employees to work from a location other than the office, usually their homes. Telecommuting is usually allowed only one or two days per week. This is not appropriate for all positions or all employees. Telecommuting works best for productive, skilled individuals who can work independently and meet deadlines without constant direction. Other things to consider are the equipment needed for telecommuters to do their jobs and whether the employer will provide it. Flexible scheduling arrangements require an element of trust. Expectations and timekeeping arrangements must be set at the onset and put into writing. This is a privilege and not a right of the employee. You should also indicate that the arrangement will be rescinded if they are found to be abusing the system.

Education Programs: A final employee benefit is the provision of tuition reimbursement. Some higher educational institutions offer tuition reimbursement for employees, their spouses, and their dependent children if they are enrolled in the institution's educational program. Other organizations might offer a training allowance or professional development funding for training, workshops, or attending professional conferences.

All of the benefits discussed here are part of the total compensation and benefit package for employees and need to be combined when determining the total package for each employee.

REFERENCES

Anderson, Thomas M. 2006. "Open Season for Health Savings." *Kiplinger's Personal Finance* 60, no. 10: 88–90.

Baldwin, David A. 2003. *Librarian Compensation Handbook: A Guide for Administrators, Librarians and Staff.* Westport, CT: Libraries Unlimited.

Ballard, Thomas H. 1982. "Public Library Unions—The Fantasy and the Reality." *American Libraries* 13, no. 8: 506–509.

Banas, Donald and Katherine Heylman. 1990. "The Right Stuff: Librarians at the Bargaining Table." *School Library Journal* 36, no. 1: 23–28.

Baugher, Phil and Maurice Freedman. 2004 "Should We Ever Work for Free?" *American Libraries* 35, no. 4: 81–84.

Bell, Allison. 2006 "Health Account Plans Pull Ahead of Indemnity Plans, Kaiser Reports." *National Underwriter* 110, no. 37: 7, 41.

Dansker, Benjamin and Pomerantz, Sherwin. 1989. "Systematic Salary Administration." *Personnel Administrator* 34, no. 3: 72–77.

"Expedia: US Workers to Skip 574 Million Vacation Days in '06." 2006. *Travel Weekly* 65, no. 22: 12.

Farley, Y.S. 2002. "Strategies for Improving Library Salaries." *American Libraries* 33, no. 1: 56–69.

Harger, Elaine and Mark Rosenzweig. 1990. "University of Cincinnati Tries Negotiation Two Ways." *Library Journal* 115, no. 5: 18.

"How Do 403(b) Plans Compare to 401(k)s, IRAs and Keoghs?" www.tiaa-cref.org/advisors/403b/403b_compare.html (accessed July 31, 2007).

Kieke, Reba L. 2006. "CIGNA Launches New Solution to Help Patients Pay for Health Care." *Managed Care Outlook* 19, no. 22: 1, 6–7.

"The Labor Union Movement in America." www.socialstudieshelp.com/ Eco_Unionization.htm (accessed February 5, 2007).

"Library Staff Covered by Collective Bargaining Agreements." 2006. *Library Worklife: HR E-News for Today's Leaders* 3, no. 6 www.ala.org/ala/ors/reports/suppl_q's_statistics.pdf (accessed February 5, 2007).

Long, Sarah. 2004. "Compensation Doesn't Add Up for Library Staff." *Library Mosaics* 15, no. 4: 18.

McLean, Carla. 2005. "The Not-So-Odd Couple: Libraries and Unions." *Aliki* 21, no. 2: 11–12.

Office of Research Statistics, American Library Association. 2005. www.ala.org/ala/ors/reports/suppl_q's_statistics.pdf (accessed February 5, 2007).

"Providence Public Library Staff Votes to Unionize." 2005. *American Libraries* 26, no. 9: 26.

"Pushing for Higher Library Salaries: Now or Never?" 2003. *American Libraries* 34, no.1: 55–57.

Pynes, Joan E. 1997. *Human Resources Management for Public and Nonprofit Organizations*. San Francisco: Jossey-Bass.

SHRM (Society for Human Resource Management). 2007. "By the Numbers: Surf, Sand and a Cell Phone." *Employee Benefit News* 21, no. 10: 66.

Singer, Paula and Jeanne Goodrich. 2006. "Retaining and Motivating High-Performing Employees." *Public Libraries* 45, no. 1: 58–63.

Smith, Shawn and Mazin, Rebecca. 2004. *The HR Answer Book*. New York: AMACOM (American Management Association).

"Survey Reports Increased Salaries." 2007. *American Libraries* 38, no. 1: 10.

Teachers Insurance and Annuity Association—College Retirement Equities Fund. 2007. "Advisor Specialists: Retirement Plans." www.TIAA-CREF.org/advisors (accessed July 31, 2007).

Turner, Anne M. 2004. "It Hurts to Ignore Work Injury Roots." *Library Journal* 129, no. 1: 64.

"When Does COBRA Coverage Begin Under the New Regulations?" 1999. *COBRA Advisory* 3, no. 1: 4–5.

EVALUATION AND PERFORMANCE APPRAISAL

The formal mechanism through which employers evaluate job performance is called performance appraisal, performance evaluation, or performance review. Managing this process may be awkward or difficult; however, it is a necessary management function. Chapter 6 will discuss various types of evaluations, tools, time involved, and individual vs. team evaluation.

Performance appraisals as we know them today began in 1842 when Congress required some department heads in the United States Civil Service to compile service reports (Goodson, 1997). This requirement was due to external pressure from Congress to make employers accountable for their performance.

The creation of the Equal Employment Opportunity Commission (EEOC) in 1965 to enforce federal legislation prohibiting employment discrimination greatly impacted the workplace environment (Johnson, 2004). Performance appraisals were closely scrutinized by the Commission and employers had to ensure that performance appraisals could withstand any allegations of discrimination. The performance appraisal needed to be a formal, uniform process with concrete examples of performance, with standards communicated to all staff. This set the tone for today's performance appraisals.

Managers and supervisors in every organization must, in some ways, determine how well employees function in their jobs. If you have been told to conduct performance evaluations, it is because the authorities in your organization realize that a performance evaluation system can deliver important benefits and improve the success of each employee, each department or unit and, ultimately, the entire organization.

WHAT IS THE VALUE OF A PERFORMANCE EVALUATION SYSTEM?

If done properly, performance appraisal can motivate employees to perform better and help identify ways in which they can develop and grow. It can also increase employee morale and improve the respect employees have for their managers and senior management. It can foster good communication between the employee and the supervisor. Proper appraisal can identify poor performers, identify methods to improve their performance, and lay the groundwork to legally and fairly terminate performers who do not improve. In the absence of a formal performance appraisal system, individual's performance will be judged informally and arbitrarily (Baldwin, 2003).

The flip side of performance appraisals is the anxiety created both for the employee and the supervisor. Supervisors often feel that the review is just added work for them and do not participate fully in the process. Too often, the review is based on their opinion of the employee and review of the individual's actual work is glossed over. I, unfortunately, have even seen supervisors simply repeat their last review of the individual changing only the date and period evaluated. Employees often are made to feel unimportant, mistreated, and unappreciated for the work that they have done. What is written in an evaluation can have a great impact on the employee-supervisor relationship. It can lead to resentment and serious morale problems if not handled appropriately.

WHAT IS THE PURPOSE OF A PERFORMANCE EVALUATION?

The true objective of performance appraisals is not to blame, reward, or praise, but to develop. Some more progressive organizations have termed this activity as a personal development plan to help lessen anxiety. Conducting appraisals properly will help people form an objective view of their past performance.

The purposes of a performance evaluation are many and varied, serving both the employee and organization as a whole. These purposes include:

- Providing a formal opportunity for supervisors to discuss performance with their subordinates
- Helping the employee understand levels of expected performance
- Providing feedback on the extent to which the employee is meeting performance expectations
- Identifying areas of performance that need improvement
- Recognizing outstanding performance
- Providing information for human resource decisions such as promotion and, in academic libraries, tenure decisions

- Identifying structural or managerial problems including quality of supervision and the effectiveness of the system of rewards and punishments, and
- Providing documentation for work references, or in cases of challenges to employment decisions

Performance evaluations occur in between 74 percent and 89 percent of private organizations. Approximately 75 percent of city governments and 100 percent of state governments reported some type of evaluation (Gedeon and Rubin, 1999).

Appraisal interviews provide the opportunity to discuss both external and internal matters. You should not limit yourself to just issues of personal performance. Remember that all employees are sources of ideas and opinions. Take note of the ideas that you think would benefit the organization and consider implementation.

The appraisal process also provides an occasion to assess staff motivation. Look to telltale signs of failing interest or lack of enthusiasm either in the organization or in personal career ambitions. If the signs are apparent, try to determine how to reverse the process and renew motivation. A competent performer will do better when they are fully engaged.

WHAT CAN AN ORGANIZATION DO TO MAKE THE PERFORMANCE APPRAISAL POSITIVE AND YET ADDRESS PERFORMANCE ISSUES?

When done correctly, a performance appraisal is a process, not a document. Evaluations can ensure that all jobs are assigned and that workloads are equalized. This is also an opportunity to make sure that the work being done is aligned with the mission of the library and to plan objectives and goals towards that mission. Proper performance evaluations also provide legal protection. Most lawsuits arise from the emotional state of an employee (DelPo, 2005). Employees who feel that they have been treated unfairly or are unaware of their poor performance until review time may be more likely to complain or bring a lawsuit against the supervisor and/or the organization. An appropriate performance appraisal system includes observation, documentation, and communication.

You may already have an appraisal system in place. Terms vary as do systems so the discussion here may not always match your system. Be aware of the differences and follow whatever your organization uses as most of these variations are merely cosmetic. All performance appraisal systems should share the same basic qualities.

WHAT ARE THE BASIC ELEMENTS OF A PERFORMANCE APPRAISAL SYSTEM?

A good evaluation system should include support, motivation, communication, collaboration, fair treatment, documentation, formality, accountability, and be consistent with the organization's core values and purpose or mission.

Support and motivation revolve around the work. The level of trust in an organization is a crucial element in employee performance and organizational success (Kane-Urrabazo, 2006). Trust goes both ways. Supervisors and managers must have trust in their employees to do their tasks. Likewise, employees must have trust in their managers and supervisors, that they are leading them according to the organization's standards and goals. Trust also includes knowing that a support ladder is in place, which will help motivate employees to do their job well. Trust is always an issue when organizations begin downsizing and is a key factor during the evaluation process, especially in organizations experiencing such a change. Many employees feel that performance evaluations validate their perceptions of their own performance, like report cards and gold stars as a symbols of approval from an instructor.

Employees will look to their supervisor and his/her attitude surrounding the whole concept of performance appraisals. If the supervisor presents an attitude that the performance evaluation is a waste of time, that attitude will affect both the employee being evaluated and the evaluation process itself. Performance appraisal systems are often viewed by managers and supervisors as a necessary evil. Other library managers have a strong need for organizational control, and performance evaluations, from their perspective, help them maintain that control. Some library managers go through the motions of evaluation but do not really connect it with the mission and goals of the institution. They may not be considering customer needs or the resources their employees need to meet those needs. They are just aware that they will be judged on whether they have conducted the performance evaluations. They are missing the point of evaluating and improving the system as a whole. Most researchers have strong beliefs in the value of performance evaluations, but often express doubt or have concerns with the simple use of mechanics for performance evaluations (Aluri and Reichel, 1994).

Communication is another key element in a performance appraisal system. The process begins by communicating that an important part of the performance appraisal is to tie the employee's efforts to the organization's goals and mission (Baldwin, 2003). Emphasizing this connection conveys the message that each employee plays a part in the overall mission of the organization and is valued and necessary.

The performance appraisal is a structured form of communication and provides an opportunity for discussion and questions from either participant. The evaluation begins with a detailed job description, which should include both standards and expectations. It should be designed by both employee and supervisor to ensure understanding and agreement. Victoria Jarosz says that managers should include goals for themselves to help employee performance (Bailey, 2002). Successful performance management includes clear performance measures so that everyone knows where they stand at the present and has a road map for the future.

The most effective performance review processes occur year-round. The annual evaluations are supplemented with ongoing feedback so that everyone has a solid understanding of how his or her work is perceived, minimizing potential surprises. Feedback also helps employees adjust as circumstances change. The importance of certain goals may shift, obstacles may appear, or employees may lose motivation or focus. Feedback will assure them of what is important, how they can adjust, and what they can do to achieve their goals.

Developing measures between supervisor and employee also produces collaboration. Research also indicates that when employees are involved in the goal setting process, they tend to set higher goals for themselves (DelPo, 2005). Collaboration is important to teamwork and helps align goals of individuals with one another.

When developing performance measures, be sure to establish a uniform set of performance standards for all staff. There will be slight variations, but you want to evaluate the same general factors. Fairness across the organization will greatly affect morale.

Documentation is also crucial. It should occur for positive actions as well as for inappropriate or negative actions. It provides a clear presentation of performance without having to rely on memory. Too often, supervisors and managers depend on their memories and the evaluation is based on the current past rather than the total review period. Training supervisors and managers in the performance review process is another way to provide consistency (Baldwin, 2003) and ensures that supervisors have at least been exposed to the same principles of performance evaluation.

Accountability is the basis for most performance evaluations. Organizations want to know if their employees are contributing to the success or the failure of their mission and goals. Demming feels that performance evaluations hold individual employees accountable for problems that exist in the system (Aluri and Reichel, 1994). However, bringing any problem to the surface through a performance evaluation can only be seen as a possible way for improvement. The search for the perfectly reliable and bias-free performance evaluation method will continue, as it does not yet exist, but performance evaluations will not go away just because they are not perfect. The supervisor must do his or her best with the knowledge and training he or she has to provide the best evaluation possible for employees.

Finally, the performance appraisal system should be consistent with the organization's core values and its purpose or mission. These values are usually an expression of the culture of the organization. Examples might include innovation and risk taking, attention to detail, focus on results or outcome, focus on techniques and processes, team orientation, competition, and stability. If a library supports innovation and risk taking, the performance appraisal should reflect that and not be punitive to innovative individuals.

Figure 6-1 provides an example of one library's vision statement, mission, and values. The performance appraisals for individuals in the organization should reflect these elements.

Vision

- To be the innovative leader among urban university libraries

Mission

- To promote excellence in learning
- To serve as a gateway to information vital for research and scholarship
- To create unique scholarly resources with an emphasis on philanthropic studies, campus generated research, and materials relating to the community it serves
- To enhance the availability of scholarly information for the residents of central Indiana

The mission of the XXXX University Library is derived from and aligned with the XXXXX Mission Statement.

Values

XXXXXX University Library is committed to:

- Creativity and innovation
- Collaboration and teamwork
- Individual and organizational learning
- Trust

- Diversity
- Opportunity
- Accountability
- Academic and intellectual freedom

Figure 6-1. Vision, Mission, and Values Statements

HOW SHOULD THE PERFORMANCE EVALUATION FORM LOOK?

Simplicity is the best rule to follow with performance evaluation forms. You may decide to have more than one type of form in your organization. This is especially true in academic libraries where librarians may be evaluated on the same standards as faculty and require areas beyond performance for evaluation, such as professional development (research) and professional service. Effective forms should contain the following elements: clear standards by which the performance will be measured, an appropriate rating scale, space for comments by the supervisor, a section for employee self-appraisal, suggestions and specifics for employee development, objectives set by the employee and supervisor at the last appraisal and a rating of their results, objectives to be met by the next appraisal date, and approval by all of the necessary levels. Let us look at each of these elements a little closer.

Figure 6-2 is a sample page of a generic evaluation. The appraisal would continue to evaluate job skills, participation in training and workshops, service orientation, goals, and other attributes for the position. There would be space to describe any unique features and areas not adequately covered by the listing. The employee's goals for the next review period would be included as well as any suggestions for improvement. Both supervisor and employee would sign and date the document.

Performance Review for:

Employee name _____ Date _____

Position _____

Supervisor completing the evaluation _____

Evaluation Period _____

Category 1: Performance of Job Skills

1a) The employee's quality of work is high.

   (Rating Scale)

   _____ Very good   _____ Good   _____ Needs Improvement

Comments: **(Space for comments)**

This item means: The work done by the employee meets the standards of the organization. The work is done well with a minimum of ongoing supervision. The individual takes pride in doing the job well. You can be proud to distribute the work of this employee to people in and out of the organization. The work does not have to be redone by others. **(Clear standards)**

1b) The employee's quantity of work is high.

   _____ Very good   _____ Good   _____ Needs Improvement

Comments:

This item means: The employee produces the amount of work needed by the organization. You can expect work to be done within an amount of time reasonable for the assignment, and comparable to the time it takes others to do similar jobs.

1c) The employee's work is accurate.

   _____ Very good   _____ Good   _____ Needs Improvement

Comments:

This item means: The employee checks work for accuracy before sending it on. You can count on the employee to be accurate and take pride in being accurate. A supervisor does not need to constantly check the employee's work for accuracy. If the employee has questions about the task, he/she asks the questions rather than guessing.

Figure 6-2. Sample Page from an Evaluation

Clear standards—Standards will include a list of the specific competencies or skills being measured, with examples of success. Using the abilities listed in the job description is a good start. There will be additional standards that apply to all positions, such as timeliness, accuracy, ability to prioritize, and positive attitude.

Appropriate rating scale—The purpose of the rating scale is to provide an objective way to determine whether an employee is meeting performance standards. Some organizations use a numerical system, e.g., 1–5. Other organizations use descriptive ratings such as Excellent, Good, Fair, and Unacceptable. Be sure to indicate clearly what rating constitutes an acceptable performance and which rating falls below acceptable standards.

Space for comments—In addition to using a rating scale, you should encourage supervisor comments and require them for both excellent or very poor ratings. You do not want the appraisal to be a mechanical checking of boxes without clearly describing the situation and supervisor responses. Encourage your reviewers to carefully review performance of the individual and not personalities.

Employee self-appraisal—Employees should be able to assess their own performance. Often, the self-appraisal is done before the actual meeting and given to the supervisor in advance. Self-appraisals can increase employee buy-in to the process and assist supervisors in their focus. The self-appraisal may also identify areas where employees' perception of their performance may differ from that of the supervisor and can generate a discussion about the difference.

Suggestions for development—The review may identify areas where the employee could benefit from training: internal or external training events, educational training, or further on-the-job experience that will enhance the employee's performance and growth.

Objectives set by the employee/supervisor previously—Reviewing the goals and standards set at the previous performance review allows for consistency. This is a good time to discuss what goals were achieved and which ones were not and why.

New objectives for the next period—The new objectives may include prior ones that were not met if they need to be achieved. How goals should be achieved and what is needed from both the employee and supervisor to do this should be central in this discussion.

Approvals—All appraisals should be reviewed by at least one person in the organization who is familiar with the goals of the process. When supervisors submit reviews that do not meet the organization's performance management objectives, they should be coached on the appropriate way to complete the appraisal and required to redo the document. This is why training in the appraisal process is important. The training should include information about why the organization values performance appraisals and how individual performance benefits the organization. The structure of the process and how it relates to compensation should be covered in training as well as the meaning and application of the rating criteria. Supervisors should be trained on how to develop goals that are specific and measurable, how to give feedback, both positive and negative, and how to coach an employee. Training should also provide an opportunity for supervisors to practice their written and verbal appraisal skills.

WHAT ARE SOME OF THE PITFALLS IN PERFORMANCE EVALUATIONS?

Supervisors often run into performance evaluation pitfalls without realizing it. They include strictness/leniency errors, central tendency, halo effect, and evaluator's biases. When a supervisor is consistently strict or lenient in rating all of their employees, the ratings all fall within the same range and they have not been individually considered. The central tendency refers to evaluators who are unwilling to give unusually high or unusually low ratings. They tend is to give everyone midrange ratings. The halo effect refers to remembering the most recent achievements and ignoring any past failures during the evaluation period. The supervisor's biases cover a range of situations. The supervisor may have a practice of sharing or not sharing the evaluation with the employee. The reputation of the employee being either excellent or difficult might bias the supervisor's evaluation. Past evaluations might also bias the results. It is difficult to rate someone lower when past evaluations have been consistently high.

Changes in management, management philosophy, or organizational objectives (once acceptable performance is no longer sufficient) can also affect the evaluation process. The standard-setting method of evaluation has been criticized on the basis that employees tend to set safe goals so that they will look better at the time of evaluation instead of setting challenging goals and taking risks of failure (Aluri and Beichel, 1994). One way to combat this is for the supervisor and employee to prepare the goals together. This also provides another opportunity for discussion between the employee and supervisor.

DO PERCEPTIONS OF TASKS MAKE A DIFFERENCE IN EVALUATION?

The tasks in a library vary widely from those that are extremely complex to those that are simple. Perception of ease or difficulty of these tasks is also important. When the perceived task is considered easy, people are given less credit for successful performance. This will always be somewhat subjective to the reviewer.

How the employee perceives the task difficulty also needs to be considered as well as how the task relates to the mission or goals of the organization. If the task measured is not meaningful to the employee, the task may not be done with as much commitment as other tasks (Taber and Alliger, 1995). This could also affect the assessment of the task achievement by the supervisor.

DOES GENDER PLAY A ROLE IN THE EVALUATION PROCESS?

Some researchers indicate that gender-based evaluations occur and such bias is a recognized problem in evaluation processes (Gedeon and Rubin, 1999). Often women are evaluated differently and to their detriment. There is also indication that even when women are rated more highly than men, they are still not promoted over men (Shore, Tashchian, and Adams, 1997). In this same vein, certain tasks may be gender typed. Studies in the mid-70s found that characteristics attributed to "successful managers" (e.g., leadership, self-confidence, ambition, objectivity) were more strongly associated with men than with women (Shore, Taschian, and Adams, 1997). Women employees are more likely to receive less favorable evaluations than men in stereotypically male jobs. Data from the American Library Association supports this pattern. In the late 1980s, females comprised approximately 69 percent of the academic librarian workforce, while only 48 percent of the librarians in director, assistant director or deputy director positions were females (Office for Library Personnel Resources, 1986). In addition, the mean salary of female academic librarians in ARL (American Research Libraries) libraries is below that of the male academic librarians (Kyrillidou and Maxwell, 1996).

It has been suggested that men and women are rated differently for identical performances. Studies have found that women are less likely to explain their successes in terms of ability but are more prone to explain performance, whether successful or not, in terms of luck. Men, on the other hand, view themselves based on their ability to succeed and expect to do so. This would indicate that women need to review their own self-perceptions and abilities in order to present themselves as more capable and confident individuals.

As an HR professional, should you suspect a gender or other bias in a supervisor's evaluation, you do need to take action. Such supervisors may need one-on-one coaching or exposure to some role playing. This is not a situation you can afford to ignore. Additional training might also be required. You might want to see how they conduct their appraisals as well. If they tend to conduct these evaluations back-to-back, you might want to suggest that they space out their evaluations more. Sometimes when evaluators complete one review and then immediately do another, they unconsciously compare the second person to the first.

ARE THERE ALTERNATIVE METHODS OF EVALUATION?

Alternative methods of evaluation come in and out of vogue and could be considered. They often supplement the traditional one-on-one performance review rather than replacing it.

One alternative method is called the 360-degree feedback. In this method, an organization may use several sources for review rather than just the supervisor. The evaluations generally contain four or five rating scales with space for comments, with between eight and fifteen respondents assessing each employee. It is important to train the participants on the system, to use at least six evaluators to preserve anonymity, and to communicate the timetable (DelPo, 2005). It can be very useful in organizations with cross-functional teams or relationships but may not work in every organization. It usually involves assessment from peers, subordinates, managers, and sometimes even customers. The implementation of this type of system can be daunting due to the number of individuals involved in the process.

The balanced scorecard is a method of evaluation that uses four specific balanced perspectives to measure performance: financial, customer, internal business processes, and learning and growth. While this tool can be adapted to rate individuals separately, it is really a tool for assessing the overall organizational performance. This is often used in organizations who use process improvement techniques.

Forced ranking systems place employees along a curve of performance or in categories of percentiles. The best performers would, for example, be placed in the top 20 percent, with a large group in the middle at 70 percent, and the worst performers in the bottom ten percent. The ranking is "forced" because there is a requirement that 10 percent of the employees be given the lowest rating regardless of whether their reviewers would have rated them that way. The system has been used to provide greater rewards for top performers and specific deadlines for performance improvement for the lowest-ranking employees. Although this process can help an organization by reinforcing goals and objectives, it can be demoralizing for the rest of the workforce and promote competition and individual performance over teamwork.

SPEAKING OF TEAMWORK, HOW DO YOU ASSESS INDIVIDUALS WHO WORK IN TEAMS?

The University of Arizona Library redesigned its organizational structure from a traditional, multilayered hierarchy to a flattened, team-based organization. One challenge in this process was to develop a performance evaluation that supported the team-based philosophy (Russell, 1998). The traditional system of appraisal focused on the individual and reinforced the idea that individuals compete against each other. For a brief period, the library did not conduct performance appraisals. Staff and librarians were exempt from the annual appraisal mechanisms so they could create a new evaluation system for the team structure (Russell, 1998). The library appointed a cross-functional project team, composed of three librarians and four library staff members, to sketch out a new system. The new documentation, packaged as a team-member portfolio, would be both summative and formative in nature. All team members would engage in a team review of each member's portfolio to provide input and feedback. Completed portfolios would record team member past achievements and future commitments to learning and to the team. As much as possible, team and team member objectives would be tested with internal and external users to determine if needs were being met. Using a variety of performance measures, teams could document their contributions to the university community.

The project team worked with Charles R. McClure, distinguished professor of information studies at Syracuse University, to build a program in which performance measurement methodologies were integrated into team planning, objective setting, and team review. The project team drafted the Performance Effectiveness Management System (PEMS) curriculum to focus teams on system implementation (Russell, 1998, 162). The curriculum included assignments for each team to draft specific reports according to a schedule and share them with the rest of the library. By concentrating on three to five critical areas, library staff decided their work priorities and the focus of their team review. Teams then sought feedback on these services, programs, or activities. Teams were required to share their mission-critical areas and corresponding standards with the rest of the library for input and feedback. The teams would also develop a method to gain customer feedback and then respond to this feedback. Team members would be evaluated on their individual portfolios and librarians also evaluated by their peers for post-continuing status review. This new system places more emphasis on team achievement and outcomes related to library mission and vision, while recognizing the fluid environment in which the library operates. It will take some time to determine if they have met their goals of transforming the system.

While this whole process has taken quite a bit of time and effort to develop, it certainly conveys the message that team-based organizations need to seriously consider their review systems. Many team-based organizations have team members review each other. Some organizations even have other teams and users rate services provided by teams.

Work teams in a factory situation in Kentucky moved to a peer-performance review in the early 1990s (Ramsay and Lehto, 1994). They settled on a combined review with evaluation by the work team members and the supervisor review. A facilitator was brought in to conduct training to teams on conducting peer-based reviews, guide the teams through the appraisal process, and facilitate the actual reviews. The management team insisted on being first to be reviewed by peers to encourage buy-in from the other teams. In this system, the team, in the absence of the member being reviewed, discusses the teammate's performance, agrees on a rating, and produces a written review. In the feedback session, the team members discuss the rating with the review subject and encourage him/her to respond. The facilitator participates in each phase of the review. The company has the following ten standards of excellence: 1) quality of work, 2) job knowledge and skills, 3) adaptability and flexibility, 4) customer relations, 5) safety and housekeeping, 6) dependability and reliability, 7) initiative, 8) stewardship, 9) interpersonal, and 10) teamwork. The scoring system is based on a numerical rating system.

Team members discuss expectations, both of the team member and the team itself. Through the appraisal process, the expectations are communicated in specific terms to the review subject and to the team. A critical aspect of this peer-review process is observable behavior. Peer reviews need to be based on actual observations; opinions and feelings do not count. Team members are required to provide specific information on a peer's performance and must include actual examples or statistics. Following this change in the Kentucky system, one manager said, "All of my people are happy, getting along, and coming up with ideas. I don't know what happened, but I like it" (Ramsay and Lehto, 1994).

Important factors in building an effective team-based, peer-performance review system include selecting and reviewing models of peer-performance review systems; your organization's standards of excellence; the rating system and criteria for each score; establishing expectations for teams as a whole and for each team member; ensuring that ratings are based on observable behavior; defining good documentation and how to produce it; helping participants overcome a lack of knowledge about other team member's jobs; incorporating supervisors' and managers' input as peer input; determining the meaning of consensus and ways to achieve it; and committing to "no surprises." Require team members to be continuously supportive of each other. It is also critical in a team culture to support the belief that everyone wants to improve, and the commitment of teams to help members improve.

SUGGESTIONS AND RECOMMENDATIONS

Given the importance of performance reviews, it pays to ensure that your system works well from top to bottom. What really needs to happen is an ongoing dialogue between the supervisor and the employee. The form would not make much of a difference if these ongoing conversations were not taking place.

You can get various types of performance appraisal forms at www. hr-guide.com/data/133.htm, www.hr.ucdavis.edu/Forms/All/Perf_Eval, www.princeton.edu/hr/manager/perfforms.htm, and hrweb.berkeley.edu/forms/pedescr.htm.

IUPUI University Library implemented a 90/90 process when they went to a team-based organization (Stanley, 2001). In this procedure, for every 90 days of work, an employee should have a 90-minute discussion with their supervisor regarding their performance for that time period and what adjustments are needed for the next 90 days. Many within the organization felt that this was too time consuming and settled on a semester assessment. Some teams in the organization still do the 90/90 (or quarterly) review of each of their team members. Unfortunately, this leads to inconsistency within the organization.

Richard Chang, a consultant in Irvine California, recommends quarterly, formal performance discussions (Tyler, 2005). If you have progress checks each quarter, the annual review becomes a simple process. Only about 25 percent of the discussion should be about past performance, the rest should focus on future improvements or goals.

Employees must be taught the definition of terms, what ratings mean, how to receive feedback, what to expect from their supervisors in terms of feedback, and where to turn if they are not receiving the feedback they need. Employees need to understand that they are not passive in the performance review process.

The appraisal can also be used as one step in a carefully constructed program of planning an individual's career path. The appraisal can help both the individual and the supervisor plan the next move and ensure that training and development are included. Send staff on any necessary training courses before or immediately after appointing them to a new task or position. Discuss and reach agreement on the career plan when you make the appointment and ask the staff member to sign off on what you have agreed. Provide staff the opportunity to use and increase their expertise.

Appraisal should never be a waste of time and effort. They will never be absolutely objective but consistency across the organization can be built into the process. Employee performance management is about ensuring that the right things are being measured and empowering employees to own and manage their own success.

HOW DO PROBATIONARY PERIODS WORK?

The probationary period is a time period when a new hire has the opportunity to learn how to do the job and what the company expects. Some organizations call this an orientation period. This is also a time when the employer can make sure that the new hire is going to work out. This period is a trial run of sorts and gives both the employer and the employee a chance to make sure that there is a good fit.

It is appropriate to let the employees know that there is a probationary period so that they are not surprised. Many organizations indicate this in a welcome letter or letter of appointment. (See a sample in Figure 6-3 below.)

If it is clear to either the employer or the individual that this arrangement is not working, one or the other can end the agreement at the end of probation without any detriment to either party.

[date]

[Name, address, city and state, zip code]

Dear [applicant name]:

This is to confirm your appointment as [position and rank] with [name of library] to begin on [start date] pending approval of the background check. Your starting annual salary of [salary information] will be paid [biweekly, monthly] at the following rate: [biweekly or monthly rate].

All new employees at [name of library] serve a probationary period of [term of probation]. This is intended as a period of learning adjustment and an opportunity for the organization and the new employee to evaluate the suitability of this match. Either party may decide to terminate this agreement during this probationary period if it is determined that a satisfactory match has not been made. The organization has the right to extend the probationary period if deemed necessary.

We look forward to having you join our organization and are confident that this will result in a mutually advantageous relationship.

Sincerely,

[name of human resources professional]
Address
City, state, and zip code
Telephone number and e-mail address

Figure 6-3. Sample Letter Regarding Probationary Period

It is recommended that you meet with the individual at the end of the probation period to discuss how he or she is doing and if further training and/or skill building is needed to meet the expectations of the job. Ninety days is a fairly standard length for a probation period. It is long enough to give employees a chance to learn the ropes and show their abilities. Some organizations extend the probation period if they feel an individual still has the necessary skills for the position but just needs a little more time to adjust or learn the job. Some employers do not allow their employees to use sick or vacation time during this period. If you plan to impose a waiting period, list the benefits that will not be available to new employees so they will know that at the start.

In the next chapter, we will discuss problem and marginal employees and how to handle them.

REFERENCES

Aluri, Rao and Mary Reichel. 1994. "Performance Evaluation: A Deadly Disease?" *The Journal of Academic Librarianship* 20, no. 3: 145–155.

Bailey, Laura. 2002. "Evaluations Help Set the Tone for Year-Round Performance." *Crain's Detroit Business* 18, no. 2: 12.

Baldwin, David A. 2003. *The Library Compensation Handbook: A Guide for Administrators, Librarians, and Staff.* Westport, CT: Libraries Unlimited.

DelPo, Amy. 2005. *The Performance Appraisal Handbook: Legal & Practical Rules for Managers.* Berkeley, CA: NOLO.

Gedeon, Julie A. and Richard E. Rubin. 1999. "Attribution Theory and Academic Library Performance Evaluation." *The Journal of Academic Librarianship* 25, no. 1: 18–25.

Goodson, Carol. 1997. *The Complete Guide to Performance Standards for Library Personnel.* New York: Neal-Schuman.

Johnson, Ben. 2004. "The Case of Performance Appraisal: Deming Versus EEOC." *Library Administration & Management* 18, no. 2: 83–86.

Kane-Urrabazo, Christine. 2006. "Management's Role in Shaping Organizational Culture." *Journal of Nursing Management* 14, no. 3: 188–194.

Kyrillidou, Martha and Kimberly A. Maxwell. 1996. *ARL Annual Salary Survey 1996–97.* Washington, DC: ARL.

Office for Library Personnel Resources, American Library Association. 1986. *Academic and Public Librarians: Data by Race, Ethnicity, and Sex.* Chicago: ALA.

Ramsay, Martin L. and Howard Lehto. 1994. "The Power of Peer Review." *Training & Development* 48, no. 7: 38–41.

Russell, Carrie. 1998. "Using Performance Measurement to Evaluate Teams and Organizational Effectiveness." *Library Administration & Management* 12, no. 3: 159–165.

Shore, Ted H., Armen Tashchian, and Janet S. Adams. 1997. "The Role of Gender in a Developmental Assessment Center." *Journal of Social Behavior and Personality* 12, no. 5: 191–203.

Stanley, Mary J. 2001. "Taking Time for the Organization." *C&RL News* 62, no. 9: 900–908.

Taber, Tom D. and George M. Alliger. 1995. "A Task-Level Assessment of Job Satisfaction." *Journal of Organizational Behavior* 16, no. 2: 101–121.

Tyler, Kathryn. 2005. "Performance Art." *HRMagazine* 50, no. 8: 58–63.

7 PROBLEM EMPLOYEES AND MARGINAL EMPLOYEES

We do not live in a perfect world. In almost every organization, no matter how fine-tuned it is, we can expect some employees who do not meet expectations. This chapter will attempt to identify the characteristics of and differences between the problem employee and the marginal employee and provide methods of dealing with them.

One article defines the difficult employee as "one who conducts themselves in a manner that is disrespectful and unprofessional to managers, coworkers, or customers" (Sweeney, Stone, and Cossack, 2007). The authors contend that these employees are generally able to perform the basic functions of the job but their negativity, animosity, or poor attitude has a detrimental effect on their coworkers. Problem behavior usually does not happen overnight or as a result of a single incident.

Mediocre employees are a different concept. These employees are not really problem employees; they are employees who do not live up to the performance expectations of management. They have also been labeled "marginal employees" (Curtis, 2003; Freed, 2000; Zimmerer, 1973).

HOW DO YOU IDENTIFY THE MARGINAL OR MEDIOCRE EMPLOYEE?

The marginal or mediocre employee exists in every workplace. These individuals usually do not pose major disciplinary problems, at least not at first. You can probably put a face to this type of individual if you think about your organization. Usually a marginal employee lacks personal motivation, has a real or imagined perception that management fails to address mediocre performance, and often has family problems or other distractions that keep him or her from being productive. He or she usually has a continuously poor attitude or poor performance. This is not the solid employee who becomes temporarily ineffective because of some sort of tragedy such as a death in the family (Freed, 2000). Often these individuals do not even realize or accept that they are not really performing.

When questioned, marginal employees might come back at you with questions. They usually cannot complete the tasks or responsibilities in the manner in which you expect and often are late, with numerous trivial mistakes such as spelling errors or lack of dates, page numbers, or signatures. They will have some excuse as to why they have made mistakes in their work or why the task has not been completed on time.

The all-too-human tendency is to be nice to people, especially those with whom you work and see every day. Why cause a fuss when someone is showing up and seemingly trying to work? Why not rate them as satisfactory, or at least as meeting required expectations? It is much easier to deal with the mediocre or marginal employee in this fashion, is it not?

By definition, marginal means "on the edge of" and, as one author puts it, "marginal employees exist "on the edge of being productive" (Hale, 1991/92, 23). The literature over and over again states that managers cannot deal with the challenge of underperformers and all too often pass them off with satisfactory evaluations. One significant finding is that most of these "marginal employees" want to go above and beyond and be an important part of the organization (Bates, 2004). Why are they marginal then? Often, disengagement with an immediate supervisor or a feeling that the organization does not really care about them gets in the way. The problem often lies with the supervisor and his/her reluctance to handle the situation. In addition, there will always be people who never give their best no matter how hard managers and supervisors try to engage them. Carol Kinsey Goman, president of Kinsey Consulting Services in California, contends that most employees want to commit to organizations because doing so satisfies a basic human need to connect and contribute to something of importance (Bates, 2004). The marginal employee can present a tremendous opportunity for supervisors to turn these unacceptable performers into workers who are not merely "passing."

SO WHAT SHOULD A SUPERVISOR/MANAGER DO ABOUT MARGINAL EMPLOYEES?

The first step is to begin a dialogue with the employee. The supervisor needs to pinpoint specific performance-related behaviors and results to be changed, such as attendance, on time behavior, avoiding errors, staying in the work area, or not interrupting others. Gather data about problems and how often they occur. This will give a good clear picture of what the employee is or is not doing. Trying to explain marginal behavior to an employee is difficult and having actual examples will make it hard for him or her to argue with you. The examples will also help the employee understand that this is unacceptable behavior. Often, the first behavior is overlooked and not addressed. The individual realizes that his or her behavior has not resulted in any consequences and so continues the behavior. Traditionally, supervisors tend to avoid confrontation and correction of marginal performance. They hope the performance will improve on its own. Allowing the marginal performance to continue sends the message that marginal performance is acceptable and sends a negative message to the high performers, leading to resentment, which can also affect organization morale.

One manner in which to approach the problem is with an "iron hand in a velvet glove" (Axelrod, Handfield-Jones, and Michaels, 2002). The iron hand is firmness in addressing the situation; the velvet glove is handling the delicate situation in a professional yet diplomatic manner. Successfully managing underperformers requires sticking to an action plan consistently throughout the organization. It is very difficult to tackle one marginal performer if you are not addressing all of them. This could be seen as discriminatory practice.

The manager must clearly define and communicate a time frame for the marginal employee to make improvement. He or she should also provide necessary tools and resources, whether it is further training or more up-to-date equipment. Consistency across an organization is also imperative. Giving examples of performance standards for each type of job function helps the employee to understand and know what is expected of them. Most marginal performers can improve their performance substantially if given the direction and the developmental support to do so (Axelrod, Handfield-Jones, and Michaels, 2002). The action plan should include the specific skills and anticipated improvement, a clear time frame for accomplishing these improvements, and a description of the support that will be provided.

WHAT IF THE MARGINAL EMPLOYEE DOES NOT IMPROVE?

When setting up an improvement process for marginal employees, consider: Does the employee want to improve? Does this employee have some strong skills that are valuable to the organization? Is this individual in a job that is not suited to his or her skills? Has the person been in the position for too short a time to evaluate his or her performance adequately? Is there something in the individual's personal life that is zapping his or her energy at this time? How much warning, help, and time has this employee already been given? If performance problems continue to persist after providing this action plan, it is probably best to ask the employee to leave. This should not come as a complete surprise if you have followed the process with clear expectations and support. Have a fair severance package in place to help the employee.

According to David H. Freed, President of the Overlook Hospital in Summit, New Jersey, the top ten reasons that organizations do not fire marginal employees in a timely manner are (Freed, 2000):

1) the hope that things will get better
2) firing someone means that a wrong hiring decision was made
3) anyone can be trained to do better
4) the employee has a family to feed
5) it is really unpleasant
6) this is not the right time
7) someone is better than no one
8) the employee may sue
9) this is a nice, collegial environment, and
10) separation costs are too high

All of these reasons give management a way of not dealing with the situation. The environment will not stay in harmony if these poor performers are overlooked and continue non-performance. Others will have to assume their tasks on top of an already busy workload, creating animosity and resentment. The need for termination is regrettable, but excuses do not solve the problem. Once it is determined that improvement cannot or will not take place, the employee needs to be let go.

In one case at a large law library, a clerical employee who had been in charge of the mailroom applied for a higher position preparing books and journals for the bindery. Because this was a promotion to a different grade level, the individual was again placed on probation. At first, things seemed to be working well. The individual learned the process quickly and seemed motivated by the new challenge. After several months, problems began to appear. The individual could not seem to meet the deadlines for the bindery pickup. The supervisor discussed the issue with the employee and both agreed that the employee needed to try harder to meet these deadlines. This employee was not lazy and was very dependable. He arrived at work on time and worked diligently throughout his work period. It soon became apparent that this was not working and so the two met again and it was agreed that on the days when the load was larger than normal, another employee would help process the materials. This became a written warning and both the supervisor and the employee signed the document, which clearly expressed the situation and intended goals. This new process worked for a short time but the bindery preparation again fell behind and several more deadlines were missed. This meant that journal issues were unavailable for use because they were in the process of getting bound. Usually, journals were unavailable for a period of about three to six weeks. Missing the deadline by even one day could make them unavailable for up to twelve weeks' time. It was clear that this was simply a job that this employee was unable to handle. The employee was eventually terminated. This was most difficult as the employee was very likeable.

In the termination interview, the supervisor, the head of the department, and the human resources manager met with the employee. The HR manager went over the entire process from his promotion, training, the addition of another individual to help with the heavy workload, the several opportunities to improve, and his inability to meet the performance standards. The employee was asked if he had any comments or thoughts. He said that he thought we had been fair through the process and understood that he was not able to meet the performance standards. He thanked the supervisor and the department head for the opportunity to try and apologized for not making it work. He was given until the end of the day to gather his personal belongings and turn in his keys and other library resources.

This was a mild termination interview. All parties involved were calm, which is not always the case. In some termination interviews I have conducted, there have been heated discussions. The human resources manager must always remain neutral and calm in these situations. It is best to end the interview by accompanying the employee to gather their belongings and then walk them to the door. With so many opportunities for a terminated employee to do damage when they are upset, this is usually the best practice.

WHAT IS THE DIFFERENCE BETWEEN A PROBLEM EMPLOYEE AND A MARGINAL EMPLOYEE?

The marginal employee is fairly dependable. The problem or difficult employee is much different. These employees possess varying degrees of competence and present problems for organizations in a variety of ways, including abusing sick time, coming to work with their own agenda (i.e., conducting personal business at work), creating conflicts between staff members, bullying, poor work performance, and other interpersonal problems (Weitzel, 2004). Some may even display violence in the workplace. They can have a great effect on coworkers, supervisors, and the entire workplace environment.

When ongoing problems are not addressed, the impact on the work environment is quite significant. Failure to address problems leads other employees to lose motivation and feel undervalued. Employees do not necessarily want a coworker to be dismissed, but they want that individual's work and behavior to improve so that their own work environment is more positive.

Sometimes, the supervisor may not want to admit that they have a problem employee for fear that it will reflect poorly on them. In other cases, the employee may exhibit such exceptional skills in certain areas that the supervisor is willing to overlook problems in other areas. Or a supervisor may have a personal friendship with the problem employee and fear that reprimanding him or her will affect their friendship. In some cases, the supervisor may simply feel so overwhelmed with professional responsibilities or personal crises that they choose just to ignore the problem employee.

To determine whether or not an individual is a problem employee, supervisors/managers can ask a number of questions, including, but not limited to, the following:

- Have you received negative feedback from others in the organization about the individual's demeanor or attitude?
- Have you received complaints about how the employee treats coworkers?
- Do you need to regularly check the employee's work?
- Do scheduling problems arise because the employee fails to show up?
- Do you frequently spend time doing tasks that you should feel comfortable delegating to the individual?
- Does the employee rarely complete work on time?
- Does the employee frequently give reasons why assignments cannot be done or why they cannot be done within the time frame given?
- Do you find it difficult to get your own work done because of the time you spend on the problems and mistakes of this individual?
- Do you rarely give this employee important assignments?
- Does the employee usually offer excuses or blame others for mistakes?
- Does the employee occasionally lie or stretch the truth?

A positive answer to any of these questions could indicate a problem employee, especially if it touches on an area of particular importance to the supervisor. An affirmative answer to two or more of these questions definitely identifies the individual as a problem employee.

Problem employees do not necessarily lack competence. After all, they were hired because they presented themselves as capable of doing the work. However, when factors such as a bad attitude, poor motivation, or an inability to get along with others are present to an extent that negatively influences performance, the organization will suffer (Weitzel, 2004).

The problem employee most often fits into one of seven categories.

- *Hostile aggressives*, who, when things do not go their way, bully and overwhelm others with snide comments or tantrums
- *Complainers*, who gripe continuously but never take action to improve the situation they are complaining about
- *Silents or unresponsives*, who respond to requests with a "yep," a "nope," or a grunt
- *Super agreeables*, who appear outgoing, personable, and supportive in the supervisor's presence, but then do not produce what they promised or what was expected
- *Negativists*, who respond with a negative spirit to every suggestion for improvement
- *Know-it-all experts*, who have a condescending and superior attitude and try to make the supervisor feel foolish
- *Indecisives*, who have difficulty making any decision and cannot let go of anything until it is perfect, which means never (Bramson, 1981).

To determine why problem employees behave in such manners, one should first consider what motivates them. Needs and values drive everyone (Kravitz, 1995). A needs motivation is an individual's need for security, love, and growth. If these needs are not met, the individual will respond negatively or problematically. Values are driven by ethical standards. When conflict with these standards or values exists, the individual will behave in a negative manner. Behavior may also reflect the employee's self-esteem. Generally, people with a low self-esteem display a "me-versus-them" mentality, which will certainly affect performance. Negative attitudes also affect employee behavior and interactions with others. The way people were raised shapes how they determine normal behavior. Consequently, individuals who grew up in negative families will tend to be negative (Kravitz, 1995).

It is the responsibility of the manager or supervisor to be aware of problems in the workplace. By continuous coaching and communication with each staff member, the supervisor should be able to identify problems. If they are ignored or avoided, the situation will only get worse. When you have an underperforming employee or a problem employee, do not let things slide. The longer you let people do something, the more they think they can get away with it. The more this happens, according to Ian Jacobsen, president of Jacobsen Consulting Group in Sunnyvale, California, "the more their performance deteriorates" (Perry, 2004). Usually, the problem employee is visible to everyone, not just to the supervisor. If the problem is not addressed, there is apt to be more grumbling and gossip and morale will decline.

Document every event that reflects a problem. A written record will be invaluable later. In conducting the performance analysis, supervisors must be prepared to pinpoint exactly where the problem behavior lies. Supervisors must remain fair in their documentation, including instances of both effective and detrimental behavior, stating facts and not opinions. All documentation should be consistent with oral comments and actions. Too often, the supervisor may generalize the employee's performance instead of concentrating on specific areas that need improvement. If the problems are not narrowly defined, it will be difficult to convey to the employee the exact issues. It is always helpful to include positive behaviors in the discussion. Focusing only on the negative aspects of the employee's performance can aggravate the problem, alienating the employee and discouraging him or her from improving.

Worth Repeating: Document, Document, Document!

Document every step of the disciplinary process. Have the employee and supervisor sign each of the warnings and steps taken. This could be very important if a lawsuit arises from the incident.

WHAT HAPPENS DURING THE MEETING WITH THE PROBLEM EMPLOYEE?

Conduct a scheduled meeting with the problem employee and be prepared. The meeting should be private. People do not want to be humiliated in front of others. There may be private matters affecting a person's attitude and performance and these should not be discussed openly. Supervisors need to listen to the employee's version of the situation and find out whether he or she is aware of the problem, whether he or she cares about the problem, and whether external personal problems are the cause for the problem behavior.

If during the meeting it is determined that the problem is caused by the employee's actions, discuss ways to eliminate or correct the behavior. The objective here is to develop a mutually agreed upon plan of action for the employee to follow (Foltz and Fulton, 2005). The employee should be given a time frame to improve, except where flagrant violations of policy dictate termination.

During the meeting, set observable and measurable outcomes. For instance, "In your next four assigned tasks, three must be done on time and the fourth no more than one day late." Or, "You must return phone calls within two hours of receipt no matter what." The appropriate approach is determined by the severity of the situation. At the conclusion of the meeting, the employee will fully understand what the expectations are, as well as the consequences, including termination, of not meeting those expectations.

HOW DO YOU FOLLOW UP AFTER THE MEETING?

After a stated period of time, conduct a follow-up interview with the employee. This will determine whether the employee has attempted to carry out appropriate actions. More interviews should occur, if appropriate, to ensure that the employee continues to make progress. It is imperative to continue to monitor the situation and follow up. If the employee makes positive changes, it is important to give the employee positive feedback. If there is no change in behavior, you must take appropriate action. Failure to do so will send a message to all employees that problem employees are not punished, which could lead to further disruptive behavior. Depending on the severity and type of problem, a supervisor might deal with the employee in a variety of ways. Examples include oral or written reprimand (warning), shadowing by a fellow coworker, moving the employee to another work area, suspension, or termination.

HOW SHOULD SUPERVISORS HANDLE INTERPERSONAL CONFLICTS?

It is natural for conflicts to occur. Different working styles and different personalities may case some conflicts. It has been suggested that organizations need to adopt a philosophy that employee conflict is a relatively normal, healthy aspect of productive workplace development (Cottringer,

2003). Having said this, conflict should not be encouraged but should be anticipated. Some conflicts can be resolved easily between the individuals and others may require the assistance of a supervisor or neutral party. Encouraging employees to try to solve the problems between themselves will help empower them. Supervisors should also note that conflicting parties may not always be aware that there is a conflict. We will discuss conflict resolution in more detail in Chapter 8.

HOW CAN THE EMPLOYEE ASSISTANCE PROGRAM HELP PROBLEM EMPLOYEES?

Many organizations provide an employee assistance program (EAP) for their staff. Such programs are an important resource for employees who may be going through significant personal crises. Observation of a sudden change in an employee's performance or behavior may signal that they might need such assistance. EAPs help employees deal with problems related to substance abuse, stress due to personal problems, depression or other mental health concerns, family support, grief, and marital problems. They provide safe and unbiased support for staff. If an employee is reluctant to talk to his or her supervisor about personal problems that are leading to poor performance at work, the EAP may be able to help resolve the issues.

For the program to work properly, employers should issue regular reminders to staff of the EAP's existence and its confidential nature. Training supervisors on how to identify employees who might benefit from using an EAP is another possibility but very sensitive as employees often feel vulnerable if someone knows they are using the service.

HOW DO YOU HANDLE THE PROBLEM OF ABSENTEEISM?

Absenteeism includes absences because of illness, injury, and personal reasons, which, though involuntary, are preventable to some degree; plus absences for which there are no valid reasons, which are considered voluntary absences. Absenteeism does not include vacation and other leave for which permission has been granted. Rather, it is unscheduled leave which forces supervisors to make last minute changes in work distribution or schedules for the day, week, or month. It does include family, weather, and other emergencies that become first priority for staff members. Voluntary absences are a significant part of the overall absenteeism problem (Anonymous, 1997). It would be rare for an employee to call in and say, "I do not want to work today." Instead, they might call in and say, "I am sick," or "I hurt my back," or "the babysitter did not show up." Employee absence can result in loss of output or service, other employees' work being disrupted to fill in, overtime costs to fill in for the absent workers, sick benefits and workers' compensation payments, and other intangible costs. The amounts may vary from one organization to another but they can easily reach 1½ times the level of the employee's wage for each day absent (Anonymous, 1997).

Absences planned in advance generally do not cause the employer undue problems. The real problem is with absences that just occur and may be of indeterminate length. These situations throw a great strain on the organization to provide work cover at very short notice and often at considerable extra cost. This could be extremely taxing on a small organization where staffing schedules are particularly tight. Most organizations require a medical certification for any illness over three to five days. However, the greater problem is absences which are in the one to two day range but frequent. The US service sector loses 2.3 percent of all scheduled labor hours to unplanned absences (Easton and Goodale, 2005).

Many organizations are somewhat hesitant in dealing with the absenteeism problem for fear of legal liability under the Family and Medical Leave Act (FMLA) or the Americans with Disabilities Act (ADA) (Falcone, 2000). An employer does have the right to discipline and fire employees with excessive absenteeism within certain guidelines. The first step in addressing excessive absenteeism is a review of your organization's policy.

Many organizations put caps on annual sick leave allowances. Others refuse to do so for fear that that will limit their ability to deal with employees on a case-by-case basis. It is also difficult for organizations to determine parameters around such leave. In academic organizations, librarians are often classified with faculty and are governed by a different set of rules.

When creating a new absenteeism policy, consider the following questions:

- Will you measure actual days or incidents (i.e., an uninterrupted series of days off from the same illness or injury)?
- What serves as the performance measurement time period: a calendar year, or other time frame?
- Are you consistent throughout the organization?
- Would a no-fault or an excuse-based system be most effective?

If you plan to change an existing policy or practice, notify employees in advance and in writing.

You might want to begin your policy with the something like the following: "Maintenance of good attendance is a condition of employment and an essential function of your job. To minimize hardships that may result from illness or injury, our organization provides paid sick time benefits. However, periodic sick leave taken on a repeated basis may be viewed as abuse of the system. It is your responsibility to establish legitimate illness or injury to receive sick leave pay." This sets the tone around the issue of repeated sick leave taken but you must follow through with consequences and be consistent among all staff.

Most staff members have legitimate reasons for absence. Others stay away because they feel their jobs lack challenge or are just boring. Watch for those warning signs and try to keep staff members engaged. Look for patterns of absence. Errant employees are easily identified because their absenteeism often follows a pattern. It may coincide with major events or be tacked onto weekends. The person often phones with an excuse, but you may find it increasingly difficult to believe the excuse that is offered. In this situation, maintain a record of patterns of absence. That information will be essential when you choose to confront the employee about the problem. You will need such evidence to prove that you did not discipline or terminate for discriminatory reasons. Do not let suspicious absences go by without an interview. Ask for a second explanation of the absence, which will trigger to the employee that you are skeptical of the excuse offered. Often, the simple act of calling attention to absences results in improved attendance (Muir, 1994).

If absenteeism does not improve and you are not convinced of the legitimacy, meet formally with the employee and reveal the evidence. Do you discipline or terminate? Whatever is decided, take firm action to eliminate or reduce the problem. If counseling or skills training is appropriate, schedule a session right away. If a warning is called for, make sure you record that warning and notify the employee in writing. If possible, have the employee sign the warning notice. If more firm action is required, do not balk at taking it. The situation will undoubtedly make its way through the grapevine and all employees will be aware of management's firm stand on unwarranted absenteeism, lessening the problem throughout the organization.

Let us consider the case of Agnes, who is an excellent performer when she is actually at work. The problem is that Agnes has a tendency to call in sick frequently. When she calls in sick, it occurs around regularly scheduled weekends and holidays.

The best defense lies in a well-crafted and consistent policy. Review your organization's past practices which would include any disciplinary actions related to unauthorized absences in the past two years. Remember that you have the choice to change a policy or practice by notifying employees in advance and in writing.

When you address the issue with Agnes, list the dates and days of the week of any absences. In addition, document the negative organizational impact resulting from her unauthorized absenteeism. For example, "Our library defines a pattern as a frequent, predictable, and observable employee action that repeats itself over time. All five of your occurrences were taken off around your regularly scheduled weekends and holidays. This patterning therefore violates our library's absenteeism policy."

Next, document your organization's expectations, provide a copy of the policy, and include the consequences of inaction. "Agnes, I expect you to immediately improve your attendance by minimizing any future occurrences of unscheduled, unauthorized absences. A copy of our attendance policy is attached. Please read it thoroughly today and meet with me tomorrow morning if you have any questions. If you meet these performance goals, no further disciplinary action will be taken. In addition, you will develop a greater sense of accomplishment by helping our department meet its goals while minimizing staff rescheduling and last minute overtime costs. Please understand, however, that failure to provide immediate and sustained improvement may result in further disciplinary action, up to and including dismissal."

While this does not guarantee that the employee will improve, the ground rules have been clearly laid and will allow you to replace this individual if absenteeism continues.

WHAT DO YOU DO WITH THE EMPLOYEE WHO SHOWS UP SICK?

The flip side of absenteeism is the employee who reports to work but demonstrates poor performance because they are physically or emotionally ill (Milano, 2005). This is becoming known as "presenteeism" (Milano, 2005). Presenteeism includes bad colds, minor injuries, seasonal allergies, or a nasty headache. An employee might also be distracted because of child care or elder care issues, financial or marital problems. In one survey conducted among 29,000 employees, one in eight reported coming to work in pain or physical discomfort at least once in any two-week period (Milano, 2005). Their condition caused them to lose concentration, to actually start working later than normal, to do tasks over because of lack of concentration, and to not really accomplish anything. Nearly half of all American employees admit being at work at least one to four days a year when they are too ill or stressed to be productive.

How dangerous is this? Think of a bus driver who has to be 100 percent attentive to his job responsibilities. He could actually be endangering the lives of many individuals who ride his bus. The risk of human error from employees working while ill can have a major impact, from loss of life to millions of dollars to the organization. Sleep deprivation can also lower productivity and raise risk factors. Often, chronic conditions contribute to people reporting to work in compromised conditions. These conditions include allergy/sinus problems, chronic back pain, arthritis, flu, migraines, and asthma. These conditions will not go away but employees should be encouraged to stay home when they are at their worst. During flu season, organizations should specifically ask individuals not to come in when they are ill.

Encourage employees with emotional issues to seek help. You can identify these individuals when you notice a sudden change in the employee's behavior. Individuals who interact on a regular basis with other employees may suddenly become withdrawn, or they might fly off the handle at the slightest incident. They probably will not want to talk about what is driving their behavior but you can certainly acknowledge what you have observed and suggest that they might want to seek some help from the EAP. Directing the employee to the appropriate agency or service will be valuable. For employees with financial issues, you can get them in touch with a local credit counseling service. One trucking organization that initiated wellness programs at its institution saw absenteeism decrease by 20 percent in one year (Milano, 2005). Managers feel that the preventive programs had a big impact on keeping employees healthy and productive.

HOW DO YOU DEAL WITH THE BULLYING EMPLOYEE?

Bullying is verbal or social behavior intended to result in power over another person. A growing body of literature describes this inappropriate workplace behavior (Namie, 2003). A survey found that 80 percent of the victims of bullying are women, with an average age of 43 (Namie, 2003). In this same survey, it was reported that only 23 percent of bullies chose to do the bullying themselves and 77 percent enlisted others to help. Among the most prevalent reasons targets reported for being bullied was that they had been seen by their bullies as threatening, either because of superior work skills or social skills.

Another study on bullying at work identified bullying as a "repeated and persistent negative action towards one or more individuals which involves a perceived power imbalance and creates a hostile work environment" (Lutgen-Sandvik, Tracy, and Alberts, 2006). Victims suffer long-term, sometimes permanent, psychological and occupational impairment. Some bullying overlapped with sexual harassment. Bullying at work affects more than just the individuals targeted. It also affects witnesses; these individuals could be seen as secondary targets. Generally, one-time incidents do not constitute "bullying." Bullying is when one or more individuals are on the receiving end of negative actions persistently over a period of time.

Responsibility for dealing with this behavior initially lies with the frontline staff. Reporting to the supervisor can trigger an exploration of the incident to determine whether the report is legitimate or not. The process can be supported by a strong policy against workplace abuse embedded in the mission and values of the organization.

In one situation I encountered, the bullying individual was not evident until the situation reached a crisis level. Two employees who worked in different locations in the library were involved. The male employee apparently did not approve of the female's behavior with other employees of the library. He made remarks to her when no one else was around to witness the harassment. She did not come to the HR department because she thought she could handle it on her own. The situation became full blown one day when he brought a dead bird into the library and dumped it on the employee's desk. Another employee witnessed the incident and was also outraged at this behavior. Both the female and the witness came to human resources to relay what had happened. The female employee then told us of other incidents.

The "bullying" employee was requested to come to human resources and asked for his version. He tried to pass it off as a joke but was warned that this behavior was inappropriate and that further behavior of this manner would not be tolerated. The bullying behavior stopped, and he eventually left for another position. While still at the library, he treated the female employee civilly and no more complaints occurred.

IS VIOLENCE IN THE WORKPLACE AN ISSUE IN LIBRARIES?

Employers do not want to think that their workplace is potentially violent, but violence does exist. According to the National Crime Victimization Survey conducted by the US Department of Justice, there are almost two million assaults and threats of on-the-job violence each year (Smith and Mazen, 2004; Gupta and Kleiner, 2005). Workplace violence can be devastating to employees and to the organization through negative publicity and potential lawsuits. It would be impossible to prevent or predict all violent incidents but organizations can take certain measures to ensure safety. Carefully screen potential hires for past violent behavior. Look for warning signs that may indicate potential violence and pursue steps to analyze this behavior. Train all employees in observation of warning signs and what steps they should take should violent behavior occur.

Common warning signs include, but are not limited to, explicit threats or verbal abuse, displays of anger such as screaming, slamming doors, or throwing things, a continual disgruntled attitude, paranoid behavior, wide mood swings, unexplained attendance problems, or other erratic behavior. Studies indicate that employees do not become violent overnight; it is a slow and gradual process (Gupta and Kleiner, 2005). Other traits that might indicate a potentially violent individual are: 1) he/she blames others for everything and portrays him/herself as a victim, 2) he/she does not take criticism well and becomes agitated when criticized, 3) he/she seems obsessed with guns and talks about weapons being the solution to everything, 4) he or she has no interest in doing his/her job and does not seem to care about anyone's feelings, 5) he/she is often absent, 6) he/she has a substance abuse problem, 7) he or she cannot control anger and hits walls or furniture when upset. Often the violent individual has financial or family problems. He or she may appear depressed or angry, shouting louder to be heard. Most of these problems could be solved by referring the individual to the EAP.

WHAT CAN YOU DO TO COPE WITH A POTENTIALLY VIOLENT EMPLOYEE?

Choose your words carefully. Avoid referring to yourself, (i.e., "I believe you should..." or "I'm going to recommend..."). This can push the employee's pent-up rage. Instead, make your company's policy the scapegoat ("Company policy requires you to...," "the procedure states that you must contact our EAP for counseling...") Keep your comments and behavior neutral and nonjudgmental.

Inform higher management immediately of threats or physical acts. Record the date, time, location, names of witnesses, and other relevant details of the incident. Encourage your staff to report all threats or acts of violence. Assure them that their names will be kept confidential to prevent reprisals. Emphasize that they are not being traitors or tattle-tales. The safety of everyone in the workplace could be compromised by a misplaced sense of loyalty or failure to speak out. Keep open communication with everyone in your work environment. Listen, do not just hear.

All organizations should have clearly defined written policies on workplace violence. Training can have a huge impact on handling potentially violent employees. According to one survey, 20.2 percent of supervisors responded that they have reduced violence in their workplace because of the training they received on how to spot troubled workers and what to do about them (Gupta and Kleiner, 2005). The companies involved had reported an increase in workplace violence prior to the training.

Negotiation training can be very important if you are caught in a potentially violent situation. You should not argue with them, hit them, shout, or threaten them as this will only agitate the person and you want them to relax and calm down (Rainham, 2003).

Although it is impossible to completely eliminate workplace violence, it can be significantly reduced. Organizations should hold training programs, especially for supervisors. There should be written policies about acts of violence and organizations should have zero tolerance of violence and guns at the workplace. Prospective employees should be carefully screened within the legal guidelines.

REFERENCES

Anonymous. 1997. "Many Ways to Reduce Absenteeism, Cut Costs." *The Worklife Report* 10, no. 3: 14–15.

Axelrod, Beth, Helen Handfield-Jones, and Ed Michaels. 2002. "A New Game Plan for C Players." *Harvard Business Review* 80, no. 1: 80–88.

Bates, Steve. 2004. "Getting Engaged." *HRMagazine* 49, no. 2: 44–51.

Bramson, Robert M. 1981. *Coping with Difficult People*. New York: Anchor Press.

Cottringer, William. 2003. "Employee Conflict." *Supervision* 64, no. 20: 3–5.

Curtis, David. 2003. "Learning from Jayson Blair: Having Marginal Employees Is Situation to Address ASAP." *Fort Worth Business Press* 16, no. 23: 41.

Easton, Fred R. and John C. Goodale. 2005. "Schedule Recovery: Unplanned Absences in Service Organizations." *Decision Sciences* 36, no. 3: 459–488.

Falcone, Paul. 2000. "Tackling Excessive Absenteeism." *HRMagazine* 45, no. 1: 139–144.

Foltz, John and Joan Fulton. 2005. "Dealing with Problem Employees." *Feed & Grain* 44, no. 4: 38–41.

Freed, David H. 2000. "One More Time: Please Fire Marginal Employees." *Health Care Manager* 18, no. 3: 45–51.

Gupta, Vick and Brian H. Kleiner. 2005. "How to Recognize and Handle Potentially Violent Employees." *Management Research News* 28, no. 11/12: 60–69.

Hale, Dwight. 1991/92. "Supervising the Marginal Employee: Dilemma and Opportunity." *Management Quarterly* 32, no. 4: 23–30.

Kravitz, Michael S. 1995. *Managing Negative People*. Menlo Park, CA: Crisp Publications.

Lutgen-Sandvik, Pamela. Sara J. Tracy, and Jess K. Alberts. 2006. "Burned by Bullying in the American Workplace: Prevalence, Perception, Degree and Impact." *Journal of Management Studies* (in press). Available: http://bullyinginstitute.org/res.html (accessed February 21, 2007).

Milano, Carol. 2005. "Being There: Can Coming to Work Be a Risk?" *Risk Management* 52, no. 11: 30–34.

Muir, John. 1994. "Dealing with Sickness Absence." *Work Study, London* 43, no. 5: 13–14.

Namie, Gary. 2003. "The Workplace Bullying Institute 2003 Report on Abusive Workplaces." Available: http://bullinginstitute.org/res.html (accessed February 21, 2007).

Perry, Phillip M. 2004. "Problem Employees: Get Your Poor Performers Back on Track." *Executive Housekeeping Today* 25, no. 11: 23–28.

Rainham, David. 2003. "How to Deal With a Violent Employee." *The Record (Kitchner-Waterloo, Ontario)* June 27: (Life) D-2.

Smith, Shawn and Rebecca Mazin. 2004. *The HR Answer Book*. New York: AMACOM.

Sweeney, John, Angela Stone, and Naomi Cossack. 2007. "Skills Data, Retirement Benefits, Difficult Employees." *HRMagazine* 52, no. 1: 49–50.

Weitzel, Thomas Q. 2004. "Managing the Problem Employee: A Road Map for Success." *FBI Law Enforcement Bulletin* 73, no. 11: 25–32.

Zimmerer, Thomas W. 1973. "Increasing Productivity Among Marginal Employees." *Industrial Management* 15, no. 1: 1–3.

CONFLICT RESOLUTION/ MANAGEMENT, PROGRESSIVE DISCIPLINE, AND RIF

Chapter 8 will review the challenges of conflict resolution and reduction in force (RIF). Sexual harassment will also be covered in this chapter.

The traditional approach to conflict assumed that conflict was bad. Conflict was used synonymously with terms such as violence, destruction, and irrationality (Robbins, 2000). In the early 1970s, conflict was regarded by management theorists as an essential and necessary fact of organizational life (Kathman and Kathman, 1990). Under this theory, conflict arises due to the rapidly changing environment and allows for organizational growth, with both positive and negative outcomes. This view has been labeled the human relations view.

A more current view, the interactionist view, "encourages conflict on the grounds that a harmonious, peaceful, tranquil, and cooperative group is likely to become static, apathetic, and nonresponsive to needs for change and innovation" (Robbins, 2000: 169). It sees conflict as not necessarily good but as an instrument for an organization to develop further and be more innovative.

WHAT IS CONFLICT?

According to the *American Heritage Dictionary*, 2nd ed., "Conflict is a state of disagreement and disharmony or a state of open fighting." It "refers to a clash, physical or figurative, involving two persons, or a small group, or to a struggle for a cause." This definitely applies to clashes in work environments.

No matter how well an organization is run, disputes, conflicts, and grievances will inevitably arise. All individuals have their own ideas and goals. In pursuing these goals, they will sometimes be at odds with others who have differing viewpoints and objectives. The increasingly diverse workforce, new technologies, and pressures to meet new demands all cause stress, which can often lead to conflict. The positive or negative results of conflict depend on the organization's ability to identify healthy and unhealthy conflict and to manage and resolve disputes and grievances before they get out of hand.

While healthy conflict resolves around the vigorous exchange of ideas in the best interests of the organization, unhealthy conflict is based on anger, frustration, and personal animosity (Smith and Mazin, 2004). The key to effective conflict management is to create an environment that encourages employees to challenge ideas but does not allow them to attack others' ideas. In organizations that effectively manage conflict, protocols guide individual and team behavior. Conflict management (as opposed to conflict resolution) presents conflict as an opportunity for individuals and organizations to move closer to achieving their goals (Kathman and Kathman, 1990).

Individuals come to the workplace from a variety of backgrounds. While this is a positive thing, conflict emerges when individuals try to inflict their viewpoints on others. The key here is to accept differences and emphasize the strengths that each person brings to the environment.

Even within an organization, different areas may have different standards and values. Whether a library is traditional or team based, library services usually include reference, circulation, interlibrary loan, acquisitions, cataloging, library instruction, technology, and administration. These units operate very differently and conflict may arise when one area tries to enforce its standards on another area.

For example, accuracy is a valued principle for original cataloging, and an extended period of time is often needed to catalog material to accuracy standards. On the other hand, reference wants the function completed quickly to satisfy the needs of the users. Conflict between these two areas could arise if one area makes demands of the other without consideration of its values and standards. Each is concerned with important issues. How can one compare the two and determine which unit takes precedence?

Another potential source of conflict for library organizations is the fine line between job roles (Kathman and Kathman, 1990). For instance, reference assistants often work side by side with the librarians at the reference service point. They may be answering some of the very same questions as librarians and yet the two roles are very different. The librarian may assume other roles such as classroom instruction, program development, or collaboration and negotiation with nonlibrary personnel. The assistant, when not on desk duty, may compile statistics or other data or even shelve library materials. Conflict can arise if paraprofessionals perceive that their tasks are the same and yet salaries and other benefits differ greatly. This type of conflict often occurs in a team-based organization when team members working side-by-side yet at different ranks or levels believe that they are less valued than other members of their team.

Other possible avenues of conflict come from internal and external environmental factors. Many libraries are asked to do more with fewer resources. Staff members may be required to take on more responsibility and yet are not given additional funds or time to do so. Changes in leadership can cause anxiety and conflict among the staff. Technology changes can also cause tensions as staff members adapt.

Most days, individuals can cope with the varying factors that influence their role and job responsibilities. Other days, the stress may be too much and conflict happens.

HOW DOES ONE HANDLE CONFLICT? IS MANAGEMENT RESPONSIBLE FOR ALL CONFLICT?

Each situation must be considered separately. However, leaders or supervisors can provide a model with their approach to conflict management, emphasizing that conflicts are a normal part of the workplace but that resolving them successfully is the main goal. Employees need to be encouraged to be tolerant of differences. The value of having a diverse workforce should be emphasized. Training employees (and supervisors) on basic conflict resolution techniques is recommended (Cottringer, 2005). This type of training is offered by numerous training facilitators.

The management literature recognizes five ways of dealing with conflict: competing, avoiding, accommodating, compromising, and collaboration (Robbins, 2000; Kathman and Kathman, 1990). Which method to choose depends on the situation, the nature of the conflict, the parties involved, the relationships between the individuals, and time restraints.

WHAT IS THE DIFFERENCE BETWEEN THESE APPROACHES TO CONFLICT?

Competition or using one's position to maintain control is when one party seeks to achieve certain goals or to further personal interests regardless of the impact on the parties to the conflict. This is a win-lose situation. An example might be a librarian who does not feel that keeping the reference hours is important but policies indicate that certain hours must be covered. In most libraries, this is not a negotiable issue and policies and norms must override the librarian's view.

Avoidance occurs when both parties withdraw from addressing the issue or postpone the discussion. The individuals involved may separate themselves but interact when needed for organizational tasks and functions.

They suppress the issue rather than totally withdraw. This approach merely puts the conflict on the back burner. It will undoubtedly resurface at a later time.

Accommodation is when the conflicting individuals seek to appease each other. In order to maintain the relationship, one party is willing to be self-sacrificing and put the other's interests above their own. You often see this type of resolution when one librarian steps in to cover another one's absence at the reference desk or instruction session. Another example would be if one staff member assumes the tasks of another even though it increases his or her workload.

Compromise occurs when each party must give up something. There is no clear winner or loser. In negotiations between unions and management, compromise is required in order to reach a settlement and agree upon a labor contract. Compromise might also be used in a conflict over limited resources such as allocating travel funds in a library.

Collaboration is when those involved in the conflict search for a mutually beneficial outcome through cooperation, requiring full consideration of all alternatives. This is considered a win-win situation. Counselors and behavioral scientists are strong advocates for this approach. Collaboration requires a shared commitment to solution of the conflict. The only drawback is the time involved in settling the dispute.

HOW CAN AN ORGANIZATION DEAL WITH CONFLICT?

There are some basic skills that you can use in managing conflict.

1) Bring the conflicting parties together in a neutral place. Treat the meeting as a serious occasion and do not allow any phone calls or interruptions. Let them know that you have observed or been informed that there are difficulties between them and ask to hear each side of the story. Emphasize that each party will be allowed to speak in turn. Listen carefully and empathetically.

2) Do not show a bias toward any individual's point of view. If you show sympathy with one of the individuals, the other will lose trust in the process and will withdraw from further engagement. As mediator, your role is not to judge or decide the solution but to assist the individuals in expressing their differences and help them work toward a meaningful solution.

3) Keep the discussion focused on the conflict. If the participants begin to ramble or drift off topic, gently bring them back to the issue. Focus on the present conflict and not past occurrences or gripes. Do not allow personal attacks such as "he is lying" or "she is stupid." Do not interject your own opinions or experiences. The discussion is about the parties in conflict.

4) Clearly define the problem or issue. Where is the problem really coming from and is the problem important to the organization? Who is affected? Is this problem the same for everyone in the organization? Disagreements are often fueled by interpersonal differences and these issues must be addressed.

5) Do not ignore emotions. It is not wise to dwell on the emotions involved but it is important to acknowledge them. Expressing emotions often helps the parties to move on.

6) Work with the conflicting employees to find a way to achieve resolution. The plan does not have to be a complete compromise but it should be acceptable to both individuals. Encourage them to suggest alternatives and record all suggestions. The participants will feel that they are part of the process and not being judged. This could lead to ownership of a final decision by both. An agreement may not be reached at the first meeting. If the meeting becomes pointless, stop the meeting and resume at another point giving the individuals time to think over what has been discussed. When they have reached an agreement, put the plan in writing so each one has something to refer to and work with.

7) Follow up periodically. If the conflict is significant, resolution may not happen overnight. Look for indications that the individuals are acting on the plan as agreed and taking steps forward. Emphasize that it is okay to take smalls steps and recognize their accomplishments as they attempt to work through their differences. Both employees must refocus their individual energy toward accomplishing organizational goals and objectives.

Other employees will be watching to see if management is serious about resolving this dispute in a professional manner. Successful supervisors will create a work environment where unnecessary anxiety and tension are minimized and disputes or conflicts are resolved.

Sometimes mediation may be the only way to work through the issues (Cote and Pistorio, 2001). A mediator does not have the authority to impose a solution on the individuals involved, but can impartially help them achieve positive outcomes. A settlement through mediation can help reduce legal and court costs for organizations (Cote and Pistorio, 2001). Many larger US corporations use mediation and arbitration before seeking legal recourse. This method is probably best used when unions are involved.

Informal mediation can occur when disputing parties request the intervention of a third party. HR personnel are often called in to perform this type of mediation. Here is one such case that I experienced.

One department had had three different heads in five years due to retirement, promotion, and a spouse transfer. As a result of this constant change, the support staff had learned to managed their workload on their own with little supervision. When the latest head of the department was appointed, she made several changes to the workload distribution and assignments. Immediately, one of the clericals who had more or less assumed a management role became disgruntled. After several months, a request for an informal mediation meeting was made by both the head and this employee.

The scheduled meeting took place in a quiet "safe" area where no interruptions would occur. Ground rules were set. This included an agreement that each party would be allowed to speak without interruptions. They both agreed to paraphrase back what the other had said to ensure understanding.

I had to intervene several times when the individuals forgot the ground rules and wanted to interrupt each other. After several false starts, the discussion became calmer and the participants actually listened to each other. I reiterated what each of the participants were expressing. The head felt as if she was not being allowed to try a new approach and the employee felt that if the way they were doing business was working, why change it? The next stage was negotiation, where the participants discussed what steps could be taken. Both were asked to present some possibilities and these were written down to make sure that all aspects could be considered. The final stage or closure was actually deciding which avenue they would take. They determined that they would give this process a month and then reevaluate to see if it was working. This was an outcome that they both could live with. We met again a month later and both participants agreed that it was working nicely.

Not every negotiation and mediation session is going to have a win-win outcome. Sometimes you have to accept that both parties are going to leave the table equally unhappy. Some conflicts simply are not resolvable. You might determine that a mediator from outside of the organization or library might better suit the situation. Smaller libraries might want to check state or regional associations to see if there is someone available within your jurisdiction that could assume this role.

In larger libraries, someone from the HR administration unit might be more appropriate.

WHAT HAPPENS WHEN EMPLOYEES LEAVE BECAUSE OF CONFLICT?

Sometimes the organization makes every effort to create a positive work environment but the employee still decides to leave after conflict resolution. The most important thing to do in this situation is to conduct a structured exit interview. The results of the exit interview might help determine if there are underlying problems that are causing people to leave. This might provide an opportunity to build a strategy for improved retention. Ask questions that will elicit information about your organization as a place to work and that will help identify trends developing in any specific area or with a specific individual. To maintain confidentiality, keep exit interview data separate from the employee's personnel file.

Sound employee relations are important in all phases of the employment cycle, including departure. Try not to make the departing employee feel uncomfortable about his or her decision or treat them as an enemy. A former employee can be an advocate for your organization for potential employees and customers. You may even end up hiring this individual again in the future.

Figure 8-1 is a sampling of questions that might be asked during the exit interview.

---

1) What factors contributed to your accepting a job with this organization?

2) Did you understand the job expectations of the position when you were hired?

3) Did you receive the support of the organization in meeting these expectations?

4) What did you enjoy most about working for this organization?

5) What did you like least about working for this organization?

6) What is your reason for leaving the organization?

7) Could this organization have done something to prevent your leaving?

8) If asked, would you recommend employment at this organization to a prospective employee?

9) Please comment on any other areas that you believe would improve the workplace quality of this organization.

Figure 8-1. Potential Questions for an Exit Interview

WHAT DO YOU DO WHEN THE PROGRESSIVE DISCIPLINE AND TERMINATION PROCESS FOR EMPLOYEES JUST IS NOT WORKING?

A formal progressive discipline process helps protect both the employee and the employer. Progressive discipline is a term that often has a negative connotation, but discipline is a fact of life in the work environment. One definition of discipline is "training that is expected to produce a specific character or pattern of behavior, especially training that produces moral or mental improvement" (*Webster's Ninth New Collegiate Dictionary*, 1989, 360). This is the principle upon which "progressive discipline" is founded. Progressive discipline is intended to change an individual's behavior so that they can be successful in the organization. However, we cannot force people to change their behavior. They can only change if they want to (Gasaway, 2007).

In the ideal world, employees would always be positive, do the right thing, and follow all of the rules of the organization. Unfortunately, many organizations will have to travel the road of progressive discipline. The progressive discipline philosophy addresses unacceptable behavior in three stages: preventative, corrective, and adverse (Terwilliger, 2005a).

WHAT IS THE PREVENTATIVE STAGE?

The first stage, the preventative phase, is informal and ongoing. It is based on the premise that creating and maintaining the appropriate environment will diminish the need for corrective and adverse disciplinary procedures. A good working environment entails comfortable physical surroundings, supportive administration with good leadership skills, clear direction and job standards, and pleasant interpersonal relationships with fellow employees.

According to some researchers, there are four factors in a healthy work environment: 1) a conscious organization with distinct goals and objectives, 2) a creative space which incorporates a culture that is accepting and allows for work to be flexible, 3) a consultative leadership where employees are given the requirements to succeed, and 4) an open work climate with high levels of participation, respect, and confidence in each other (Arwedson, Roos, and Bjorklund, 2007). This sounds very similar to the preventative stage of progressive discipline.

While organizations can provide some of the tools for a suitable work environment, the employees themselves must be accountable, too. If the employees feel that the management is fair and supportive, they are more likely to be motivated and pursue their role as a productive, happy team member. This is based on the assumption that the majority of your employees want to be competent and effective in performing their job responsibilities and maintain good relations with other employees.

Sooner or later, you can expect that someone will unwittingly, thoughtlessly, or willfully violate the standards of conduct and job performance. If these situations are not addressed or corrected within a reasonable period of time, additional problems will arise. Morale within the organization will be affected and other employees will lose motivation to perform their jobs well. This will move the organization to the second phase, or corrective stage.

WHAT IS THE CORRECTIVE STAGE?

It is imperative that an organization has a formal discipline program in place and that employees are made aware of the process and the consequences. Discipline is a difficult and stressful process, but if not conducted, the problems will persist and get worse.

Before imposing discipline, investigate the alleged incident or problem to determine whether a breach of workplace rules has occurred. Employees need to know what the problem is and what they must do to fix it. In addition, employees need to have a reasonable period of time in which to fix the problem and understand the consequences of inaction.

Give the employee an opportunity to defend him or herself and then consider all aspects of the situation. What has the employee's previous record been? Do you have firsthand knowledge of the facts regarding the incident and will you be able to prove these facts? Documentation must show that the employee acted unreasonably (Falcone, 2000). Was the employee informally notified about the unacceptable behavior when it occurred and allowed to correct the behavior? The employee should have the opportunity to correct the behavior before the corrective stage begins. If the employee's behavior continues to be unacceptable, then the corrective stage should ensue.

The corrective interview is not an annual performance review and is not a form of punitive action. It is a formal meeting between the supervisor and the employee to develop an action plan to change the employee's unacceptable behavior. It is an attempt to avoid formal undesirable action further down the road. Most infractions fall into one of these four categories: policy and/or procedure violations, performance transgressions, behavior or misconduct infractions, and absenteeism or tardiness (Falcone, 2000). It is important to classify the unacceptable behavior in your documentation. For instance, an employee's first warning might be for a performance-related issue. If the employee then develops a tardiness problem, this is a different infraction from the first one. You must be careful to be very clear about what you are addressing with each step. Be sure that you are consistent. It never hurts to have legal or administrative counsel in on your process to ensure that you are following the process correctly.

HOW DO YOU PREPARE FOR THE FIRST CORRECTIVE INTERVIEW?

Once you have decided that a first corrective interview is warranted, prepare and make sure that everything is in order. Plan to conduct the session in a confidential location that will allow for no interruptions. This will demonstrate to the employee that this is a serious and important matter. Set aside the appropriate amount of time for the discussion.

Decide what issues and topics are to be covered. Use the following principles to guide your behavior during the interview:

- Remain calm and objective throughout the interview.
- Focus on the issues and the inappropriate behavior and state this clearly.
- Do not exaggerate the problem behavior or apologize for having to do the interview.
- Do not wander from the issues at hand and use examples relating to the issues.
- Make sure that the employee understands what they have done that was unacceptable.
- Avoid debating the issue with the employee or weakening on your decision.
- Maintain control of the discussion and do not let the employee direct the discussion.
- Be helpful and encourage the employee while respecting his/her dignity and viewpoint.
- Inform the employee what will happen if the behavior does not improve.
- Do not inhibit the employee from taking this to the next level of supervision.

Both positive and negative aspects of an employee's performance should be discussed. Identification of problems is a positive thing because it results in teaching, coaching, and growing. Criticism helps employees to get back on track and stay there. Discuss how your expectations differ from the employee's performance. The goal is to solve the problem and maintain a good relationship with the employee.

This first corrective interview is also called an "oral warning." Take notes and include an adopted plan for change. Have the employee sign and date the report of the meeting. Make a copy for the employee and retain a copy for the employee's file. Acknowledge that the signature does not indicate agreement but does demonstrate that the employee has seen and read the documentation.

Establish a time frame for when the expected change should be accomplished. As part of the action plan, schedule follow-up meetings with the employee to assess the progress being made. When the designated period of time for improvement is reached, send a memo to the employee indicating whether or not the behavior has improved and whether the behavior is acceptable or not. If the issue is resolved, keep the positive letter in the employee's file for one year. If the situation is not resolved, the negative letter will be part of the evidence that indicates further action is needed. Positive or negative, the follow-up memo should be signed and dated by the employee (Terwilliger, 2005b). If the employee refuses to sign the summary or the follow-up memo, indicate this on the documents. It is advisable to have witnesses verify that the employee refused to sign the documents.

WHAT IF THE FIRST CORRECTIVE INTERVIEW FAILS TO IMPROVE THE EMPLOYEE'S BEHAVIOR?

The first corrective interview's purpose is to gain the employee's agreement to change (Christie and Kleiner, 2000). The employee who agrees to make changes, even grudgingly, is more likely to do so than the one who is told they must change. If this interview fails to work and the employee's behavior is still unacceptable, the supervisor will be forced to conduct the next step, the letter of warning. Written warnings are for unacceptable performance that is repeated or considered to be severe but not requiring immediate termination. This letter advises the employee of the continued deficiencies and the consequences of what happens if he or she fails to correct them within a designated time period.

This "letter of warning" is placed in the supervisor's working file and is also placed in the employee's personnel file for three years. The employee may submit a rebuttal, which can be attached to the letter of warning.

The letter of warning should indicate the deficiencies and identify previous corrective actions taken to correct the behavior. The time frame should be appropriate for the expected actions. Always include a specific date on which the progress on the plan will be reviewed. Follow up on this plan and notify the employee as to whether the work performance or behavior has been improved to the acceptable level or not. This notice will also serve as evidence and documentation for future action. The written reprimand should include what the supervisor is willing to do to assist in correcting the problem. If the unacceptable behavior continues following one or more written reprimands, suspension is the next logical step.

WHAT IF THE EMPLOYEE IS PART OF A LABOR UNION AND REQUESTS REPRESENTATION AT THE INTERVIEWS?

The employee technically does not have a right to representation during the corrective phase or during routine business communication unless formal adverse action is a possibility (Terwilliger, 2005c). However, your organization should allow a representative to be present if the employee requests it. Usually the employee will not request representation at the first interview or oral warning. At the second or written warning stage, you should inform the employee of his/her right to have representation and, if requested, postpone the meeting until representation can be present. If the organization has followed correct procedures, there should be no problem with having representation. In fact, if the unacceptable behavior continues and could lead to future adverse action, it would be wise to have the representative present.

WHAT IS THE ADVERSE STAGE?

Suspension is part of stage three or the adverse stage. This suspension serves as an additional warning and should clearly specify that discharge or termination will be the result of another such infraction within a stated period of time (Dhanoa and Kleiner, 2000). Suspensions are issued when written warnings have not resolved the unacceptable behavior of the employee and the employer is still hopeful that the employee will improve and change unacceptable behavior or performance. Again, as with the other warnings, a specific date for improvement following the suspension should be indicated. Often after a suspension, one more infraction of the unacceptable behavior will be the limit before termination or discharge.

Suspending an employee is very serious and sends a strong message. This is the first step toward termination. Suspension may be with or without pay. The duration of the suspension is best determined by the seriousness of the infraction. The employee may not care about the organization, but he/she may care about the money and his/her responsibilities. How the employee reacts to this measure will give you some idea about how effective this measure will be.

WHAT IS THE BEST WAY TO HANDLE DISCHARGE OR TERMINATION?

Discharge or termination of an employee follows continued or repeated failures in work performance or behavior. Sometimes exceptionally serious behavior, i.e., involving theft or sexual harassment charges, may warrant immediate discharge.

When you choose this path, you are no longer using progressive discipline. You have determined that the employee is no longer salvageable and you are ready to move on. Make sure that the employee has had every possible opportunity to correct his/her behavior. Once the decision to terminate an employee is made, the action should be taken immediately. Sometimes, it is possible to obtain a negotiated resignation, which often is less bothersome and is in the best interests of both the employee and the employer (Christie and Kleine, 2000)—the progressive discipline process is a tool and not a weapon. At the time of dismissal, the employer should remove the employee's name from all eligible lists and technology access. An organization is responsible to see that the dismissed employee receives all income due to him/her.

Adverse employment action or termination may result in legal action (Gasaway, 2007). It is wise to have your HR department or organization attorney review such actions before they are administered. It is better to be prepared for such action than to be surprised.

WHAT DO YOU DO ABOUT SEXUAL HARASSMENT? DOES IT WARRANT PROGRESSIVE DISCIPLINE?

The appropriate response to sexual harassment depends on the situation and each incident must be viewed on its own. The best approach might be discipline combined with strong remedial counseling and/or training ("Training or Punishment," 2001). Choosing the appropriate degree of discipline for an employee who has been charged with sexual harassment can be difficult. It is important to consider all factors surrounding the situation when determining whether this behavior was a one-time incident or whether the employee will harass again.

Most organizations recognize and address obvious instances of sexual harassment but many do not adequately educate their supervisors that sexual harassment includes much more than inappropriate physical contact or threats. A hostile work environment claim can be made based on sexually charged jokes, pictures, and overtures when that environment interferes with an individual's work performance. Claims can also be made on subtle behaviors such as uninvited letters, phone calls, and gifts. In order to minimize the risks of sexual harassment claims, all employers should review and strengthen their anti-harassment policies and complaint procedures. All employees should be trained on the policies and procedures, and supervisors should be held accountable for preventing such activity. Any complaints that are brought to their attention should be addressed immediately and reported.

Incidents should be investigated thoroughly before any formal charges are made. The US Equal Employment Opportunity Commission views discipline in terms of proportional punishment ("Training or Punishment," 2001). A person making a few off-color remarks but having no prior record could be verbally reprimanded. Severe or continued harassing behavior should probably be dealt with by suspension or termination. All reprimands should be documented which technically transforms a verbal warning into a written one. The warning should state that the behavior must not be repeated or else the employee faces further consequences up to and including termination.

IS THERE A CLEAR-CUT TEST FOR TERMINATING A FIRST OFFENDER?

Any sexual physical contact is normally considered dischargable behavior by the employer community and the courts ("Training or Punishment," 2001).

Not every incidence of touching warrants discharge. There have been a few cases where people brush against one another and a claim is made that it was a deliberate act when in fact it was accidental. Another "iffy" area is affectionate hugs or patting the back or shoulders. These are not normally considered adequate grounds for termination on a first offense unless the complainant has had to reject unwelcome behavior repeatedly.

Offensive words may also be cause for discharge depending on the coarseness and severity. Using a four-letter word to proposition a coworker or saying something very explicit and offensive could be probable grounds for dismissal. This needs to be pursued very carefully. Other facts to consider in dismissal cases are whether the offender had previously used unreported crude language or has had previous rule violations or misconduct warnings.

HOW DO YOU HANDLE REDUCTION IN FORCE OR RIF?

At some point, an organization may have to use RIF as a strategy for dealing with budget cuts. A RIF is defined as elimination of a permanent position that results from a lack of work. Another term for this process is "downsizing." Strategies must be in place to work through this difficult task.

Some organizations who want to avoid confrontation associated with progressive discipline look to the no-fault layoff (Falcone, 2000). This is not the best route for an organization to pursue. A layoff eliminates positions, not individuals. Written records must reflect that a position is being eliminated because of a lack of work or other financial constraints. You cannot arbitrarily select someone for RIF because they are your weakest performer.

The practice of layoffs can be detrimental to an organization in that the action creates uncertainty about the future of the organization, the security of other jobs, and the degree of trust (Zatzick and Iverson, 2006). If employees who are terminated believe that they have been treated callously, anger and retaliation can result. Even survivors of the cuts can become angry and distrustful and retaliate toward the organization because of perceived unfairness and coldness in the termination of their coworkers (Cangemi and Miller, 2004). Some researchers have reported that high-performing employees often take jobs elsewhere in order to avoid uncertainties in a downsizing environment (Zatzick and Iverson, 2006).

A reduction in the workforce is usually the last resort for an organization. In many libraries today, funding has been substantially cut, contributing to decisions to cut the workforce. Organizations must take into consideration several legal aspects. These statutes include the National Labor Relations Act, the Civil Rights Act of 1964, the Americans with Disabilities Act, the Age Discrimination in Employment Act, the Older Workers Benefit Protection Act, the Employee Retirement Income Security Act, and the Worker Adjustment Retraining and Notification Act (Kuhn and Stout, 2004). Any terminated employee who feels his/her rights have been violated to any of the listed statutes may bring a legal action against the organization. If the investigation finds reasonable cause to believe a violation has occurred, the first step involves seeking conciliation with the employer. If that fails, the EEOC can either sue the employer or give the employee permission to pursue the claim in court. Costs in both time and litigation can be severe.

Alternatives should also be considered before going the route of RIFs. One team that was formed to study the most effective way to make a reduction came up with the plan that all employees, including the leadership group, would work four days a week, cutting payroll by 20 percent (Cangemi and Miller, 2004). Everyone shared in the pain and the mood and atmosphere within the organization remained upbeat and optimistic because the employees had a voice in the solution to the problem. Other alternatives might include voluntary retirement and/or buyouts.

Organizations must clearly consider all of the ramifications of downsizing before choosing this option. Is downsizing worth the potential loss of reputation among future employees or current customers? Potential applicants might think twice about joining an organization that has downsized. Employees within the organization often face expanded roles and increased workloads, elevating stress levels and uncertainty. Organizations can take specific steps to ensure that downsizing has as little negative impact on employees as possible, such as providing financial help to individuals losing their jobs, including severance packages, outplacement, and continuation of medical benefits (Kammeyer-Mueller and Liao, 2006). Another important factor is the extent to which the organization has provided advanced warning. Communication demonstrates that an organization is upfront and honest in interacting with the employees and signals organizational support.

In this chapter, we have explored conflict and its resolution, progressive discipline procedures, downsizing, and termination. These are all difficult situations. Conflict often erupts because of unintended miscues and blind spots. Leaders and human resources professionals are in a unique position to help employees focus on these blind spots and disconnects and lead them into needed changes. Turning conflict into confrontation and successful outcomes takes skill and practice. Library managers and HR professionals must strive to promote civility and create a workplace that is conducive to bring out the best in all employees.

One significant factor in conflict resolution and other problematic issues is supportive communication, which is nonjudgmental and sensitive to everyone's needs. In Chapter 9, we will explore the many facets of communication and how it affects the organization.

REFERENCES

Arwedson, Ingrid L., Susanne Roos, and Anita Bjorklund. 2007. "Constituents of Healthy Workplaces." *Work* 28: 3–11.

Bernardi, Lauren M. 2003. "Nine Steps to Effective Discipline." *Canadian Manager* 28, no. 4: 19–20, 30.

Cangemi, Joseph P. and Richard L. Miller. 2004. "Exit Strategies." *Journal of Management Development* 28, no. 10: 982–987.

Christie, Betsy and Brian H. Kleiner. 2000. "When Is an Employee Unsalvageable?" *Equal Opportunities International* 19, no. 6/7: 40–44.

Cote, Sylvie and Marc Pistorio. 2001. "Resolving Disputes." *CMA Management* 75, no. 7: 18–19.

Cottringer, William. 2005. "Adopting a Philosophy on Conflict." *Supervision* 66, no. 3: 3–5.

Dhanoa, David S. and Brian H. Kleiner. 2000. "How to Conduct Due Process Discipline." *Management Research News* 23, no. 7/8: 89–94.

Falcone, Paul. 2000. "Employee Separations: Layoffs vs. Terminations for Cause." *HRMagazine* 45, no. 10: 189–196.

Gasaway, Richard B. 2007. "The Purpose of Discipline." *Fire Engineering* 160, no. 1: 12–16.

Kammeyer-Mueller, John and Hui Liao. 2006. "Workforce Reduction and Job-Seeker Attraction: Examining Job Seekers' Reactions to Firm Workforce Reduction Policies." *Human Resource Management* 45, no. 4: 585–603.

Kathman, Jane M. and Michael D. Kathman. 1990. "Conflict Management in the Academic Library." *Journal of Academic Librarianship* 16, no. 3: 145–150.

Kuhn, Dennis M. and David E. Stout. 2004. "Reducing Your Workforce: What You Don't Know Can Hurt You." *Strategic Finance* 85, no. 11: 41–45.

Robbins, Stephen P. 2000. *Essentials of Organizational Behavior*, 6th ed. Upper Saddle River, NJ: Prentice-Hall.

Smith, Shawn and Rebecca Mazin. 2004. *The HR Answer Book*. New York: AMACOM.

Terwilliger, Michael S. 2005a. "A Supervisor's Guide to Progressive Discipline, Part 1." *Fire Engineering* 158, no. 5: 105–109.

Terwilliger, Michael S. 2005b. "A Supervisor's Guide to Progressive Discipline, Part 2." *Fire Engineering* 158, no. 6: 97–102.

Terwilliger, Michael S. 2005c. "A Supervisor's Guide to Progressive Discipline, Part 3." *Fire Engineering* 158, no. 7: 85–92.

"Training or Punishment: Which Path Should You Take?" 2001. *Fair Practice Guidelines*, September 1, 2001: 535: 5–6.

Webster's Ninth New Collegiate Dictionary. 1989. Springfield, MA: Merriam-Webster.

Zatzick, Christopher D. and Roderick D. Iverson. 2006. "High-Involvement Management and Workforce Reduction: Competitive Advantage or Disadvantage?" *Academy of Management Journal* 49, no. 5: 999–1015.

9

COMMUNICATION: VERBAL, WRITTEN, AND ELECTRONIC

We spend nearly 70 percent of our waking hours in communication through writing, speaking, or listening (Robbins, 2000). It is no wonder then that employees view faulty communication as the source for many issues in the workplace. It is only through communication that information and ideas can be conveyed. Chapter 9 will deal with communication and how it affects the workplace environment.

Effective communication hinges upon individuals understanding your meaning and replying in terms that move the exchange forward. Communication is always a two-way process. Individuals involved in communication may have different wants, needs, and attitudes. These differences can present barriers if they conflict with those of the other party. All communication must overcome such barriers if it is to be successful. The first step is to recognize that barriers exist. Breakdowns in communication can lead to misunderstandings, costly errors, and low morale. Let us review how communication functions in a work environment.

Communication serves four major functions within a group or organization: control, motivation, emotional expression, and information (Scott and Mitchell, 1976). Job descriptions, policy and procedures manuals, and supervisors are examples of the control function of communication. All organizations have formal guidelines for employees to follow and a reporting line of authority, which control employee behavior by providing what they are supposed to be doing, how they are supposed to behave, and to whom they report.

Communication fosters motivation through good leadership. Great leaders are usually good communicators. They understand that real communication is two-way, with information, reactions, and feedback flowing in both directions (Sebastian, 2004). The formation of specific goals, feedback on progress towards the goals, and reinforcement of desired behavior all stimulate motivation and require communication.

For many employees, the work environment is their primary source for interaction with others. The communication that occurs within the group or team is a fundamental means by which members show their frustration and feelings of satisfaction. Communication in this sense provides an avenue for expression of emotions or feelings and also provides a fulfillment of social needs.

The last function that communication performs is the provision of information. Through information, individuals can make decisions, plan strategies, and achieve goals.

All of these functions are equally important. For employees to perform effectively, they need to maintain some form of control over other members, stimulate or motivate others to perform effectively, provide a means for emotional expression, and make choices based on information. Every communication interaction performs one or more of these four functions.

HOW DOES COMMUNICATION FLOW WITHIN AN ORGANIZATION?

Communication can flow either vertically or laterally (Robbins, 2000). Vertical flow can be downward or upward. Communication that flows from one level of a group or organization to a lower level is considered downward communication. This is used by team leaders or supervisors to assign goals, provide job instructions, inform employees about policy and procedures, identify areas for work improvement and offer feedback about performance.

Upward communication flows to a higher level in the team, group, or organization. Upward communication provides feedback to higher-ups, informs them of progress toward goals, and relays any problems. Upward communication enables supervisors to know how employees feel about their jobs, coworkers, and the organization. Upward communication can also be a way for those at higher levels to receive ideas on how things can be improved.

Lateral communication refers to the communication that takes place among members of the same work group or team, supervisors or managers at the same level, and administration or management members at the same level. Lateral communication helps facilitate coordination and can save time. Lateral communication can also be seen as harmful when it is used to circumvent the system by going around superiors to get things done or when decisions are made without approval from the next level.

HOW DO MEMBERS OF AN ORGANIZATION TRANSFER INFORMATION OR COMMUNICATE WITH OTHERS?

There are basically three methods of communication: oral, written, and nonverbal communication, which might be a symbolic gesture or a visual image. The three methods can also be combined. Oral communication examples are one-on-one conversations, group or team discussions, speeches, and the informal rumor mill or grapevine gossip. The advantages of oral communication are speed and instant feedback. A verbal message can be expressed and a response received in a minimal amount of time. If the receiver is unsure of the message, immediate feedback allows for clarification and correction of the message from the sender. Oral communication is the chief means by which organizations work on a day-to-day basis.

The major disadvantage of oral communication is that the more individuals a message has to be passed through, the greater the chances are for distortion. As in the game "telephone," distortion can occur in organizations when individuals pass along information and relay what they perceive the message to be.

Written communications include memos, letters, electronic mail (e-mail), fax transmissions, organizational periodicals or newsletters, and notices placed on bulletin boards (Robbins, 2000). Generally, both the sender and the receiver have a record or copy of the communication. The message can be kept for an indefinite period of time, which is useful for later reference. Individuals are usually more careful when preparing written communications to make sure that the information is concise, clear, and understandable. The disadvantage to written communication is that it takes more time than the spoken word. Another disadvantage is that there may not be any feedback. One way to ensure feedback is to ask the receiver to summarize what you have written. This will give evidence that the message has been received and understood.

Nonverbal communication is the most difficult to interpret and understand. Nonverbal communication includes gestures, facial expressions, intonation or emphasis of words, body movement, and actual physical space between the sender and the receiver. Nonverbal communication may be sent unconsciously and can often complicate the verbal communication given. Research indicates that 60 to 70 percent of communication is nonverbal (Wood, 2006). One researcher indicates that the percentage of nonverbal communication is as high as 93 percent (Rosenthal, 2006). This researcher goes on to identify nonverbal attributes such as posture, height, gestures, eye behavior, facial expression, weight, attractiveness, tone of voice, and proximity to others. Upright posture and height, even if they are an illusion, impart authority. In one study on nonverbal cues, participants were asked a series of open-ended questions about recent shopping experiences that involved interactions with salespeople (Wood, 2006). The most common nonverbal cue mentioned was the "dress and/or attire" followed by "smile." Numerous studies indicate that the outward expression of a smile, even if it is only for a brief second, is perceived by receivers on an unconscious level (Ekman, 1997; Gladwell, 2005). Actions and body language profoundly but unconsciously affect individuals. The receiver uses these nonverbal cues to reach judgments about the intentions of the sender. In order to establish a good relationship, the receiver must perceive that the sender had positive intentions.

There is evidence that librarians who are trained in nonverbal communication can replace negative perceptions of themselves with positive ones (Sampson, 1995). This has been a concern of those who work in libraries because they are sometimes viewed as being distant and not helpful. Sampson, a specialist in personal communication skills, discusses the five linked elements of personal perceptions—appearance, body language, communication style, presence, and reputation and suggests way to promote a positive image. One of the drawbacks of nonverbal communication is that culture also plays into what the receiver perceives. An example is the handshake. In Denmark, handshakes of short duration are likely to be perceived positively, but the opposite is true in Italy (Peterson, 2005). And in some cultures, a handshake would be an offensive gesture.

Worth Repeating: Actions Speak Louder Than Words

Remember that most communication is done through nonverbal cues such as gestures and facial expressions rather than through written or oral communication.

WHAT BARRIERS ARE THERE TO EFFECTIVE COMMUNICATION?

A number of barriers can distort effective communication.

Nonverbal Cues—Nonverbal communication is almost always accompanied by oral communication. As long as the two are in agreement, they reinforce each other. When nonverbal cues are inconsistent with the oral message, the receiver becomes confused and the message suffers.

Filtering—Filtering refers to a sender who purposely manipulates information so that it will be seen more favorably by the receiver. For example, when an employee tells his supervisor what he feels the supervisor wants to hear, he is filtering information. The greater number of vertical levels in the organization, the more opportunities there are for filtering. You can expect some filtering whenever there are status differences.

Selective Perception—The receiver sees and hear things in a selective way based on his needs, motivations, experience, background, and other personal characteristics. The receiver also projects his interests and expectations into communication. Individuals do not always see reality; they interpret what is seen and call that interpretation reality (Robbins, 2000).

Gender Styles—Men and women use oral communication differently; consequently, gender becomes a barrier to communication between the sexes (Booher, 1999; Hale, 1999). Women's language tends to be indirect, discreet, tactful, and even manipulative. Women tend to give fewer directives and use more courtesy words with those directives. Men's language tends to be more direct, powerful, blunt, and at times, offensive. Women talk to build rapport with others, exploring their own feelings and opinions. Men tend to view conversation as a means of exchanging information or solving problems. They discuss events, facts, happenings in the news, sports, or other topics not directly related to themselves. Men may complain about women talking on and on about their problems. Women criticize men for not listening. Women present a problem to gain support and connection, not to get the male's advice.

Emotions—The mood or emotional state that the receiver is in at the time of receipt of a communication message will influence how he or she interprets it. The same message received when you are angry or upset is often interpreted differently than when you are in a positive state. Extreme emotions such as elation or despair are most likely to hinder effective communication. In these states, we are most prone to disregard our rational and objective thinking processes and substitute emotional judgments.

Language—Words may have different meanings to different people. Language will be influenced by age, education, and cultural background. Various departments within organizations also have their own jargon and individuals in each of these will use terms and phrases unique to their area. In libraries, catalogers, instruction librarians, and technology specialists all use different terms related to the work that they do. Senders tend to assume that the words and terms they use mean the same to the receiver as they do to themselves.

Cross-Cultural Communication—People from different cultures see, interpret, and evaluate things differently and act according to their own interpretation. Cross-cultural communication clearly creates the potential for increased communication problems (Robbins, 2000). The greater the differences in backgrounds between sender and receiver, the greater the differences attached to particular words or behaviors.

Different cultures like to receive information and trust information they receive from different sources in different ways. In some cultures, information that comes directly from a manager is not trustworthy. Instead, they prefer that the word comes from a leader of the employee group, a headman, or a shop foreman (Ribbink, 2002). And in some cultures, employees do not feel comfortable being singled out for praise in front of an entire employee group, a typical method used in the US. These employees prefer quiet praise in a private office.

Broad generalizations are often made about a culture's use of word and gesture. In an article discussing the variations of various cultures, the following observations were noted: Some Japanese and other Asians find it easier than some Europeans to be silent; the Germans, Nordics, and British are generally less talkative than many people in the Latin nations and are often more restrained in gesture; some British seem to avoid saying what they mean while Australians may disconcert others by forcefully saying exactly what they mean; and many Americans can also be very straightforward (Varner, 2001). Library staff need to be aware that these cultural differences exist as they work with others.

A large metropolitan public library is likely to employ a variety of individuals from various countries. Even though most of these employees speak fluent English, they may still retain their culture's preferences in communication. For example, in one such library on the West Coast, there were a significant number of Hispanic employees both at the professional level and the support staff level. As in many of the larger library systems today, day-to-day communication is primarily done through e-mails and written memos. They are read, responded to, and saved in relevant folders. However, one of the Hispanic librarians rarely responded to any of the e-mail conversations conducted by his teammates. Finally, in exasperation, his team leader scheduled a meeting with him to find out why he was not involved in the discussions related to team goals and projects.

During the meeting, the librarian informed his team leader that he had, in fact, responded to all of the e-mails but had done so through face-to-face meetings with his teammates. He went on to relay that he felt very uncomfortable discussing important issues electronically and preferred discussing these items orally. After conferring with the other team members, the team leader found that what the librarian had said was true. The team leader realized that this was a culture issue rather than one that needed disciplinary procedure. After discussing this with the librarian and team members, it was decided that they would schedule face-to-face meetings for the really important decision making, and other issues as appropriate. The librarian agreed to respond to and actively participate in e-mail discussions, too. The end result was a win-win situation for the team.

WHAT CAN SUPERVISORS OR MANAGERS DO TO OVERCOME THESE BARRIERS?

Many communication problems can be attributed directly to misunderstandings and inaccuracies. One way to lessen these is to use feedback. Feedback can be oral, written, or nonverbal. If a supervisor or manager asks, "Did you understand that?" the response is "Yes" or "No." A better way to approach this is to ask the individual to restate the message or communication in his or her own words. If the supervisor then hears what he/she intended, the communication was received and understood.

Feedback does not have to be oral—actions speak louder than words. If all employees were to complete a report or form by a certain date, failure of some employees to comply with this request is a form of feedback. This could indicate that not all employees received the message or it could indicate that there is an issue that needs to be addressed. When you give a speech to a group, you can tell by their eye movements and other nonverbal cues, such as nodding in agreement, whether they are getting or understanding your message. This type of feedback is very important to performers who prefer to perform in front of a live audience. The immediate response of laughter or applause, or the lack of either, lets the performer know whether he or she is being acknowledged or not.

Since we know that language can be a barrier, messages should be structured in such a way that they are clear and understandable. Words should be chosen carefully. Simplify the language used and consider the audience or receiver to whom the message is directed so it will be received and understood. Slang and jargon might be deterrents when the receiver does not understand the meanings of the terms used.

Active listening has long been an important facet of effective communication. Many of us are poor listeners; we may hear what is said but we are not really listening. Hearing is passive while true listening is an active search for meaning (Robbins, 2000). Active listening requires total concentration. Think about the last conversation that you had with someone. In the time when the other individual was talking, were you actively listening or were you simply hearing? If you were thinking of how you were going to respond to the individual when he had completed his thought, then you were probably only hearing what he was saying, but your focus was on how you were going to reply.

Active listening involves the following steps:

- Listen patiently. Make a conscious effort to block out distracting thoughts and focus your undivided attention on the words and nonverbal cues presented by the sender.

- Pause before responding to the individual and let his or her words sink in deeply. This will help you understand the emotions as well as the words actually spoken.

- Restate or reiterate the main points of the message in your own words.

- Ask for clarification on points that seem confusing to you and phrase your questions in a non-threatening tone.

- Exhibit affirmative head nods and appropriate facial expressions to convey to the speaker that you are listening.

- Avoid distracting actions or gestures such as shuffling papers or playing with a pencil. This could make the speaker feel that you are bored or uninterested.

- Avoid interrupting the speaker. Let the speaker finish his or her thoughts before responding. Do not try to interject where you think the speaker's thoughts are going.
- Stay unattached emotionally as logic often disappears when emotions surface. Even if you disagree, do not judge or take offense.
- Most of us would rather voice our own ideas and thoughts than listen to what others say. It is impossible to talk and listen at the same time. The good listener recognizes this and does not over talk.
- Take notes if possible. When you write down an employee's comments, he/she feels taken seriously and that comments are valued.

These steps open up the lines of communication with your employees. The goal is to improve one's ability to receive the full meaning of a communication without having it distorted by premature judgments or interpretations (Sebastian, 2004).

Other things that prevent barriers to communication are constraining emotions and watching nonverbal cues. Emotions can severely cloud and distort the meaning of both sent and received messages. Gestures and other nonverbal cues can distract from the communication and prevent it from being received and understood.

A final barrier is grapevine gossip. One cannot eliminate the grapevine but supervisors or managers should try to use it and make it work for them rather than against them. To reduce the potential dangers of the grapevine, managers and supervisors should make good use of formal channels by relaying information that is relevant and accurate, often and with clarity.

HOW CAN I MAKE MEETINGS MORE EFFECTIVE?

A recent survey of 38,000 people found that, on average, they felt that 66 percent of the time they spent in meetings was wasted (Moran Jr., 2006). If this is a common complaint among the employees within your organization, the situation needs to be improved. There are many how-to books for effective meetings available. However, continual dissatisfaction with meetings signifies that these tools are not sufficient.

Communication at meetings is much more difficult than one would surmise. Meetings are small to large group interactions with group dynamics. Unspoken assumptions, emotions, word choice, attention, and external factors can contribute to misunderstandings and confused communication in meetings.

Each day, workers in the United States attend about 11 million meetings, according to a 1998 MCI Conference White Paper (Rogelberg, Scott and Kello, 2007). The average employee spends about six hours per week in scheduled meetings, with supervisors spending more time in meetings than nonsupervisors. Senior employees spend nearly 23 hours in meetings each week and those in larger organizations tend to spend more time in meetings than those in smaller organizations.

If effective communication between two people can be complicated, a discussion involving six or more individuals will be even more so. The presence of others may limit a speaker's willingness to be straightforward. When someone asks for clarification, the response still may not be clear but the discussion moves on because of time pressures. Some may be intimidated to admit that they still are not clear on the message. Emotions often surface during meetings and they need to be neutralized before accurate listening can take place. Meeting room environments are generally a lot nosier than the environment where a one-on-one conversation takes place.

Generally, two types of meetings occur in the workplace. One type is held to inform the participants regarding work-related matters. The content of these meetings consists of announcements, updates, and reports. Participants are expected to listen and understand and ask questions when they need clarification. This type of meeting is also known as an information sharing meeting. The second type of meeting is to reach a conclusion on agenda topics. The end result may be a solution to a problem or an action plan for a new activity. In this type of meeting, participants are expected to understand the issues, evaluate the suggestions or recommendations, and then participate in the choice of one of these. This is called a decision-making meeting (Moran Jr., 2006).

Effective meetings should begin with basic preparation skills. First, an agenda should be created and sent to participants in advance along with any relevant background materials (Nadler, 2007). When appropriate, other agenda items should be solicited from the participants. The agenda should suggest time estimates for each topic, both to promote efficiency and to convey that each item will get sufficient time (Rogelberg, Scott, and Kello, 2007).

Establishing clear ground rules is essential. Define roles and expectations for both leaders and participants, including clauses about confidentiality and interruption rules. Begin the meeting by stating its purpose and objectives. Some portions of the meeting may be just information sharing. Others may require participants' input so that a decision or strategy can be reached. Try to make sure that you have everyone's input and acknowledge individual contributions to the discussion and decision making. Sometimes it is useful to hold meetings in new environments to break monotony and established ruts and stimulate creation of new ideas.

Another critical part of effective meetings is time management. Meetings should always start and end at the time announced. Starting late wastes the time of individuals who arrive on time and sends an inappropriate message about the value of the meeting. Times assigned to agenda items should also be honored. Allow enough time for winding up a meeting. Summarize the discussion and check that others agree with your account. Make decisions about unfinished business and run through the decisions made or the actions that will be taken. Assign each action to an individual and attach a target time for completion. To increase the effectiveness of meetings, attendees should periodically critique the meeting's effectiveness. Many organizations use the "plus/delta" process to assess the meeting.

Successful organizations do not treat meetings as a necessary evil but as a way to solve problems and build a better organization. Those willing to understand meeting dynamics, to prepare well for each meeting and to commit to good meeting management will have more effective and efficient meetings.

The time is 9:55 a.m. and Betsy, human resources professional at the Mystic Public Library, is rushing to the conference room for her biweekly meeting with her staff. This 10:00 a.m. meeting is to establish goals and projects for the ensuing year. She forgot to send out the agenda ahead of time or the materials for the team to read in advance. By the time she reaches the conference room, the rest of the staff is already there. She enters and begins passing out the materials and agenda. She then proceeds to write the agenda on the chart pad so that all can see it as well. There is a lot of commotion in the room as everyone is talking.

The meeting finally gets underway about 10:13 a.m. Betsy asks the staff if there are other items to add to the agenda but reminds them that the agenda is pretty full because of planning items. Several staff members raise their hand and add a few frivolous items to the agenda. Betsy decides to approach these added items first as she assumes they will be quick to deal with. One item concerns recognition of staff anniversaries and whether to acknowledge this on the day of the anniversary for each staff member or at a general meeting of all staff once a month. What Betsy thought would be a simple item turns into a full-blown discussion and takes approximately 45 minutes. Now there are only about 30 minutes left and work on next year's goals and projects has not even started. To add to the dilemma, the staff have not had the opportunity to review the materials that Betsy wanted them to read before beginning the planning session. She asks them to quickly review the materials and tries to begin a discussion on setting priorities. No one is prepared and the meeting ends abruptly. Betsy goes back to her office, frustrated and upset over the meeting failure.

This scenario is fictional, but I have often seen meetings conducted in this fashion. What should have been a very important meeting ended up being a waste of time for everyone. Betsy is a good example of someone doing everything the wrong way. She is setting a poor example for others to follow and her carelessness sends a message to her staff that the meeting was not really that important. She should have had the agenda ready ahead of time and also requested any additional items before the meeting began. In addition, any materials that she wanted the staff to be prepared to discuss should have been distributed well in advance, allowing them the opportunity to read them before the meeting. Betsy started the meeting late and did not facilitate the meeting in a fashion that would have allowed the important items to be discussed first. Effective and efficient meetings need to be organized and conducted in a fashion that expresses the importance of meeting management.

HOW CAN I COMMUNICATE EFFECTIVELY OVER E-MAIL?

Electronic mail has become one of the most popular conduits for communication in the workplace. According to the December 2006 Pew Internet and American Life Project Tracking survey, 70 percent of American adult Internet users, about 141 million people, use the Internet on an average day. Of them, 91 percent were using the Internet to either send or read e-mail.

It is easy to make mistakes or violate societal norms of the electronic world. E-mail, while easily written, may not be as easy to understand. Humor, sarcasm, anger, joy, and other emotions are not always conveyed in an e-mail. When speaking face to face or over the telephone, nonverbal gestures and changes in voice tone signal to the listener the intent of the message. With e-mail, we need to carefully review before we hit that send key. Writing an e-mail to someone should be done with the same care as a telephone call or a written letter.

It is easy to send an e-mail when you are angry, and it only takes a few seconds to reply to an e-mail when something has triggered a reflex of emotion. Making a telephone call gives you a few seconds to cool off. Walking to someone's office gives you more time to think about what you are going to say. E-mail is instantaneous and, once sent, there is virtually no way of retrieving it without the recipient knowing. A better way of handling this instant reaction is to go ahead and write the e-mail when you are angry but then delete it. Then think carefully about what you want to say and write the real one.

One should not be rude or insensitive just because of the electronic format. Do not write your messages in all caps. This is the electronic version of yelling. Most individuals with e-mail accounts receive jokes in their mailboxes. It is not necessary to forward every joke you receive. Jokes take up bandwidth and time. If the joke is in the form of an attachment, then the size is even larger. Many mailboxes get overloaded from too many such e-mails.

The most effective way to improve the speed and quality of communication and information flow in the electronic world is to control the quantity. Whenever you send a message, ask yourself whether you really need to—if not, do not send it. Keep messages brief, because the shorter they are, the faster they can be processed. Check regularly to see if anything can be shortened or eliminated. Will anyone really notice if some regular communications are no longer made? Finally, do not procrastinate over responses. It is better, faster, and more efficient to answer immediately and keep your mailbox clear.

Also remember that when you send or forward something, your name may be forever attached to the mail. If the joke is insensitive or politically incorrect, you must be prepared to have your name associated with the material. You have no control over the next person who will receive it after you send it.

HOW DO LISTSERVS, CHAT ROOMS, AND MESSAGE BOARDS AFFECT WORKPLACE COMMUNICATION?

A listserv is an automated e-mail system organized by subject matter. When one individual sends a message to the operator, it is routed to the e-mail addresses of all other subscribers. In libraries, listservs might include reference, instruction, cataloging, acquisitions, interlibrary services, and circulation, to name a few. Subscribing is usually as simple as sending an e-mail to the appropriate address with the word "subscribe" in the subject heading or body of the message. According to *TechEncyclopedia*, there are over 10,000 listservs in existence (Sloboda, 1999). Depending on the nature of the listserv, there could be anywhere from a few messages a week to dozens a day.

Most listservs are moderated to prevent flame wars and off-topic messages. One should only send items related to the topic of the listserv. Be careful of grammar and spelling as it will reflect on your credibility. Listservs can be a very effective way to recruit for library positions, which makes them a useful tool for the HR professional.

Chat rooms allow interested participants to engage in real-time discussions. Various Web sites host this venue of communication. For example, many television news programs offer the opportunity to pose questions and chat with one of their analysts or news reporters. In libraries, chat reference has emerged to provide new ways of interacting with library users (Tenopir, 2006). As with face-to-face reference, some librarians and users are better at it than others. Libraries have also found chat rooms convenient for discussions with other staff members. The chat room is probably best described as instant messaging for groups. It is like a group of people sitting around a room having a conversation except that it is online. The drawback is that employees could get so involved in the chat room discussions that they might neglect library duties. Some libraries designate an individual to monitor the chat room discussion to ensure that this does not become a problem. Chat relies on the written word although emoticons such as smiley faces, Internet abbreviations, and boldface type are used to convey some nonverbal cues. Negative chats can happen when there is confusion between individuals involved in the chat room, resulting in flame wars with the use of ALL CAPS or shouting. This could also lead to problems in the workplace.

Instant Messaging (IM) is usually limited to two individuals. Kresge Library in Michigan tried using IM with their staff members as part of a movement towards using similar technology at the reference desk (Doan and Ferry, 2006). The majority of their staff had never used this form of technology before. After three months of using IM among their staff, a survey was conducted. The staff was divided on whether the use of IM reduced their amount of e-mail. The library determined some IM best practices. They found the file sharing capabilities of some IM clients to be slow and cumbersome. They also felt that if it required more than four sentences, individuals should just go and talk with each other. IM can be a way to get responses quickly but should be used carefully.

Message boards are a hybrid of listservs and chat rooms. Individuals post messages to a single location; however, it is not done through e-mail. The individual posts on a Web page that hosts the message board. To read messages, the individual goes to the same place. Everything is done in one central location like the chat room. The message board does not have the ability to host real time discussions.

HOW IS TELECONFERENCING OR VIDEOCONFERENCING USED FOR WORKPLACE COMMUNICATION?

Jeffrey Katzenberg, CEO of DreamWorks Animation, used to fly from Los Angeles to the company's office in Bristol, England, once every three weeks. This constant travel was very hard on him and he challenged his tech team to come up with a way to bring his group together virtually (Crockett and Tucker, 2007). The system created mimics a typical boardroom, with a large conference table. Meeting participants sit on one side of the table and their remote colleagues sit opposite them, behind a similar wood table reflected on three giant flat screen monitors. If the meeting was held over the telephone, participants would have no idea who was present at the conference except through voice contact. This system is very elaborate and expensive and beyond the type of videoconferencing that most libraries use today. Not everyone wants or needs a full-blown conference room setup, but video systems' costs will begin decreasing, allowing more organizations to use them.

With the costs of travel increasing and library budgets decreasing, videoconferencing becomes more appealing when groups of individuals from different locations need to meet. Teleconferencing was the first step towards gathering individuals virtually and did allow some of the nonverbal cues that are missed in e-mail. Videoconferencing allows all participants to be involved with the nonverbal cues present as well. Currently, a technician is usually needed to make sure that the conference is executed without trouble. As the systems become more stable and efficient, a simple press of the button will launch the videoconference.

Webcasting, although similar to Web conferencing, is a one-to-many communications medium that utilizes media and video to enable high impact communication and education that can be tracked, analyzed, and refined based on audience behavior and feedback (Pulier, 2007). Web conferencing is more a recording of the meeting. In Webcasting, tools such as PowerPoint, screen captures and interactive features make its quality far beyond what can be accomplished in Web conferencing. The detailed tracking available in many Webcasting tools can be invaluable for information about the viewing audience.

Further developments in technology and how they affect the work environment will be discussed in the next chapter.

REFERENCES

Booher, Dianna. 1999. "Communicate With Confidence." *Enterprise, Salt Lake City* (November 29), no. 23: 15.

Crockett, Roger O. 2007. "The 21st Century Meeting." *Business Week* (February 26), no. 4023: 72–79.

Doan, Tomalee and Kristine Ferry. 2006. "Instant Messaging (IM): Providing Services and Enhancing Communication." *Journal of Business & Finance Librarianship* 12, no. 2:17–22.

Ekman, Paul. 1997. *What the Face Reveals: Basic and Applied Studies of Spontaneous Expressing Using the Facial Action Coding System (FACS)*. New York: Oxford University Press.

Gladwell, Malcolm. 2005. *Blink: The Power of Thinking Without Thinking*. New York: Little, Brown.

Hale, Mary. 1999. "He Says, She Says: Gender and Worklife." *Public Administration Review* 59, no. 5: 410–435.

Moran, Jr., Robert F. 2006. "Meetings: The Bane of the Workplace." *Library Administration & Management* 20, no. 3: 135–139.

Nadler, Reidan S. 2007. "Are You a Meeting Menace or Master?" *T & D* 61, no. 1: 10–11.

Peterson, Robin T. 2005. "An Examination of the Relative Effectiveness of Training in Nonverbal Communication: Personal Selling Implications." *Journal of Marketing Education* 27, no. 2: 143–150.

Pew Internet and American Life Project Tracking Survey, December 2006. Available: www.pewinternet.org/trends/Internet_Activities (accessed May 17, 2007).

Pulier, Greg. 2007. "Select the Right Tool for the Job: Video Webcasting Can Reach a Variety of Internal and External Audiences." *Communication News* 44, no. 7: 12, 17.

Ribbink, Kim. 2002. "Seven Ways to Better Communicate in Today's Diverse Workplace." *Harvard Management Communication Letter* 5, no. 11: 3–5.

Robbins, Stephen P. 2000. *Essentials of Organization Behavior*, 6th ed. Upper Saddle River, NJ: Prentice-Hall.

Rogelberg, Steven G., Cliff Scott, and John Kello. 2007. "The Science and Fiction of Meetings." *MIT Sloan Management Review* 48, no. 2: 17–21.

Rosenthal, Roseanne. 2006. "Stand and Think tall: 93% of Communication Is Nonverbal." *Illinois Music Educator* 66, no. 3: 58–59.

Sampson, Eleri. 1995. "First Impressions: The Power of Personal Style." *Library Management* 16, no. 4: 25–28.

Scott, William G. and Terrence R. Mitonell. 1971. *Organization Theory: A Structural and Behavioral Analysis*, 3rd ed. Homewood, IL: R. D. Irwin.

Sebastian, Don. 2004. "Effective Communication in the Workplace." *Executive Housekeeping Today* 25, no. 12: 16–17.

Sloboda, Brian. 1999. "'Netiquette'—New Rules and Policies for the Information Age." *Management Quarterly* 40, no. 4: 9–33.

Tenopir, Carol. 2006. "What Chat Transcripts Reveal." *Library Journal* 131, no. 4: 34.

Varner, Iris I. 2001. "Teaching Intercultural Management Communication: Where Are We? Where Do We Go?" *Business Communication Quarterly* 64, no. 1: 99–111.

Wood, John Andy. 2006. "NLP Revisited: Nonverbal Communications and Signals of Trustworthiness." *Journal of Personal Selling & Sales Management* 26, no. 2: 197–204.

10 THE ROLE OF TECHNOLOGY IN HUMAN RESOURCES MANAGEMENT

Most libraries today have online catalogs, various research databases, and a multitude of computer resources for the staff and clientele. In addition, many human resources functions can now be performed electronically. Not only has technology enhanced human resources functions, it has added new meaning to the primary rights of the individual employee. In this chapter, we will review the impact of electronic human resources functions. The chapter will also discuss some technology related problems that might have to be addressed.

Many HR activities are now conducted using technology. Like other professionals, some HR professionals worry that advancing technology will mean that they will be replaced or criticized. HR professionals and librarians who are wary of using new technologies might consider that new technology will not only assist them in doing a more efficient, cost effective job, but also has the potential to elevate their value in the organization (Brooks, 2006).

Human resource information systems (HRIS) allow the human resources professional to become a more strategic player in the organization (Hussain, Wallace, and Cornelius, 2007). HRIS are systems used to acquire, store, manipulate, analyze, retrieve, and distribute information about an organization's human resources (Ball, 2001). The HRIS system helps provide quality information to management for decision making and also helps the HR professional perform his or her job more effectively (Ball, 2001).

HR professionals need to determine how the system can best aid them in their roles rather than fear its use.

WHICH HR FUNCTIONS CAN BE CONDUCTED USING TECHNOLOGY OR HRIS SYSTEMS?

According to popular belief, human resources professionals are far behind in the use of technology. In reality, technology was being used for payroll, benefits administration, and employee record holding as far back as the

1960s (Ball, 2001). Information was held on a mainframe system with retrieval from the database using simple keyword searches.

With newer systems, a variety of HR functions are now more streamlined. One popular system, PeopleSoft, boasts applications in the following HR content areas: eBenefits, eDevelopment, ePay, eRecruit, eCompensation, eProfile, eRecruit Manager Desktop, eCompensation Desktop, and eProfile Manager Desktop (Florkowski and Olivas-Lujan, 2006). It also includes several self-service areas for employees, allowing them to change addresses and names, choose benefit packages, or make changes in their pensions or health plans.

Using PeopleSoft, Indiana University Purdue University Indianapolis created a bridge to their HRIS system called eDoc. This bridge allows departments to initiate and process employee activities by connecting to Administer Workforce, another PeopleSoft module. According to Juletta Toliver (2007), IUPUI human resources administrator, "one main advantage in using this electronic system would have to be the eDoc component, as it replaced paper and incorporates workflow which, in essence, is an electronic approval structure."

Recruitment software includes each sequential stage of the recruitment process: applicant screening, applicant tracking, interview management, skills matching, media response analysis, and budget control (Ball, 2001). Figure 10-1 lists a few popular recruitment software packages.

---

www.pcrecruiter.com: PCRecruiter Web helps manage your candidates and positions in a single, relational database.

www.people-trak.com: People–Trak software helps manage employees and HR strategy.

www.taleo.com: Aids in filling jobs faster with eRecruiting solution.

www.fasttrack.net.au/home: FastTrack's VMS solution lets you control contingent workforce management.

Figure 10-1. Recruitment Software Web Sites

Through these technologies, individuals can apply online, complete application forms, and attach resumes or other applicable information in one step. The human resources professional can then review applications and determine if there are matches to available positions. Units or department personnel could also connect to the database. The electronic recruitment process saves a great deal of time and paperwork for those involved in recruitment. Once the individual is hired and his or her data is put into the system, he or she is automatically added to the payroll system.

Payroll is another function that has been streamlined with advances in technology. The more than 130 million people in the US workforce receive some four billion paychecks each year, according to the American

Payroll Association (Kahan, 2001). That is a lot of payroll processing if one has to manually complete each transaction. An electronic payroll system is one of the most common forms of automation in the HR world (Grensing-Pophal, 2005). One of the most well known payroll services is ADP. They do contract services for payroll and benefits administration and can be found at www.adp.com. A couple of other systems are Payroll Systems at www.payroll-us.com and PrO Unlimited at www.pro-unlimited.com.

Smaller libraries especially have found that using outsourcing for payroll is much more cost effective than doing it in-house. Many payroll processing services have moved their services online. The user gains the ability to manage payroll at any time and from any location. In addition, the vendor can make instantaneous changes or updates to the software, reducing the number of support calls and allowing users to conduct business seamlessly and without interruption.

A payroll package should be easy to access and kept current with changes in laws and rates. It should handle direct deposit and flexible payments. Security is a must as they collect and make use of exactly the kind of information actively sought by identity thieves (McClure, 2005). Most systems require the use of VPN (virtual private networking) to access the system. This is an authentication for accessing and is often used with a smart card system. This isolates your network behind a firewall and allows you to control which specific computers have access to your system. Another type of security measure is to encrypt the data that is transferred to the payroll system. The only way to read the data is with the correct decryption key for both the data and the network.

Some smaller organizations prefer to install their own desktop payroll software and process their own payroll (Bland, 2007). These desktop payroll software licenses cost a few hundred dollars plus a couple of hundred dollars per year for support and upgrades, a great deal less than online payroll services. 2020 Software compares the top 21 payroll solutions at www.2020software.com. This comparison includes module details, technology, advantages, and pricing per number of employees, as well as a free demo.

Cost is the not the only reason that some organizations prefer to do the payroll in house. Many organizations fear for the security of payroll information hosted at an off-site location (Bland, 2007). Although the in house system might provide more security, it will not have all of the functionality of the larger HRIS systems.

Timekeeping or attendance functions are generally tied into the payroll system and can streamline payroll preprocessing and ensure accuracy of reported hours (Katz, 2006). HRIS systems handle employees who work varied shifts, in varied job roles, and at varied pay scales, making the processing of their payroll much easier for the payroll personnel. They can also prevent inevitable human error. The systems mentioned above for payroll also have timekeeping features.

HOW CAN A LIBRARY PREVENT AN EMPLOYEE CLOCKING IN ON THE COMPUTER FOR A FRIEND?

The problem of an individual clocking in for someone else compromises data integrity; however, there are systems developing that can eliminate this problem. Biometric technology might be the answer (Katz, 2006). Biometrics is technology that uses any unique, measurable physiological or behavioral characteristic to recognize or verify an individual's identity. Fingerprinting is a form of biometrics. More advanced biometric technology was shown in the film *Minority Report*.

The most reliable and cost effective biometric system would identify through voice patterns, iris or retinal patterns, or visual pattern recognition, including facial, hand, and full body identification (Katz, 2006). The comparison would occur each time an individual logged into the system. Ideally, the features would match 100 percent, and when this does not occur, the system refuses the log in and also indicates that an unauthorized individual is attempting to use the system.

Software packages come bundled with a sensor or other data collection device and many are priced at low entry costs with upgrades available for organizations that have more than 50 employees. This may be the wave of future for many organizations. Some employees may resent this type of log in procedure, comparing it to "big brother." The verdict is still out on biometrics.

Naperville Public Library in Ohio plans to switch from cards to finger-scan readers so patrons can log on to the library computers by themselves (L.B., 2005). The library contracted with US Biometrics to install the software and the reader devices for $32,000 plus an additional $8,000 for a four-year maintenance plan. The scanning is optional, but patrons who refuse to offer their fingers for scanning will need a librarian to log them on the computers. The library did this in an effort to decrease card swapping among children whose parents had not given them permission to use the computers. The deputy director of the library believes that as users become more comfortable with the system, they will use it more. Naperville is only the second library in the country to implement biometric technology.

HOW DO WEB-BASED PENSION AND BENEFIT PROGRAMS WORK?

Web-based benefits administration provides greater service to the employees, ease of administration, and reporting mechanisms. Calculation of benefit coverage is conducted, employee contribution amounts are calculated, benefit plan participation history is tracked, and employee benefit statements are produced. The system can produce flexible benefit enrollment forms and interface with third-party administrators for 401(k) pension programs. It can also administer COBRA eligibility and participation as well as tracking pension plan investments. In Figure 10-2, a list of potential administration software is given. You can find out more about these systems at www.pensionportal.com/admininstration_software.htm.

ASC's Defined Contribution/401(k) & Compliance Testing System   Handle plans with virtually any scenario, in less time, by eliminating time-consuming manual processes.

BasicFlex   Commonly perceived for Fortune 500 companies, the BasicFlex benefit administration system is a turn-key system of documents, software, and tax filing for employers with as few as two employees.

Benefits on the Web—The benefits.com system   Employee benefits on the Web. Automated HR administration with benefits and investment packages to recruit and retain employees.

BeneSoft   The elegant solution for benefits administration software.

Blaze SSI Corporation   Pension, 401(k), 403(b), plan design and administration software.

Byrne Software Technologies   VisualHCS includes modules for contribution and eligibility, health claims processing, premium billing, pension, EDI, Web self-service, and online contribution reporting.

Cascade   Cascade's corporate mission is to develop and support strategic software systems for the employee benefits and human resource community. Their focus in on the development and maintenance of their application software.

Centora   developers of HRight for data management, benefits and payroll administration, and support.

CMG Consulting, Inc.   Provides corporate benefits administration and consulting services, including financial and retirement planning. Offers D-Access, an online employee structured retirement plan.

Corbel   Provides total solutions for the employee benefits industry with software for retirement plan documents and recordkeeping of daily or traditional plans.

CPAS Systems, Inc.   Complete administration of defined benefit pension plans.

Cyborg Systems   Client/server-based human resources management system (HRMS), payroll, benefits, and time and attendance software suite.

DATAIR Employee Benefit Systems, Inc.   DATAIR has been a leading provider of software for employee benefit professionals since 1967, offering a full range of PC-based solutions for documents, proposal, administration, reporting, and client management.

Facts Services, Inc.   Provides automated and intergrated software and hardware solutions for employee benefit administration, specializing in health claims processing, risk management and managed care systems.

F.A.S. Pension Manager   Group and individual, defined benefits and defined contributions, pensions administration, fund management and actuarial valuation (multi-user, multi-scheme or self-administration available; network or stand-alone PC).

Incompass Administrative Software   Administrative software for record keeping and compliance testing for defined contribution/401(k) and defined benefit plans.

Integrated Benefit Solutions   IBS assists companies with employee benefit plan administration and recordkeeping software such as the SunGard OmniPlan and OmniPlus systems.

LVadmin   Lynchval's Internet/PC-based defined benefit pension administration software for TPA's and plan sponsors. Supports single-employer qualified and nonqualified plans, public plans, multi-employer/union. DB systems consulting also available.

McCamish Systems   Benefit plan administration software. McCamish Systems uses innovative technology to provide proven solutions and world class services for the administration of life insurance, annuities and nonqualified employee benefit plans.

Figure 10-2. Benefits Administration Software

P+W Software   Benefit software for human resources, managing Section 125, FSA, and cafeteria plans.

PENAD PX3000   PX3000 streamlines the administration of DC and DB pension plans and puts Member information on the Web.

Pension Assistant   Pension software for defined benefit pension plans.

PensionGold   Retirement Solutions; Levi, Ray & Shoup, Inc. (LRS) is the defined benefit retirement industry's leading provider of pension administration software and services. Since 1987, our innovative suite of products and services has kept pace with the rapidly growing and increasingly complex demands placed on defined benefit plan sponsors.

ProAdmin   ProAdmin is designed to greatly enhance the efficiency of the pension plan calculation setup process, improve quality and lower operational risk. What used to take months of programming can now be accomplished in a matter of days.

PTAS Pension Transfer Agent System   Fully integrated, full featured, multi-user, multi-currency, real-time share registration/unit trust system that offers an effective and versatile management system, with E*TAS, the Web interface.

TACS Pension Administration Software   TACS, municipal pension software, vocational rehabilitation software, pension software, contributory retirement administration, defined benefit plans, case management software, client payroll, case note.

Total Service Manager (TSM)   TSM is an integrated recordkeeping information processing, and administration product specifically developed for the defined contribution industry.

Travisoft Software   Cobra software from Travis Software automates HIPAA and employee benefits management.

Ulysses Software   Pension software that provides mainframe power with PC ease of use. Connect to your networks, control your priorities, administer your plans, communicate with employees.

UltiPro   Provided by the US Group (Ultimate Software), featuring tax, 401(K), and time clock interfaces. benefits administration, COBRA, ad hoc reporting.

VisualHCS Pension   Visual HCS is a fully automated defined benefit/defined contribution pension administration system. Features include a custom pension calculation, Web interface, ACH and account management.

Vitech Benefits Administration System   The Vitech Benefits Administration System is the nation's leading software for multi-employer and public retirement fund administration.

Figure 10-2. Benefits Administration Software *(Continued)*

Administration software also benefits employees. With little or no training, employees can access information or make benefits selections online. Safeguards and controls help prevent errors by making sure a particular employee is only presented with benefit plans for which he or she is eligible. The system flags typos or other errors in real time so the employee can correct errors before submitting the forms to HR.

HOW DOES TECHNOLOGY AFFECT TRAINING?

A key function in any HRIS is the monitoring of training programs and employee skills. Common features include monitoring and administration of classes taken; storage of course administration; and evaluation information

(Ball, 2001). Most monitoring systems are not connected to the actual training program but simply monitor when individuals take the course, how they did on the course, and perhaps their evaluation of the course.

There are many new vendors and products in this market. Do not use an outside custom developer unless you have really experienced the technology. There are many off-the-shelf content packages out there to try ("Is Your Company Ready...," 2002).

The convenience and fairly low cost of "e-learning" is inviting to organizations both large and small ("E-Learning Takes Hold...," 2002). Blending online and offline classes allows the organization to tailor the learning to meet goals and objectives. When organizations move from off-the-shelf training programs and want to customize e-learning for their own employees, they usually turn to authoring tools. You will need good IT support and experts in authoring to take advantage of this type of tool.

Some libraries develop their own training materials and then post them on the Web for staff to access. One such program in Ohio has a training course consisting of six self-paced training modules that include resources, examples, quizzes, and exercises (Balas, 2005). Other libraries look to workshops and online conferences for training. This is done through satellite downlinks and some are even offered in a package to libraries unable to provide desktop access. Figure 10-3 lists some online resources available to libraries.

ALA—Are You Ready for Online Learning?
  www.ala.org/ala/alcts/alctsconted/alctsceevents/webcources/WebCTready.htm

ALA—Fundamentals of Acquisitions Web Course
  www.ala.org/ala/alcts/alctsconted/alctsceevents/webcourses/alctsfundamentals.htm

Cataloger's Learning Workshop (Library of Congress)
  www.loc.gov/catworkshop

Webjunction—Learning Center
  http://webjunction.org/do/Navigation?category=372

Marketing the Library Staff Training
  www.olc.org/marketing

Orientation for New Employees, Ohio Library Council
  www.olc.org/orientation

ORE (Ohio Reference Excellence) on the Web, Web-based training for Reference Service from Ohio Library Council
  www.olc.org/ore

ALA—Webcasts
  www.ala.org/Template.cfm?Section=userservices&template=/ContentManagement/ContentDisplay.cfm&ContentD=80123

College of DuPage Software and Special Services: Library Teleconferences
  www.dupagepress.com/COD/index.php?id=5

LibrarySupportStaff.com: Free Online Learning Sites
  http://librarysupportstaff.com/ed4you.htm#Online%20Tutorial

Figure 10-3. Online Training Resources

Training administration can be used for scheduling and registration, for training sessions, as well as tracking what employees have completed. Employees are positive about the ease of registration and taking classes online without having to leave their office area or workstation (Grensing-Pophal, 2005).

HOW DOES AN ORGANIZATION CHOOSE AN HRIS SYSTEM?

In these times of tight budgets, getting approval for a new HRIS system may be a real challenge. The first step in the process is to analyze all of the human resources' needs. How are HR activities being performed? Is the current system meeting those needs? Other questions that need to be considered are ("Checklist Helps HRIS Pros," 2001):

- What personnel information are people requesting?
- How is this personnel information obtained?
- How long does it take to provide this information once it has been requested?
- What human resource management needs are not being addressed and handled properly?
- How effective is the HR support to the budgeting and planning processes?
- Where do you stand in complying with COBRA, ERISA (Employment Retirement Income Security Act), FLSA (Fair Labor Standards Act), and other statutes and regulations?
- What tasks are the HR department or personnel being asked to do?
- How well are these tasks being performed?
- What programs, services, and management support must the HR department and/or personnel department provide to help the organization meet its goals?

As vendors demonstrate their products, carefully review the depth and quality within each functional or technical area of the system. Using a checklist can be helpful, but remember that a checklist does not provide complete answers. See the sample checklist in Figure 10-4.

Management will want to know costs as well as the potential benefits. Often, the library organization will already have some of the necessary components: computers, database licenses and telecommunications networks. The major cost components will be the HR software license, ongoing IT support, and user training.

Indicate the extent to which the following capabilities and features are provided in the basic system

Employment and Staffing

___ Tracks I-9 compliance

___ Administers new hire processing

___ Administers termination processing

___ Maintains skills inventories

___ Tracks internal/external work experience

___ Tracks status history (leaves of absence, layoffs, etc.)

___ Administers requisition fulfillment

___ Monitors position control and budget data

___ Facilitates career and position planning

Compensation

___ Administers salary change requests

___ Creates salary change history

___ Tracks unlimited salary change history

___ Stores and reports on W-2 and other payroll earnings

___ Tracks salary change forecasts

___ Tracks unlimited performance evaluation history

___ Administers bonus plans

___ Administers stock option plans

___ Evaluates/grades jobs

___ Tracks job descriptions

Benefits

___ Administers benefit plan participation

___ Tracks benefit plan eligibility

___ Calculates benefit coverage amounts

___ Calculates employee contribution amounts

___ Calculates benefit premium payment amounts

___ Tracks benefit plan participation history

___ Produces employee benefit statements

___ Administers COBRA eligibility and participation

___ Interfaces with third-party administrators for 401(k) pension

___ Tracks 401(k) pension plan investments

Benefits *(Continued)*

___ Administers flexible benefits

___ Produces flexible benefit enrollment forms

___ Administers flexible spending account balances

EEO/Affirmative Action

___ Prepares EEO-I (or applicable) report

___ Generates promotion and transfer analysis

___ Creates pay equity analysis data

___ Creates utilization analysis data

___ Supports source-of-hire analysis

___ Generates termination analysis

Training and Development

___ Administers training enrollment

___ Tracks training class participation

___ Tracks training costs

___ Evaluates training requirements

___ Schedules training classes

OSHA/Safety/Industrial Health

___ Tracks first reports of injuries

___ Calculates sick time use and leave balances

___ Prepares OSHA 200 report

___ Generates illness and injury data

___ Tracks individual safety history

___ Maintains safety training record

___ Tracks medical and rehabilitative activities

___ Calculates costs associated with illness and injury

___ Monitors workplace hazards

___ Monitors hazardous exposures

Employee and Labor Relations

___ Maintains union rosters

___ Tracks seniority rankings

___ Generates job opening notices

___ Supports bid/bump process

___ Tracks grievances

___ Calculates impact of negotiable alternative scenarios

Figure 10-4. Choosing an HRIS System

System Requirements, Features, and Capabilities

1) What hardware is recommended or required to operate the system?

2) What is the anticipated cost of the hardware, using industry standard suppliers?

3) What local area networks are fully compatible with the system?

4) What is the maximum number of employees?

5) Is the system written in a commercially available relational database, or it it written in programming language(s)?

6) What is the estimated processing time to generate a standard 10-field employee roster listing, including age, annual salary, and years of service for 500 employee records?

Fields

1) How many named, predefined fields are in the standard system?

2) How many named, predefined fields are there when all modules are included?

3) How many user-definable fields are in the standard system?

4) Can the nontechnical user easily create new fields, in addition to the user-definable fields?

5) What training is required to create totally new fields?

6) Can the user modify or create:
   a. Field names
   b. Field lengths for on-screen display purposes
   c. Field lengths for reporting purposes
   d. Create multiple versions of the same field with differing field lengths for reporting purposes
   e. Field edits and validations
   f. Screen prompt/display name
   g. Column headings for reports
   h. Alpha/numeric characteristics of each field
   i. Required/optional characteristics of each field
   j. Display format/output conversions for fields, and/or
   k. Set default values for fields to simplify data entry
   l. Inactivate unnecessary fields
   m. Reactivate fields not previously used
   n. Connect fields to tables

Tables

1) How many tables are provided in the standard system?

2) Can a nontechnical user easily add tables to the system?

Tables *(Continued)*

3) How much training is required to add a table to the system?

4) Can the nontechnical user modify table characteristics?

5) Can a nontechnical user easily add fields to a table?

6) Can table contents be accessed using a "hot" key and reviewed in a "pop-up" window during data entry without interrupting the data entry process?

7) Can tables be updated during data entry?

Reporting Capabilities

1) How many standard reports are provided with the standard system?

2) Can a nontechnical user easily modify the standard reports?

3) Can the nontechnical user change the sorting and selection criteria for standard reports when the reports are run?

4) How many sorting and sequencing levels may be defined for a report?

5) How long would it take for a nontechnical user to add two new fields to a standard report and delete one existing field?

6) Is there a fully prompted report writer that allows a nontechnical user to easily create new reports?

7) Does the report writer allow the nontechnical user to "point and pick" fields for the report and to create the selection of records for the report?

8) How many files can be accessed on a single report?

9) Does the system provide the ability to develop matrix-style reports with user-selected statistical data in each matrix cell?

10) Can the system produce mailing labels in any format?

Security and Audit

1) Can a unique security profile be established for each user?

2) How many unique user security profiles can be established?

3) Can each individual user be restricted from:
   a. Specific records or groups of records?
   b. Specific fields of information?
   c. Specific commands?
   d. Specific files of information?
   e. Specific screens and menus?
   f. The ability to update tables?

Figure 10-4. Choosing an HRIS System *(Continued)*

Security and Audit *(Continued)*

4) Can the nontechnical user easily define what fields will be subject to audit tracking?

5) Does the system validate data as they are entered for consistency with other data?

6) Does the system display descriptive error messages whenever a data entry or operational error occurs?

7) Can the nontechnical user easily modify "help" messages?

8) Are automated backup procedures included to prevent loss of data?

Utilities and Other Features

1) Does the system automatically build historical records as changes are entered?

2) How many historical entries may be maintained for any single field?

3) Is there an "import and export" utility to allow movement of data between systems?

4) Does the system incorporate a built-in word processor?

5) Will the system internally merge data into form letters and documents, or must the information be "exported" to another system?

6) How many days of training are required to achieve normal operating efficiency?

Utilities and Other Features *(Continued)*

7) Can the nontechnical user easily modify screens and menus?

8) Can the nontechnical user easily create new screens and menus?

9) How much training is required to create new screens and menus?

10) Are all system features and utilities fully documented?

11) Is the documentation indexed?

12) Is technical information (e.g., field names and definitions; database file structure) documented in the user's manual or in an appendix?

Costs

1) What is the price of the recommended basic system?

2) What is the price of any recommended module(s)? What, if any, additional costs are there to meet the needs described?

3) What is the cost for first-year maintenance?

4) What are the costs for first-year training and implementation support?

5) What are the costs for the anticipated customization?

6) What are the estimated recurring annual maintenance (and other) costs after the first year?

Figure 10-4. Choosing an HRIS System *(Continued)*

The savings benefits are generally much more difficult to calculate than the costs. Improvements in time and data content of reports needed by management will definitely be of great value. The data in a system tends to be more accurate since it comes from a single source (Safran, 2006).

WHAT ARE THE USER ISSUES INVOLVED IN IMPLEMENTING AN HRIS SYSTEM?

Users should be involved in the entire process (Lapointe, 1998). There are typically three types of users. The "power" users are computer literate and expect access to "expert paths" or shortcuts. This user typically expects fast response time and streamlined navigation. The "casual" users expect user-friendly interaction with the system and want built-in help. They might be resistant to a new system. The third type, the "empowered" users are familiar with technology, recognize the benefits of the new technology, and are willing and probably eager to use the new system. Their expectations probably lie somewhere between the other two extremes.

Involving users early in the implementation will provide a sense of ownership of the new system. Users should be involved in the decision-making process and evaluation of the various systems. Users can also define their own training needs and even deliver portions of the system training that pertain to their jobs.

The power users can evaluate new systems and make recommendations from their expert viewpoint. After the software has been purchased and design phases are underway, the power users and the empowered users can provide input on process design. This can be shared with coworkers and provide a connection between the new system and the users. Experienced trainers can then work with these users to determine the best training methods, course content, and scheduling. These users will become peer trainers and "subject matter" experts.

Regular and consistent communication with all users helps bolster employee morale and reduce anxiety about the new system. Establishing a help desk for users when the system goes live is also recommended (Lapointe, 1998). The number and types of help requests received should be recorded to determine where training was ineffective and identify where refresher courses or on-the-job training are needed. Additionally, three months or so after the system has been activated, the employees who attended training should be surveyed to assess productivity and skill gaps.

The introduction of a new information system brings challenges and often fear or anxiety. Involving users throughout the process can alleviate much of this anxiety and also empower users. HR technology provides an illustration of both the positive and negative impact that HR can have on the bottom line.

HOW CAN AN ORGANIZATION ENSURE PROPER E-MAIL, INTERNET, AND COMPUTER USAGE?

These days almost all employees at professional organizations of any size have access to a personal computer and the Internet at their desks. The employer sees the workstation as a tool to boost the performance and productivity of the organization. In libraries, especially, many job tasks are

Internet related. The Internet provides employees with quick access to vital information, which is especially important for libraries.

Think about your own organization. Are you using e-mail for most of your communication now? Do you use the computer for your card catalog and for searching reference questions? Most of us have become so used to this tool that we take it for granted. It is second nature to us to turn to the computer to find answers quickly both for library users and for ourselves.

Many employees treat the company PC and Internet connectivity as if it were their own private PC and Web connection (Nesher, 2006). Some employees download music, watch videos, play games online, and send private e-mail to friends and family. Misuse can create a number of legal problems for an employer. Computers have undoubtedly changed the way people work, but they have also changed the way people avoid work and sabotage work.

E-mail transmissions are considered "documents" and can be used against an employer in a lawsuit like a written letter or memorandum (Smith and Mazen, 2004). In recent court cases, employee e-mail messages have been presented as evidence in claims of discrimination, sexual harassment, and other illegal activities. Even when users delete messages, they remain in the organization's electronic archives. Deleted messages can be recalled and an improper message can come back to haunt an employer months or years after the message was transmitted.

A recent survey of 192 companies found that 92 percent of managers check employees' e-mail and Internet use at work ("E-Mail and Web Monitoring," 2003). Most organizations do permit reasonable personal use of the Web and e-mail, although less than half define what they consider to be reasonable. Considering the fact that most employees spend more time at work than they do at home, it seems reasonable that they would have to conduct some personal business during the normal work week. It only becomes a problem when the employee is spending more time doing personal business than doing their actual work. Twenty-five percent of the organizations have no procedures or safeguards to ensure that monitoring is not abused and almost 50 percent of the respondents lack written guidelines, policies, or procedures for monitoring.

Employers could violate their monitoring privileges and monitor employees' online activities all the time, not just when something gives them a reason to investigate. By not having guidelines in place about when and why they would monitor, employees are at their mercy.

Organizations must develop and communicate a policy regarding online issues, which should apply to all employees with access to these tools. Often, just reminding the employees about the use of the computer and that most of the information resides there for an indefinite period of time is enough for them not to abuse their computer rights. However, there will be some employees who do try to take advantage of the system. They might go as far as trying to use the computer for their own business as a sideline to their regular job. The organization policy should be clear about such abuse and the consequences for it.

DO EMPLOYEES HAVE THE RIGHT TO PRIVACY IN THEIR COMPUTER USAGE?

Typically, an employee sending personal e-mails in the workplace and using organization-supplied Internet access does **not** have the right to privacy, nor does a right to privacy exist related to Internet use or personal files stored on the organization's computer system or server. The electronic mail systems and computers are the property of the organization. As an employer, you have the right to expect that employees will use these tools for proper business purposes and the right to monitor employee activity for potential violations. As mentioned, e-mail messages and computer files can be used as evidence in a court of law and organizations have the right to take steps to minimize the risk that an employee may create documentation that is discriminatory, harassing, or otherwise illegal or improper.

However, there is a limited exception to the general rule that employees have no expectation of privacy in the workplace. Under the laws of some states, if an employer is found to have created for its employees a "reasonable expectation of privacy," employees may be able to legitimately claim that employer monitoring violates their privacy rights (Smith and Mazen, 2004).

The best way to protect the organization is to directly let employees know, both verbally and in writing, that they have no right to expect privacy in any of their activities related to organization e-mail, Internet, and computer use. Make it clear that all of these systems are company property. Even if your organization is not currently conducting electronic monitoring, do not promise employees that you will not do so in the future.

SHOULD AN ORGANIZATION MONITOR EMPLOYEES' COMPUTER ACTIVITY?

There is no single answer. Many organizations do not monitor their staff computer usage. It does take a fair amount of time to go through all of the data stored and most organizations feel that it might not be worth the effort. Most monitoring systems are done through software installed on the machine. A few monitoring software packages are: www.watchdog

pc.com; www.pearlsw.com/index.html; www.track4win.com/Monitor_Internet_Usage.asp; and www.spectorcne.com/intro.html.

Organizations have a strong interest in ensuring that their confidential and proprietary information is not being sent out of the company without authorization. Many library employees take organization "secrets" with them when they leave their jobs, ranging from e-mail contacts to strategies for future electronic use. This has the potential to do serious damage if this information falls into the wrong hands. Memory sticks and even MP3 players have been used to remove intellectual property and company secrets (McConnell, 2006).

IT-savvy employees can wreak even more havoc. They can develop "back-door" software programs that allow remote users to control a computer or they can place a virus on the organization's network or server. One disgruntled ex-employee of a major professional services organization planted a "remote login" and had access to his former employer's network many months after leaving, although the employee had set out to obtain revenge on the company rather than steal data (McConnell, 2006).

When someone gives their notice to quit, organizations should consider providing them with paid leave for the duration of their notice period. The most likely time for employees to do damage or steal information is during the time from giving notice to the date of departure.

WHAT SHOULD AN ORGANIZATION DO IF THEY SUSPECT MISUSE OF A COMPUTER?

First, isolate any workstations where you think there may be suspicious activity. Preserve the evidence. In many cases, employers fail to catch the offenders because they have not preserved the evidence (McConnell, 2006). Printing off an e-mail could tarnish the evidence. Do not confront the individual or give the offender an opportunity to cover his or her tracks until you have taken the appropriate steps to secure the data. Act fairly and impartially as it could be an innocent mistake on the part of the employee. Lock out e-mail and Internet accounts and prevent external access. Record your actions and the reasons behind them.

One of the worst scenarios in a workplace is misuse involving pornographic Web sites, especially child pornography. This is criminal conduct and will result in employee discharge. An example of this happened in a large public library. This library had a shared laser printer for staff members. One of the female staff members had been working on a project and sent her work to the printer. When she gathered the papers and brought them back to her work area, she discovered among the pages of her project a printout of child pornography pictures.

Not sure what to do, she asked for advice from a fellow staff member. This staff member immediately took it to the head of security in the library. The head of security met with the head of technology and the director and ran a program to determine where the print request had originated. It was determined that it came from one of the male staff's workstations. Library security was contacted and they came and confiscated the computer workstation. The male staff member denied any knowledge of the print or use of the computer in this way. Since the computer was in an open staff area, no charges were made at that time pending further investigation. The staff member was issued a different computer to use while his former one was being investigated.

After several months, library security informed the director of much more evidence that indicated that this individual had been using the computer for seeking out other pornographic Web sites although none of them were related to child pornography. The director had no choice but to terminate the staff member for computer misconduct. On the day of giving him notice, the staff member was asked to meet with the director and the human resources professional. The staff member said that he was sorry for what he had done. At the end of the conference, the human resources professional was asked to escort the individual to his work area so that he could collect his personal belongings and then escorted him out of the building. Formal charges were made against him and he was tried and convicted but received no prison time for his actions. Library security also confiscated his second computer workstation and again found pornographic sites.

Though this is an extreme example, it shows the extent to which computer misuse can affect an organization.

HOW DOES ONE SET STANDARDS REGARDING PROPER USAGE?

A well drafted, well communicated policy related to computer usage, e-mails and Internet access will instill in employees the instinct to think twice before clicking the "send" button. Most employees that misuse these tools do not do so intentionally. Employees often do not understand that e-mail transmissions are not private documents and that inappropriate use of the system opens both the organization and the individual to potential legal exposure and personal embarrassment.

A sound policy should contain the following elements:

- a statement that the organization's e-mail system is company property to be used for the purposes of furthering the organization's business
- a statement as to whether personal e-mails are permitted, defining any limitations on personal use of the system
- an explanation of the rules governing the use of e-mail, the Internet, and the computer system
- a statement that usage should comply with all applicable laws and regulations
- a statement that employees should not transmit or receive confidential or sensitive information
- a statement that employees should not transmit or receive, discriminatory, harassing, sexually oriented, offensive, or other illegal or improper messages or Web sites
- a statement forbidding the downloading of unauthorized software onto the employer's system
- a statement explaining the organization's reasons for conducting electronic monitoring (if you intend to do so), as well as the circumstances under which monitoring will take place
- a statement that the employee has no expectation to privacy regarding any e-mails; any computer documents sent, received, or stored at the workplace; or any activities related to the Internet

Distribute the policy regularly to all employees. You might want to require that all employees sign an acknowledgment that they have received, read, understood, and agree to abide by the rules.

WHAT IMPACT HAS TECHNOLOGY HAD ON THE LIBRARY WORKPLACE?

Automation is not a new concept in the library world. Library automation was in existence as far back as 1936 when a punch card computer system was installed at the University of Texas for circulation control (Jui, 1993). The use of magnetic tapes to store information replaced the punch card system in the early 1960s. In the early 1970s, a light pen device was used to read bar codes.

At about this same time, machine readable cataloguing formats (MARC records) began to be used. Many libraries used MARC tapes to create large databases of cataloged records. As systems improved, library catalogers were able to recall and transfer a bibliographic record into their own library catalog system. This feature eliminated the labor intensive file maintenance once associated with a card catalog. Acquisition systems were developed for ordering of library materials and automated serials systems. Computers also began to be used for interlibrary loan requests.

Through personal computers, library operations have taken on a new life. Computers loaded with word processing, spreadsheet analysis, and presentation software programs have become standard fixtures on each employee's desk. Some of the workforce has become mobile, conducting business outside of the library setting through the use of PDAs, cell phones, iPods, and laptops (Vaughan, 2005).

Library users can log in to the library from home and access library materials while sitting comfortably in an easy chair. Many libraries have set up "chat reference" so that users may ask reference questions online and get immediate responses from staff.

Technology has also changed the role of the librarian at the reference desk. It is not uncommon for computer clusters to be placed in close proximity to the reference desk, so many "reference" questions have become problem-solving questions related to the computer. Some libraries have added a technical support person at this central point.

Another technology that seems to be hitting the work environment can be identified by the little earphones peeking out from sweatshirts and pockets everywhere. Millions of people are plugged into mp3 players and iPods, getting their groove on to the latest music download (Agnvall, 2006). Many organizations are purchasing these devices as a means of training. Employees can actually listen to a training workshop while still working on the job. One IBM learning consultant, Alexis Cornelias, describes this learning as "education on the go" (Agnvall, 2006).

As with e-mail and the Internet, the drawback is the misuse or overuse of the tool. With open access to music sites, employees can fill the company's hard drives with downloaded music, causing the computers to run slower and raising concerns related to copyright infringement, possibly making the organization a target for a lawsuit (Gurchiek, 2006). In many libraries, use of mp3 players while working has become an additional perk, especially for employees in nonpublic areas. Again, policies related to the use of such equipment must be clearly identified.

Videoconferencing, Webcasting, and teleconferencing are other electronic tools that are used widely in the work environment. These conferencing tools allow individuals to participate in meetings and group discussions remotely. We also have mobile phones, BlackBerrys, smart phones, and wireless PDAs, which have capabilities far beyond those of old standard telephones. One size does not fit all and the infinite customizability of technology is yet another of its strengths.

REFERENCES

Agnvall, Elizabeth. 2006. "Just-In-Time Training." *HRMagazine* 51, no. 5: 66–71.

Balas, Janet E. 2005. "Once More Unto the Breach: Revisiting Training (Again)." *Computers in Libraries* 25, no. 8: 43–47.

Ball, Kirstie S. 2001. "The Use of Human Resource Information Systems: A Survey." *Personnel Review* 30, no. 6: 677–693.

Bland, Vikki. 2007. "Painless Pay Days." *NZ Business* 21, no. 1: 50–53.

Brooks, Art. 2006. "Dispelling HR's Fear of Technology Takeover." *Employee Benefit Plan Review* 60, no. 10: 6–8.

Burak, Lauren. 2005. "Have Your Finger Ready for Check Out." *School Library Journal* 51, no. 8: 26.

"Checklist Helps HRIS Pros Narrow Choices for a New System." 2001. *IOMA's Report on Managing HR Information Systems,* no. 6: 4–7.

"E-Learning Takes Hold Among Companies of All Sizes." 2002. *IOMA's Report on Managing Human Resources Information Systems,* no. 4: 18–21.

"E-Mail and Web Monitoring Are Now a Way of Life on the Job." 2003. *HRFocus* 80, no. 12: 8.

Florkowski, Gary W. and Miguel R. Olivas-Lujan. 2006. "The Diffusion of Human Resource Information Technology Innovations in US and Non-US firms." *Personnel Review* 35, no. 6: 685–710.

Grensing-Pophal, Lin. 2005. "Automating HR." *Credit Union Management* 28, no. 2: 32–35.

Gurchiek, Kathy. 2006. "iPods Can Hit Sour Note in the Office." *HRMagazine* 51, no. 4: 30, 36.

Hussain, Zahid, James Wallace, and Nelarine E. Cornelius. 2007. "The Use and Impact of Human Resource Information Systems on Human Resource Management Professionals." *Information & Management* 44: 74–89.

"Is Your Company Ready for E-Learning?" 2002. *IOMA's Corporate e-Learning Buyer's Guide,* no. 4: 6–10.

Jui, Doris. 1993. "Technology's Impact on Library Operations." ERIC ED 389 333.

Kahan, Stuart. 2001. "Online Payroll Taking Off." *Practical Accountant* 34, no. 7: 42–44.

Katz, Judith. 2006. "Tracking Employee Time: A Long-Term Problem." *Nursing Homes Long-Term Management* 55, no. 12: 50–51.

Lapointe, Joel. 1998. "People Make the System Go . . . Or Not." *HRMagazine* 43, no. 10: 28–33.

L.B. 2005. "Have Your Fingers Ready for Checkout." *School Library Journal* 51, no. 8: 26.

Mastrangelo, Paul M., Wendi Everton, and Jeffery A. Jolton. 2006. "Personal Use of Work Computers: Distraction Versus Destruction." *CyperPsychology & Behavior* 9, no. 6: 730–740.

McClure, David. 2005. "What to Look for in…Payroll." *Accounting Technology* 21, no. 10: 13.

McConnell, John. 2006. "Fighting the Enemy Within." *Personnel Today* (May 9): 30–31.

Nesher, Raviv. 2006. "Employee Misuse Can Put Your Company at Risk." *Central New York Business Journal* 20, no. 25: 22–23.

Safran, Gerson. 2006. "Making the Case for an HRMS." *Canadian HR Reporter* 19, no. 7: 13.

Smith, Shawn, and Rebecca Mazin. 2004. *The HR Answer Book*. New York: AMACOM.

Sreenivasulu, V. 2000. "The Role of a Digital Librarian in the Management of Digital Information Systems (DIS)." *The Electronic Library* 18, no. 1: 12–20.

Tennant, Roy. 2002. "The Digital Librarian Shortage." *Library Journal* 127, no. 5: 32.

Toliver, Julietta. (April 13, 2007). E-mail message to Mary J. Stanley.

Vaughan, Jason. 2005. "Lied Library @ Four Years: Technology Never Stands Still." *Library Hi Tech* 23 no. 1:34–49.

11 MANAGING CHANGE

This final chapter will focus on managing change within the library environment. Change is unavoidable and will occur even when the staff is comfortable with the ways things are. External forces such as budget, new technologies, change in leadership, and retiring workforce produce changes. Taking a proactive approach to change is the only way to take charge of the future. Putting change in a more positive light will help build staff acceptance and commitment. The use of part-time or contractual employees will also be part of the chapter as this is one of the ongoing changes in the library world.

Organizational change has been defined as "the movement of an organization away from its present state and toward some desired future state to increase its effectiveness" (George and Jones, 2000). Organizational change is an ongoing process that has important implications for organizational performance and for the well-being of its employees. An organization must adapt to changes quickly and effectively in order to survive. The more an organization changes, the easier and more effective the change process becomes. Developing and managing a plan for change is vital.

Think back to the day when you first started your professional career. Remember that first day and all of the emotions, doubts, and hopes that you experienced as you plunged into that first job. Now think about your current professional position and the first day that you started in that position. How has your career changed from that very first professional position? How has your current position changed from the first day you started in it? Has it changed any in the last week?

Our jobs are changing so rapidly it may seem as if we are hurtling through space at warp speed. Managing change is one of the greatest challenges and frustrations that any leader in today's workforce must face (Mercurio, 2006). You can deal with change in three ways: by resisting, following, or leading. A resister tries to stay put, which is impossible in changing situations; the majority of people and organizations who start by resisting eventually find that they have to follow, trying to catch up. Overcoming resistance and gaining acceptance from stakeholders can also be challenging. The problems resulting from dealing with change are rarely a result of the change itself. In most cases, problems can be traced to one of two factors: 1) lack of understanding surrounding the purpose for the change, and 2) lack of clarity on how to implement the change. The challenge then lies in driving organizational change successfully and with as few casualties along the way as possible. Casualties of change could include positions lost, individuals demoted, or the loss of comfort from doing tasks in a familiar way.

How do we understand, cope, and even thrive in this environment? Probably the same way that we have survived in the past—by preparing, planning, and implementing. When a new change comes along, we go through the process all over again. Then we go on to the next change. As we more fully enter the information age, we must adopt the viewpoint that change is inevitable and embrace change with open arms and open minds.

Positive aspects of change may be less obvious at first than the negative aspects. New ventures, expansion, promotions, and growth often bring challenges before delivering rewards. It is wise to use change as a stimulus to encourage new ideas and gather enthusiasm for future progress.

WHAT TYPES OF CHANGE DO LIBRARIES EXPERIENCE?

Understanding the type of change you are dealing with will help you to approach change effectively and to interpret others' response to it. A gradual change occurs slowly over a prolonged period, at a steady rate or with minor fluctuations in intensity. It can involve many people or just a few, but is most effective as an unending organization-wide program to improve quality and processes, reduce costs, and raise performance or service levels. A radical change is a sudden, dramatic change with marked effects. An example for many libraries occurred when the old card catalog was "dumped" overnight and gave way to the online catalog. Though this may have been a gradual change for the library employees, it was a radical change to the library user who came in to use the old catalog and found that it had vanished. Before making radical changes of any kind, the organization should plan thoroughly, thinking through the options to minimize risks.

In one academic library, the director who had been with the library for over 25 years announced her retirement. Over the next six months a search was conducted for her replacement. The director retired and a month later, the new director came on board. For the first six months, this new director did not make any changes. He also conducted meetings with each and every full-time employee of the library.

Then, like a sudden blast of artic air, change occurred. The new director announced that the library was going to become a team organization. He declared the new teams and who the team leaders would be. Some individuals who had been heads of units suddenly found themselves in subordinate positions with their underlings now serving as their team leader. Sixteen new teams were formed out of the old six units of the library. This change was definitely handled "top down." Staff members were unsure what to think or what to do. The entire organization was in culture shock.

In an effort to develop and mold this new change, a week was set aside and dubbed Organizational Week. A consultant was invited to present a workshop on team building through effective group process skills. The workshop covered team meeting management, facilitation, and group norms or ground rules. At the end of the week, a luncheon with games and prizes was held to celebrate the week's success. Results from the week's activities were immediately noticeable in teams' meeting behavior. The senior management team felt positive about the effectiveness of this effort and decided to make an ongoing commitment to conduct one of these weeks at the end of each semester. The practice still continues today although the week has been reduced to a period of two to three days instead of five. The time is used for planning, professional development of all staff, or to hear an outside speaker with trends of the future in libraries.

WHAT ARE SOME OF THE CHALLENGES IN MANAGING CHANGE?

In times of change, organizations face major challenges such as retention and morale issues as well as maintaining high level work results (McKnight, 2006). Change is a word that strikes fear in some and excitement in others. Often the effect of change is influenced more by one's attitude about change than by the change itself. As one director put it, "embracing a change over which you have no control leaves people thinking you are really something" (Cole, 2005).

Resistance to change takes three main forms: opposition based on misunderstanding or rational objections; fear of personal consequences; and emotional distrust. You will probably encounter all three and should plan ways to deal with them. The intensity of negative response will largely depend on the existing degree of trust. Before introducing a new change, be sure to consult and communicate with everyone as much as possible to build up trust and prepare your staff for the change.

One particular challenge is staffing changes. Personnel changes are probably the hardest to get used to. Friendships are established and when someone leaves for a better job or retirement, it is bittersweet (Lutz, 2005). However, by adapting to these changes, you often develop new relationships with the individuals who fill the vacant positions.

Three specific challenges are the aging of our workforce, the diminishing state of education, and increased global competitiveness (Furchtgott-Roth, 2005). As the large baby boom generation ages, the demographic structure of the economy will shift and the proportion of Americans over the age of

55 will increase significantly. Increases in longevity will also raise the proportion of older Americans.

On the positive side, the rate of older workers participating in the labor force is rising. This is a sign that America is open and flexible to providing opportunities for older Americans. With a future labor shortage looming, human resources professionals will need to encourage their organizations to utilize this aging workforce. Phased retirement, flexible schedules, mentoring, and consulting arrangements all appeal to members of this generation who want to stay employed during their golden years. These aging workers have substantial experience and can be integrated easily into the workforce while allowing them the freedom to pursue other interests.

Experienced librarians can be a significant resource in managing change. Most libraries are not able to recruit a significant number of positions to accommodate new roles, so it is essential to include senior librarians in any plans for the support of new technology. Their knowledge of organizational history can serve an important role (Youngman, 1999). Experienced librarians are often seen as being inflexible but they often respond quite favorably to the challenge of a revised mix of responsibilities that includes new roles created by new technology. New work assignments can be motivating and serve as an excellent means of avoiding stagnation and burnout. Senior librarians are also a great tool for mentoring new librarians. As fast as change is occurring, a balance between change and stability must be maintained to ensure the best customer service, avoid burnout, and keep staff focused.

HOW DOES CHANGE AFFECT RECRUITMENT?

Many recent library school graduates have specific technology skills that did not exist just a few years ago. These specialized skills can allow an entry-level librarian to quickly become productive in a new nontraditional role while taking time to develop expertise in more traditional subject based tasks. Sometimes these enthusiastic librarians with fresh skills can spur the interest of the senior librarians and motivate them to acquire and use new technology skills.

Adding a position or recruiting to fill a vacated position also presents a chance to rethink the organization and staffing patterns in a library or department. The recruiting of a new librarian can be an excellent opportunity to review the organizational chart and revamp existing position descriptions. Careful analysis of current and projected staffing needs can create a recruiting effort that will result in a truly effective new staff member.

Today's employees change jobs frequently to find the best match and continually seek new opportunities. In 2004, out of the US labor force of 147 million, there were 51 million separations and 54 million new hires (Furchtgott-Roth, 2005). Employment data reveals the importance of education and technical skills. The more education you have, the less likely you are to be unemployed (Furchtgott-Roth, 2005). The overall unemployment rate in Fall 2005 was 5.1 percent, but varied according to education status. The unemployment rate for those with a bachelor's degree was 2.4 percent; for those with a two-year degree, it was 3.6 percent; for those with a high school diploma, it was 5 percent; and for those without a high school diploma, it was 8.2 percent. Most library staff have at least a bachelor's degree and most librarian positions require a master's degree in library science. This would suggest that library workers would then be more likely to be employed; however, as with other professions, these individuals are still part of the workforce that tends to change jobs frequently for various reasons. Many have degrees in other fields from library science and move on to the field of choice. Often, library workers move on because their spouses change jobs and move to other locations. Therefore, libraries will still be seeking new hires to fill the vacancies that occur. I recommend that libraries who have potential librarians on their staff to encourage and support these individuals in considering this career.

IS THE PART-TIME EMPLOYEE A GOOD ALTERNATIVE?

The hiring of part-timers brings issues of status, equitable compensation, and professional support to the forefront (Brustman and Via, 1988). On one hand, administrators may view part-timers as strictly money-saving devices or a scheduling convenience. On the other hand, part-timers may want to work less than a 40-hour week and yet maintain involvement in professional life and continue professional development. Well qualified professionals are seeking meaningful and equitably compensated employment that accommodates other time demands. Full-time employees may see part-timers as jeopardizing their own status and positions.

The integration of part-time workers into the culture of the organization can enhance or impede successful implementation (Sherer and Coakley, 1999). Through the use of new technologies, part-time employees might be more involved in the day-to-day operations of the library even when they are not physically at the library. For instance, most individuals check their e-mail regularly whether they are at work or not.

In one survey done among part-time employees, part-timers indicated that they experienced a significant decline in feedback from their supervisors when they moved from full-time employment to part-time employment (Sherer and Coakley, 1999). Issues such as performance reviews, benefits and compensation, training, and career development fell by the wayside. Creating opportunities for part-time employees to address these concerns can eliminate misunderstandings that might contribute to dissatisfaction.

Managers or supervisors will need to ensure that the goals of the organization in using part-time employees are attained, and at the same time facilitate positive working relationships between the full- and part-time employees. It is imperative that both types of employees are not given the impression that their status is temporary or that their value and contributions to the organization are diminished.

Part-time professionals will continue to increase. Library organizations need to be prepared and plan for a variety of individual schedules in a department or team. Specific policies and practices related to part-time employment need to be in place for this movement to be successful.

SHOULD CONTRACTUAL EMPLOYEES BE USED DURING A TIME OF CHANGE?

Temporary or contractual employees are often used when staff are needed for a short period of time. Taking on a temporary employee allows the organization to meet an increase in demand while creating the opportunity to assess whether or not it is likely to last. Many times these workers are preferred because they are excluded from costly payroll taxes and pension and benefit plans.

Researchers suggest that in the future, employees will fall into two distinct classes: 1) members of the permanent organizational group who have strong attachments to the organization, and 2) contract employees who will be less attached to the organization (Lipponen and Leskinen, 2006). The growth of temporary employees in the library sector is yet to be determined but could definitely be a possibility.

While hiring temporary employees fills a needed gap in a just-in-time situation, morale issues might arise among the permanent employees. As organizations use more and more contingent employees instead of permanent workers, some permanent employees will perceive them as competitors or at least as potentially threatening and not part of the "in-group." Managers and supervisors need to know how to reduce intergroup conflicts resulting from these attitudes.

Organizations must also be mindful of how temporary these workers are in the organization. Many employees hired as temps remain in the same job for a number of years. A growing number of lawsuits are proving that legislation governing the pension and benefits treatment of this category of contract employees circumvents the system (Cohen, 1999). In some situations, the IRS has determined that employers have replaced permanent employees with temps and not enough payroll taxes have been paid as a result (Cohen, 1999). Use caution when hiring these employees. Another factor in the use of temporary employees is cost. The cost of temporary workers has been steadily increasing for the past few years (Howard, 2003). Organizations will be faced with the reality of deciding whether they are willing to pay more for this temporary labor or whether they will decide to do the work with their permanent employees.

HOW WILL VIRTUAL EMPLOYEES IMPACT THE WORKFORCE OF THE FUTURE?

Imagine hiring employees that you have never met and are never likely to meet. You conduct your working relationships via e-mail, chat, and phone. Is this taking telecommuting too far? Most case studies to date have involved a current full-time librarian working one or two days from home or being granted a leave to telecommute for a few months. In these situations, the supervisor has already worked with the employee in person. They are familiar with the telecommuting librarian's work habits, performance, and personality and have regular discussions in person with this individual regarding work projects and performance. Would telecommuting work without this personal contact?

This is the reality at Librarians' Index to the Internet (Schneider, 2003). This is a completely virtual library with five employees and over 100 volunteers. In the virtual workplace, the normal workplace cues are nonexistent. One librarian from this virtual workplace feels that you lose the ability to read individual body language, which makes up most of the communication process. She also contends that the virtual work environment lacks the informal collegial community found in the physical workplace.

Virtual workers need to be well organized, self-starting, strategic planners who are highly comfortable with computers. They will have to contend with clearing printer jams, installing updates, and figuring out what to do when the DSL connection suddenly disappears. Virtual workers also need to address the issue of having family close by who assume that they can interrupt the worker. Too often, these workers tend to give far too much of themselves because the computer is always close at hand. Virtual employment and its impact on libraries will be discussed more later in this chapter.

HOW CAN YOU ADDRESS THE CHALLENGES OF RETENTION AND MORALE DURING A PERIOD OF CHANGE?

Organizational changes impact all employees, and affects employee relationships with not only management but also fellow employees (Decker et al., 2001). Organizational changes influence the level of trust employees place in the organization and may also affect employees' loyalty to the organization. At the time of hiring, the employer and the new employee make certain commitments to one another. Employees develop certain psychological expectations of the organization and when they are violated through restructuring or some other organizational change, distrust, resistance, and lack of loyalty may result. Employers must attempt to understand and address concerns related to change in order to help the employees through the transitional process. Most organizations have been unable to restructure without significant challenges to employee morale.

In order to help the transition, first examine why individuals resist change. The first reaction for employees who hear of an imminent change is to personalize it and ask, "How is this going to affect me?" Unsubstantiated rumors add to a situation where the worst possible scenario is perceived. The employees' thinking is based on how past changes have impacted them and others. The pain of leaving behind old habits that may have given enormous satisfaction may not be compensated by the pleasure of changing to new habits (Atkinson, 2005). Some individuals find that changing their habits is just too hard, which is why health and fitness resolutions fail and why most diets do not work.

Organizational change often means making employees do more for less, putting them under increased surveillance, and increasing job instability as the employment relationship and the psychological contract are reengineered.

Employees felt that change affected their well being in the following ways (Worrall and Cooper, 2006):

- Unmanageable workloads
- Having little control over aspects of their job
- Work interfering with home and personal life

- Not having enough time to do their job as well as they would like
- Working longer hours than they wanted to
- Having little or no influence over performance targets
- Not being involved in decisions which affected their job
- Employee's ideas or suggestions not being taken into account

All of these factors influence the employee's attitude and morale during change. Employees tend to feel that changes have been imposed upon them and that they have little say in setting targets or objectives, many of which are seen as unreasonable or unattainable.

There appears to be a direct correlation between an individual's length of time in a position and their willingness to adapt to change (Mercurio, 2006). The longer an employee remains in the same role, the more difficult it can be for the organization to gain that individual's acceptance and overcome any resistance. For individuals who have experienced success in their roles, resistance is fueled by fears of stepping outside their comfort zone and/or not being able to experience the same success.

Employees with less time in the organization are often more receptive to making adjustments to their role. Some even perceive this as an opportunity to grow and feel rewarded by the new challenge.

In many of today's libraries, the organizational structure has become flattened, which limits the ability to move upward in responsibility. Experienced or senior librarians see no other alternative but to move out of the organization. If you want to keep these experienced employees, your organization has to provide opportunities for them to stay engaged. Organizational change can provide that opportunity through new projects or a change in venue that will give them motivation to stay.

HOW HAS TECHNOLOGY IMPACTED LIBRARIES IN THIS TIME OF CHANGE?

Library work has changed dramatically in the past 25 years largely because of technology. Changes are most apparent in role definitions, tasks, organizational structures, and user expectations. Traditional production work performed by librarians a generation ago is now accomplished by machines, causing a redefinition of roles for the traditional librarian and assistant. New titles such as library technical assistant, digital librarian, and computer specialist reflect a new direction. Tasks that were once only conducted by librarians are now being accomplished by paraprofessionals and library assistants. According to some researchers, this has caused tension, devaluation of the MLS, and a blurring of work responsibilities (Poole and Denny, 2001).

The expectations of the end user have added some anxiety and tension. The convenience of unmediated searching is assumed. Clients insist on immediate personal assistance in navigating through complex databases and expect instant online satisfaction at the click of a button. Users also expect librarians to handle technicalities in downloading files, clearing paper jams, and troubleshooting computer problems.

To add to the confusion, change in technology is also inevitable. Database interfaces and formats change at the whim of the vendor, often to the disadvantage of end users. The expense of purchasing electronic information, site licensing, and accuracy of coverage adds to the pressure, along with issues relating to updating the hardware and software. Librarians and managers are uncertain about the longevity and/or accessibility of the products they purchase.

Although this technology explosion has afforded librarians the opportunity to take on new roles and visibility, reactions to technology vary (Poole and Denny, 2001). Many librarians welcome automation and expect it to enhance their job satisfaction and professional development. Others express concern about ergonomics. Most did not believe that the automation offered any major time-saving benefits. Some librarians expressed concern over inadequate training. The pressure to keep up has intensified. In one survey, new health and stress anxieties surfaced around computer related ailments. The name given to this new ailment is "technostress."

WHAT IS TECHNOSTRESS AND HOW CAN IT BE TREATED?

Technostress can be defined in a number of ways. One definition labels it as "our reaction to technology and how we are changing due to its influence" (Brillhart, 2004). According to Craig Brod, technostress is a "modern disease of adaptation caused by the inability to cope with new technologies in a healthy manner" (Brod, 1984). Technostress can also be defined as personal stress generated by a reliance on technological devices. The primary symptom of those who are ambivalent, reluctant, or fearful of computers is anxiety. This stress is generally experienced by those individuals who feel pressured to accept and use computers.

One researcher studying technostress and librarians found that the most dynamic part of technostress for librarians is their changing role

(Ennis, 2005). Technology has made it easy for individuals to enter a virtual library and the user is unaware that the site that they have entered was created by librarians. In addition, technology has also created the expectation of free, online, and full text resources for the end users. Librarians have to explain to these users that sometimes information is not free, full text, or online and the user will still have to come into the library and pull the information off the shelf. Librarians must also explain why the library cannot provide everything online.

Symptoms of technostress can include memory issues, sleep difficulties, recreational activities that are interrupted by cell phone calls and pagers, or preoccupation with to-do lists, calls, and errands. Other symptoms can be headaches, irritability, stomach or intestinal problems, and heart-related issues, such as heart attack or high blood pressure. Most of these symptoms are no different than common physiological expressions of stress. Memory issues do seem to be uniquely related to technostress (Brillhart, 2004). These problems tend to be a direct effect of the brain being overstimulated daily with no time for rest.

In the current work environment, there is rarely any down time. Individuals have a cell phone for work to keep in contact. At home, they typically have computers where they can log into work via virtual networks and access files and work as needed. When traveling or on vacation, many individuals take their laptops along in case of emergencies or to check their e-mail. All of these electronic enablers provide the means to connect to the workplace even when individuals are physically away from it.

Consider the case of Dorothy, a 40-year-old library staff member at Main Street Public Library in Smalltown, USA. Dorothy has a bachelor's degree in English from the community college but has not had the time nor funding to continue her library education degree. She has been working at the library for 15 years and has learned most of her library skills by on-the-job experience. About five years ago, the old card catalog was replaced with a new, streamlined online catalog. In addition, all of the staff members received a new computer workstation. Dorothy took to the computer immediately. She loved learning the new jargon associated with computers and was soon able to create a homepage for the library. She became the library computer guru.

Lately, however, Dorothy has noticed that she has an increasing number of headaches, is irritable, unable to sleep more than a couple of hours at a time, and has begun forgetting to do simple things. Her mind seems to dwell on work-related activities that she feels she needs to accomplish. Her coworkers have remarked that she never seems to spend time with them anymore. It is as if she were physically attached to the computer. Her workload has increased immensely because of her computer ability. Dorothy is experiencing "technostress." The good news is that Dorothy is aware of the changes that are occurring and can do something about it.

Dorothy requests a meeting with the director who also serves as the library's human resources professional. In this meeting, Dorothy describes what is happening and the director agrees with her that some changes need to be made to bring Dorothy back to a normal working schedule. Some of Dorothy's computer activities are reassigned to another library staff member. In addition, Dorothy starts taking regular lunch and rest breaks as well as taking a week's vacation. After a short period, Dorothy seems like her old self again and is learning to enjoy her work again. Dorothy has learned how to manage the technology rather than letting the technology manage her.

HOW CAN INDIVIDUALS COPE WITH AND AVOID STRESS?

Stress takes months to accumulate and affect the performance and health of an employee. The employee starts off at optimum performance and as the stress level is increased, the employee's capability is stretched. Once the employee has reached the maximum level of coping, sleeping becomes difficult, causing fatigue during the day when high performance is needed. The employee's body cannot refresh and reenergize at night. Once fatigue sets in, anxiety and depression begin to affect the employee. Then the body becomes depleted of its ability to ward off illness. After bottoming out, employees will begin to climb back up the curve. They will regain confidence as they return closer to the top of the curve and optimum performance levels return. Then the cycle will begin again.

There are several strategies that employees can use to avoid this vicious cycle. First, the employee needs to learn how to relax. Taking regular vacations is one way to prevent stress. Rest breaks during the day can also break the stress cycle. Many individuals set a timer on their workstations reminding them to stop and take a break, get up from the computer, take a brief walk, and so on. Meditation can also relieve stress and refresh your mind during the weekday.

Time management is one of the most effective ways to reduce stress in the work environment. If employees can manage their time well, they are more organized and less likely to be stressed due to the multitasking required for accomplishing their many projects. Making lists can help to manage time by lumping activities into three priority groups: critical, important, and optional. Many organizations have introduced Stephen Covey's *Seven Habits of Highly Effective People* into the work environment to aid individuals in time management and setting priorities.

Staying healthy is an optimal way to minimize stress. Exercise and good nutrition allow the body to work out frustrations and keep the body running at maximum efficiency. Exercising can also help alleviate sleep problems and other physical symptoms. Maintaining a positive attitude can also be important. Cultivating a sense of humor and being able to laugh at oneself is most helpful in reducing stress levels.

Setting realistic and attainable goals is also extremely important in reducing stress. No one individual can be an expert at everything and an individual trying to be perfect in all aspects will suffer high stress levels. Individuals also need to celebrate when they achieve goals, whether they are small in nature, or large organizational goals.

Organizations will need to develop stress and technostress reduction training programs to deal with this issue. Since technostress is related to information technology, the implementation of systems, system selection, hardware procurement, and requirements analysis should all consider the impact on the employee (Brillhart, 2004). IT projects should be implemented gradually. Training costs should be built into all system implementations, project planning, and other IT-related projects. If an organization reduces the various forms of stress in its environment, it will increase productivity, and decrease employee related costs of technostress.

WHAT OTHER WAYS CAN ORGANIZATIONS TACKLE ISSUES SURROUNDING CHANGE?

Organizations are increasingly recognizing the need for interventions to create balance in the work lives of their employees. Virtual work or telecommuting programs allow individuals to work away from central offices, reducing commuting time and providing the opportunity for employees to adapt their work hours to better suit the many different demands on their time. The basic assumption lending support to virtual work is that technology provides work schedule flexibility, allowing people to cope with conflicting work and nonwork responsibilities that are a primary source of job stress (Mamaghani, 2006). According to the Telework Coalition's Web site, in 1995 there were only 4 million teleworkers. In 2000 that number grew to 23.6 million in the United States (Mamaghani, 2006). The number of Americans who worked at home as little as one day per week increased from 41.3 million in 2003 to 44.4 million in 2004. In 2003, an estimated 137 million people worldwide worked from their homes.

For job seekers, an organization that offers flexible work schedules and/or the ability to telecommute will serve as an incentive, making those organizations that embrace technology more attractive to younger, tech-savvy potential employees. Organizations may be able to use telecommuting as a bargaining tool when negotiating with these workers.

The real challenge in initiating a telecommuting program is determining who will be the telecommuters and who will need to physically be at the library. Academic librarians often have the ability to work a few days a week from home, but cannot do so on an everyday basis. When special projects are due, some librarians are granted approval to work from home to concentrate on this project without interruption. This is often done on the condition that the employee will be available by computer or telephone if needed. Issues arise when colleagues or subordinates interpret this as "special privileges" and think that the individual is not really working but playing at home.

Virtual work is relatively new and is especially common among highly skilled and technologically capable professionals (Raghuram and Wiesenfeld, 2004). When employees work out of a fixed location, physical boundaries and standardized work hours separate work and nonwork domains. Virtual work creates a fuzzy boundary between work and home domains but individuals with strong self-control are able to work with these ambiguous boundaries. One consequence of virtual work is that the employee may feel disconnected from the organizational community and its social support.

Flexible work schedules are a morale booster but employers must be cognizant of the impact on employees who are not able to telecommute. Another consideration is the lack of peer-to-peer interaction resulting from a partially mobile workforce or work team.

WHAT IMPACT DOES CHANGE HAVE ON THE HUMAN RESOURCES PROFESSIONAL?

There have been numerous attempts to capture the changing nature of personnel roles in response to major transformations in the workplace. One researcher indicates that the role of the HR professional has altered in a number of respects and has become more multifaceted and complex (Caldwell, 2003). Today's HR professionals find themselves in a more reactive role of fighting fires. In a time of lay-offs, reductions in budget, and restructuring, they are forced to do more with less.

Technology continues to determine how work is done and HR needs to become more fluent in assisting organizations to manage work, performance, and these changes through the use of technology (Buford and Mackavey, 2003). Demographic changes are very important for HR strategy. Different tools have to be applied for an older workforce than for the younger generation. Sources of motivation also vary between women and men and among minorities. Different benefit packages and training programs will be needed for these different demographic perspectives. There are more women in the workforce than ever before and HR professionals will have to take this into consideration and help them balance careers with family roles. HR professionals will also have to face the cultural differences that need to be considered to integrate some minority staff members (Lipiec, 2001).

New paradigms in the workplace environment are forcing organizations to redefine employee competencies. Fluency in a second language may be needed. Respect of different cultural values will be important and new employees will need training and development in this area. Training and skill building has often been under the management of the human resources department or professionals. Workplaces today are becoming the primary place where adults acquire and practice skills (Von Dran, 2005).

HR professionals will have to have a holistic view of the organization. They must be able to define strategic goals, coordinate with employees to achieve these goals, and be knowledgeable about organizational finances. All changes in organizations are based on the premise that the status quo is in need of improvement. Some significant changes that affect libraries are new technologies, the proliferation of computers and access to the Internet, changes in the nature of the workforce, increased competition among vendors and publishers, and social and political trends resulting in heightened privacy and security concerns in the wake of September 11, 2001 (9/11).

Often, employees try to preserve their proven routines by continuing to support unnecessary hierarchical structures or by performing unnecessary tasks. There are several reasons for this resistance. Employees might resist change because their energies are focused elsewhere. Some examples are employees with school-age children, elderly parents, or both, and those who have reached career peaks and are anticipating retirement. These employees might reinforce each other's unwillingness to learn new routines and skills, while simultaneously defending their accomplishments and position power. Creating win-win situations requires patience, resources, and creativity as each group member's needs are different and individual solutions are necessary.

HR professionals will need to understand their own capacity for change and their resilience in coping with the inevitable stresses that result. They have to be role models for the values of the new organization.

HOW CAN THE HR PROFESSIONAL COPE DURING A CHANGE?

HR staff members are often overwhelmed by the multiple demands they face during a transition. First, HR professionals must understand what they can and what they cannot control. They can exert control by seeking information. If top management is not forthcoming, schedule an appointment and ask pertinent questions. They may or may not be able to tell you much but, at the very least, you will have established contact. You also might have data that will help them and it is very likely that they too, are overwhelmed with work and will appreciate your proactive approach. An effective blend of human resources programs and business strategy will have a profound effect on the nature and future of organizations.

Learn about what is going around. Talk with people, ask questions, get information, and try to determine the extent of the situation. Stop and listen to yourself. Find out what emotions you are feeling and what you find frightening or exciting. Determine whether you are in control of your emotions or if they are in control of you. Some individuals indicate that keeping a journal during a time of transition or change is an excellent way to understand and control their emotional reactions to organizational transitions (Marks, 2003).

Be tolerant of those around you and realize that individuals that you have relied upon in the past may not have much more information than you do. They will also be going through their own stressful reactions. Similarly, be tolerant of your own behaviors and emotions. This is especially difficult for HR professionals who pride themselves on providing top-notch service to their internal customers and colleagues. You will be challenged to learn new ways of doing things along with new ways of thinking about past practices. Recognize that you will make some mistakes as you begin doing things in a new way.

Keep communication flowing upward and downward. HR professionals can be role models for others. Contribute to building the best possible new organization and a culture in which openness and honesty prevail. Like the library profession, the human resources profession is no stranger to change. Faced with rapid and constant change, many organizations are seeking improvement in workforce productivity in order to maintain a competitive advantage and, as a result, turning to HR professionals to redesign the HR function in fundamental ways. The end result is that human resources becomes a more strategic role, not just a record keeping service (Hawthorne, 2004).

Odds are that you will go through multiple transitions in your career. HR can sponsor periodic workshops that help staff learn from a current transition how to better manage future ones. Engaging the participants in discussion about the transitions can help them apply strategies to resolve their situations. Trying to stay healthy, positive, and motivated will reduce stress and allow you to cope and help others cope with the changing environment.

REFERENCES

Atkinson, Philip. 2005. "Managing Resistance to Change." *Management Services* 49, no. 1: 14–19.

Brillhart, Peter E. 2004. "Technostress in the Workplace: Managing Stress in the Electronic Workplace." *The Journal of American Academy of Business* 5, no. 1/2: 302–307.

Brod, Craig. 1984. *Technostress: The Human Cost of the Computer Revolution*. Reading, MA, Addison-Wesley.

Brustman, Mary Jane and Barbara J. Via. 1988. "Employment and Status of Part-Time Librarians in US Academic Libraries." *The Journal of Academic Librarianship* 14, no. 2: 87–91.

Buford, Casey, and Maria Mackavey. 2003. "New Directions for Human Resources in 2002 and Beyond." *Journal of American Academy of Business* 2, no. 2: 600–601.

Caldwell, Raymond. 2003. "The Changing Roles of Personnel Managers: Old Ambiguities, New Uncertainties." *Journal of Management Studies* 40, no. 4: 983–1005.

Cohen, Dian. 1999. "The 'Permatemp' Dilemma." *Benefits Canada* 23, no. 4: 98.

Cole, Maureen. 2005. "Top 10 Reasons to Embrace Change." *OLA Quarterly* 11, no. 2/3: 3–4.

Decker, Diann, Gloria E. Wheeler, Janell Johnson, and Robert J. Parsons. 2001. "Effect of Organizational Change on the Individual Employee." *Health Care Manager* 19, no. 4: 1–12.

Ennis, Lisa A. 2005. "The Evolution of Technostress." *Computers in Libraries* 25, no. 8: 10–12.

Furchtgott-Roth, Diana. 2005. "Challenges in Staff." *HRMagazine* 50, no. 13: 69–70.

George, Jennifer M. and Gareth R. Jones. 2000. *Essentials of Managing Organizational Behavior*. Upper Saddle River, NJ: Prentice-Hall.

Hawthorne, Pat. 2004. "Redesigning Library Human Resources: Integrating Human Resources Management and Organizational Development." *Library Trends* 53, no. 1.

Howard, Simon. 2003. "The Price of Flexibility." *People Management* 9, no. 6: 59.

Lipiec, Jacek. 2001. "Human Resources Management Perspective at the Turn of the Century." *Public Personnel Management* 30, no. 2: 137–147.

Lipponen, Jukka and Johanna Leskinen. 2006. "Conditions of Contract, Common In-Group Identity and In-Group Bias Toward Contingent Workers." *The Journal of Social Psychology* 146, no. 6: 671–684.

Lutz, Amanda. 2005. "Be Prepared for Changes...Lots of Them!" *Quill Magazine* 93, no. 8: 42.

Mamaghani, Farrokh. 2006. "Impact of Information Technology on the Workforce of the Future: An Analysis." *International Journal of Management* 23, no. 4: 845–850.

Marks, Mitchell Lee. 2003. "Surviving Madness." *HRMagazine* 48, no. 6: 86.

McKnight, William. 2006. "Managing Change in Information Management." *DM Review* 16, no. 9: 56.

Mercurio, Nancy. 2006. "Managing Change Successfully." *Canadian Manager* 31, no. 2: 6–7.

Poole, Carolyn E. and Emmett Denny. 2001. "Technological Change in the Workplace: A Statewide Survey of Community College Library and Learning Resources Personnel." *College & Research Libraries* 62, no. 6: 503–515.

Raghuram, Sumita and Batia Wiesenfeld. 2004. "Work-Nonwork Conflict and Job Stress Among Virtual Workers." *Human Resources Management* 43, no. 2/3: 259–277.

Schneider, Karen G. 2003. "Managing the Virtual Workplace." *Library Journal* 128, no. 1: 24–25.

Sherer, Pamela D. and Lori A. Coakley. 1999. "Questioning and Developing Your Part-Time Employee Practices." *Workforce* (Supplement, October 1999): 4.

Von Dran, Gisela. 2005. "Human Resources and Leadership Strategies for Libraries in Transition." *Library Administration & Management* 19, no. 4: 177–184.

Worrall, Les and Cary Cooper. 2006. "Short Changed." *People Management* 12, no. 13: 36–38.

Youngman, Daryl C. 1999. "Library Staffing Considerations in the Age of Technology: Basic Elements for Managing Change." *Issues in Science and Technology Librarianship* (Fall): 24.

BIBLIOGRAPHY

Abbasi, Sami M. and Kenneth W. Hollman. 2000. "Turnover: The Real Bottom Line." *Public Personnel Management* 29, no. 3: 333–343.

Abernathy, Robert. 2005. *Smooth Legal Sailing!: Americans with Disabilities Act.* (workshop, IUPUI University Library, Indianapolis, IN).

Abernathy, Robert. 2005. *Smooth Legal Sailing!: Sexual Harassment* (workshop, IUPUI University Library, Indianapolis, IN).

ACRL Professional Development Committee. 2000. "ACRL Statement on Professional Development." *C&RL News* 61, no. 10: 933.

Addington, Mark A. 2004. "Overtime Regs: What They Mean for You." *Lodging Hospitality* 60, no. 14: 30.

"Age Discrimination in Employment Act: Equal Employment Opportunity Commission Interpretation." March 2005. *Supreme Court Debates* 8, no. 3: 67–96.

Agnvall, Elizabeth. 2006. "Just-in-Time Training." *HRMagazine* 51, no. 5: 66–71.

Albanese, Andrew Richard. 2003. "The Top Seven Academic Library Issues." *Library Journal* 128, no. 4: 43–46.

Allen, Don. 1995. "Recruitment Management: Finding the Right Fit." *HR Focus* 2, no. 4: 15.

Aluri, Rao and Mary Reichel. 1994. "Performance Evaluation: A Deadly Disease?" *The Journal of Academic Librarianship* 20, no. 3: 145–155.

Anderson, Thomas M. 2006. "Open Season for Health Savings." *Kiplinger's Personal Finance* 60, no. 10: 88–90.

Anonymous. 1997. "Many Ways to Reduce Absenteeism, Cut Costs." *The Worklife Report* 10, no. 3: 14–15.

Anonymous. 2006. "Employers Work to Retain Staff, Despite Rise in Job Seeking." *HR Focus* 83, no. 10: 8.

Arthur, Diane. 2001. *The Employee Recruitment and Retention Handbook.* New York: AMACOM.

Arwedson, Ingrid L., Susanne Roos, and Anita Bjorklund. 2007. "Constituents of Healthy Workplaces." *Work* 28: 3–11.

Atkinson, Philip. 2005. "Managing Resistance to Change." *Management Services* 49, no. 1: 14–19.

Avsec, Robert. 2006. "Grow Your Own Leaders." *Fire Chief* 50, no. 8: 38–41.

Axelrod, Beth, Helen Handfield-Jones, and Ed Michaels. 2002. "A New Game Plan for C Players." *Harvard Business Review* 80, no. 1: 80–88.

Bailey, Laura. 2002. "Evaluations Help Set the Tone for Year-Round Performance." *Crain's Detroit Business* 18, no. 2: 12.

Baldiga, Nancy R. 2005. "Opportunity and Balance: Is Your Organization Ready to Provide Both?" *Journal of Accountancy* 199, no. 5: 39–45.

Baldwin, David A. 1996. *The Academic Librarian's Human Resources Handbook: Employer Rights and Responsibilities.* Englewood, CO: Libraries Unlimited.

Baldwin, David A. 2003. *Librarian Compensation Handbook: A Guide for Administrators, Librarians and Staff.* Westport, CT: Libraries Unlimited.

Ball, Kirstie S. 2001. "The Use of Human Resource Information Systems: A Survey." *Personnel Review* 30, no. 6: 677–693.

Ballard, Angela and Laura Blessing. 2006. "Organizational Socialization through Employee Orientations at North Carolina." *College and Research Libraries* 67, no. 3: 240–248.

Ballard, Thomas H. 1982. "Public Library Unions—the Fantasy and the Reality." *American Libraries* 13, no. 8: 506–509.

Banas, Donald and Katherine Heylman. 1990. "The Right Stuff: Librarians at the Bargaining Table." *School Library Journal* 36: 23–28.

Bassett, James W. 2006. "7 Steps to Screen New Hires." *Review of Optometry* 143, no. 5: 29–32.

Bates, Steve. 2004. "Getting Engaged." *HRMagazine* 49, no. 2: 44–51.

Baugher, Phil and Maurice Freedman. 2004. "Should We Ever Work for Free?" *American Libraries* 35, no. 4: 81–84.

Baum II, Charles L. 2006. "The Effects of Government—Mandated Family Leave on Employer Family Leave Policies." *Contemporary Economic Policy* 24, no. 3: 432–445.

Bell, Allison. 2006. "Health Account Plans Pull Ahead of Indemnity Plans, Kaiser Reports." *National Underwriter* 110, no. 37: 7, 41.

Bernardi, Lauren M. 2002. "Managing Problem Employees." *Canadian Manager* 27, no. 1: 12–15.

Bernardi, Lauren M. 2003. "Nine Steps to Effective Discipline." *Canadian Manager* 28, no. 4: 19–20, 30.

Berta, Dina. 2006. "Leadership Development Bolsters Employee Retentions." *Nation's Restaurant News* 40, no. 37: 18.

Bisoux, Tricia. 2005. "What Makes Leaders Great." *BizEd* 4, no. 6: 40–45.

Bland, Vikki. 2007. "Painless Pay Days." *NZ Business* 21, no. 1: 50–53.

Bliss, Elizabeth. 2006. "Staffing in the Small Public Library: An Overview." *Rural Libraries* 26, no. 1: 7–28.

Booher, Dianna. 1999. "Communicate with Confidence." *Enterprise, Salt Lake City* 29, no. 23: 15.

Bosseau, Don L. and Susan K. Martin. 2000. "The Accidental Profession." *Journal of Academic Librarianship* 26, no. 3: 171–176.

Bouton, David. 2005. *Smooth Legal Sailing!: FLSA.* (workshop, IUPUI University Library, Indianapolis, IN.

Bramson, Robert M. 1981. *Coping with Difficult People*. New York: Anchor Press.

Brillhart, Peter E. 2004. "Technostress in the Workplace: Managing Stress in the Electronic Workplace." *The Journal of American Academy of Business* 5, no. 1/2: 302–307.

Brod, Craig. 1984. *Technostress: The Human Cost of the Computer Revolution*. Reading, MA: Addison-Wesley.

Brooks, Art. 2006. "Dispelling HR's Fear of Technology Takeover." *Employee Benefit Plan Review* 60, no. 10: 6–8.

Brustman, Mary Jane and Barbara J. Via. 1988. "Employment and Status of Part-Time Librarians in US Academic Libraries." *The Journal of Academic Librarianship* 14, no. 2: 87–91.

Buchanan, Robert. 2005. "Library Assistant Training: Perceptions, Incentives, and Barriers." *Journal of Academic Librarianship* 31, no. 5: 421–431.

Buford, Casey and Maria Mackavey. 2003. "New Directions for Human Resources in 2002 and Beyond." *Journal of American Academy of Business* 2, no. 2: 600–601.

Caldwell, Raymond. 2003. "The Changing Roles of Personnel Managers: Old Ambiguities, New Uncertainties." *Journal of Management Studies* 40, no. 4: 983–1005.

Cangemi, Joseph P. and Richard L. Miller. 2004. "Exit Strategies." *Journal of Management Development* 28, no. 10: 982–987.

Carlson, Kevin D., Mary L. Connerley, and Ross L. Mecham III. 2002. "Recruitment Evaluation: The Case for Assessing the Quality of Applicants Attracted." *Personnel Psychology* 55, no. 2: 461–491.

"Changing Roles of Academic and Research Libraries." 2006. Roundtable on Technology and Change in Academic Libraries convened by the Association of College and Research Libraries (ACRL) on November 2–3, 2006 in Chicago. Available: www.ala.org/ACRL (accessed March 20, 2007).

"Checklist Helps HRIS Pros Narrow Choices for a New System." 2001. *IOMA's Report on Managing HR Information Systems* v. 2001, 6: 4–7.

Christie, Betsy and Brian H. Kleiner. 2000. "When Is an Employee Unsalvageable?" *Equal Opportunities International* 19, no. 6/7: 40–44.

Chute, A., E. Kroe, P. Garner, M. Polcari, and C.J. Ramsey. 2002. *Public Libraries in the United States: Fiscal Year 2000*. (NCES 2002-344). Washington, DC: US Department of Education, National Center for Education Statistics. Available: http://nces.ed.gov/pubs2002/2002344 (accessed March 28, 2007).

Code of Federal Regulations, Title 29, Volume 4, Chapter XIV—Equal Employment Opportunity Commission, Part 1602, Section 1602.7—Requirement for filing of report.

Cohen, Dian. 1999. "The 'Permatemp' Dilemma." *Benefits Canada* 23, no. 4: 98.

Cole, Maureen. 2005. "Top 10 Reasons to Embrace Change." *OLA Quarterly* 11, no. 2/3: 3–4.

Cote, Sylvie and Marc Pistorio. 2001. "Resolving Disputes." *CMA Management* 75, no.7: 18–19.

Cottringer, William. 2005. "Adopting a Philosophy on Conflict." *Supervision* 66, no. 3: 3–5.

Cottringer, William. 2003. "Employee Conflict." *Supervision* 64, no. 20: 3–5.

Creth, Sheila and Frederick Duda, eds. 1989. *Personnel Administration in Libraries*, 2nd. Ed. New York: Neal-Schuman.

Crockett, Roger O. 2007. "The 21st Century Meeting." *Business Week* (February 26) Issue 4023: 72–79.

Curtis, David. 2003. "Learning from Jayson Blair: Having Marginal Employees Is Situation to Address ASAP." *Fort Worth Business Press* 16, no. 23: 41.

Dansker, Benjamin and Sherwin Pomerantz. 1989. "Systematic Salary Administration." *Personnel Administrator* 34, no. 3: 72–77.

DeBruijn, Erik and Margaret Friesen. 1996. "Investing in Human Resources: Staff Training and Development at the University of British Columbia Library." *Library Administration and Organization* 14: 63–94.

Decker, Diann, Gloria E. Wheeler, Janell Johnson, and Robert J. Parsons. 2001. "Effect of Organizational Change on the Individual Employee." *Health Care Manager* 19, no. 4: 1–12.

Deeprose, Donna. 2007. *How to Recognize and Reward Employees*, 2nd ed. New York: AMACOM.

De la Pena McCook, Kathleen and Paula Geist. 1993. "Diversity Deferred: Where Are the Minority Librarians." *Library Journal* 118, no. 18 (November 1): 35.

DelPo, Amy. 2005. *The Performance Appraisal Handbook: Legal & Practical Rules for Managers*. Berkeley, CA; NOLO.

DeMers, Allen. 2002. "Solutions and Strategies for IT: Recruitment and Retention: A Manager's Guide." *Public Personnel Management* 31, no. 1 (Spring): 27–41.

Deshpande, Satish P. and Damodar Y. Golhar. 1994. "HRM Practices in Large and Small Manufacturing Firms: A Comparative Study." *Journal of Small Business Management* 32, no. 2 (April): 49–57.

Dhanoa, David S. and Brian H. Kleiner 2000. "How to Conduct Due Process Discipline." *Management Research News* 23, no. 7/8: 89–94.

DiMattia, Susan. 2006. "Special Librarians Embrace Transformation in Baltimore." *American Libraries* 37, no. 7: 24–25.

Doan, Tomalee and Kristine Ferry. (2006). "Instant Messaging (IM): Providing Services and Enhancing Communication." *Journal of Business & Finance Librarianship* 12, no. 2:17–22.

Easton, Fred R. and John C. Goodale. 2005. "Schedule Recovery: Unplanned Absences in Service Organizations." *Decision Sciences* 36, no. 3: 459–488.

Ekman, Paul. 1997. *What the Face Reveals: Basic and Applied Studies of Spontaneous Expressing Using the Facial Action Coding System (FACS)*. New York: Oxford University Press.

"E-Learning Takes Hold Among Companies of All Sizes." 2002. *IOMA's Report on Managing Human Resources Information Systems* no. 4: 18–21.

"E-Mail and Web Monitoring Are Now a Way of Life on the Job." 2003. *HRFocus* 80, no. 12: 8.

Ennis, Lisa A. 2005. "The Evolution of Technostress." *Computers in Libraries* 25, no. 8: 10–12.

Everhart, Nancy. 2000. "Looking For a Few Good Librarians." *School Library Journal* 46, no. 9: 58–61.

"Expedia: U.S. Workers to Skip 574 Million Vacation Days in '06." 2006. *Travel Weekly* 65, no. 22: 12.

Falcone, Paul. 1992. "Power Interview Skills Will Find 'The Best' Quickly." *HR News* 69, no. 11: 14.

Falcone, Paul. 1995. "Getting Employers to Open Up on a Reference Check." *HRM Magazine* 40, no. 7 (July): 58–63.

Falcone, Paul. 2000. "Employee Separations: Layoffs vs. Terminations for Cause." *HRMagazine* 45, no. 10: 189–196.

Falcone, Paul. 2000. "Tacking Excessive Absenteeism." *HRMagazine* 45, no. 1: 139–144.

Farley, Y. S. 2002. "Strategies for Improving Library Salaries." *American Libraries* 33, no. 1: 56–59.

Fenn, Donna. 2000. "Scourpower." *Inc.* 22, no. 17: 110–117.

Fialkoff, Francine and Evan St. Lifer. 1993. "Early Recruitment Yields High Results." *Library Journal* 118: (November 1):18–19.

Fietzer, W. 1993. "World Enough, and Time: Using Search and Screen Committees to Select Personnel in Academic Libraries." *Journal of Academic Librarianship* 19, no. 3: 149–153.

Fisher, Heather. 2000. "Children's Librarians: What Are They?" *Orana* 36, no. 1: 9–13.

Florkowski, Gary W. and Miguel R. Olivas-Lujan. 2006. "The Diffusion of Human Resource Information Technology Innovations in US and Non-US Firms." *Personnel Review* 35, no. 6: 685–710.

Foltz, John and Joan Fulton. 2005. "Dealing with Problem Employees." *Feed & Grain* 44, no. 4: 38–41.

Freed, David H. 2000. "One More Time: Please Fire Marginal Employees." *Health Care Manager* 18, no. 3: 45–51.

Furchtgott-Roth, Diana. 2005. "Challenges in Staff." *HRMagazine* 50, no. 13: 69–70.

Gasaway, Richard B. 2007. "The Purpose of Discipline." *Fire Engineering* 160, no. 1: 12–16.

Gedeon, Julie A. and Richard E. Rubin. 1999. "Attribution Theory and Academic Library Performance Evaluation." *The Journal of Academic Librarianship* 25, no. 1: 18–25.

George, Jennifer M. and Gareth R. Jones. 2002. *Essentials of Managing Organizational Behavior*. Upper Saddle River, NJ: Prentice-Hall.

Gjelten, Dan and Teresa Fishel. 2006. "Developing Leaders and Transforming Libraries: Leader Institutes for Librarians." *C&RL News* 67, no. 7: 409–412.

Gladwell, Malcolm. 2005. *Blink: The Power of Thinking Without Thinking*. New York: Little, Brown.

Glynn, Gillian, Matthew T. Miklave A. J. Trafimow, A. J., D. Diane Hatch, and James E. Hall. 2001. "Legal Insight: HR Within the Law." *Workforce* 80, no. 3: 76–81.

Golian, Linda M. and Michael W. Galbraith. 1996. "Effective Monitoring Programs for Professional Library Development." *Advances in Library Administration and Organization* 14: 95–124.

Goodson, Carol. 1997. *The Complete Guide to Performance Standards for Library Personnel*. New York: Neal-Schuman.

Grensing-Pophal, Lin. 2005. "Automating HR." *Credit Union Management* 28, no. 2: 32–35.

Gupta, Vick and Brian H. Kleiner. 2005. "How to Recognize and Handle Potentially Violent Employees." *Management Research News* 28, no. 11/12: 60–69.

Gurchiek, Kathy. 2006. "iPods Can Hit Sour Note in the Office." *HRMagazine* 51, no. 4: 30, 36.

Hackett, R. D. and R. M. Guiion. 1985. "A Re-evaluation of the Absenteeism-Job Satisfaction Relationship." *Organizational Behavior and Human Decision Processes* 35: 340–381.

Hale, Dwight. 1991/92. "Supervising the Marginal Employee: Dilemma and Opportunity." *Management Quarterly* 32, no. 4: 23–30.

Hale, Mary. 1999. "He Says, She Says: Gender and Worklife." *Public Administration Review* 59, no. 5: 410–435.

Harralson, David M. 2001. "Recruitment in Academic Libraries: Library Literature in the 90s." *College and Undergraduate Libraries* 8, no. 1: 37–68.

Hauge, Mary. 1997. "Recruit for the Profession." *Book Report* 15, no. 4 (January/February): 19.

Hawthorne, Pat. 2004. "Redesigning Library Human Resources: Integrating Human Resources Management and Organizational Development." *Library Trends* 53, no. 1.

Herring, J. J. 1986. "Establishing and Integrating Employment Recruiting System." *Personnel* 63: 47–52.

Hesse, Katherine A. and Doris R. M. Ehrens. 2006. "Family Medical Leave." *Benefits Quarterly: Third Quarter 2006* 22, no. 3: 57–58.

Hicks, Sheila, Mary Peters, and Marilyn Smith. 2006. "Orientation Redesign." *T&D* 60, no. 7: 43–45.

"The High Cost of Pain." *HR Focus* 73, no. 10(October 1996): 19.

Hill, Jean M. 1984. "Absenteeism: Effect of Employee Counseling in the Library." *Journal of Academic Librarianship* 9, no. 6: 342–344.

Holt, Glen E. 1999. "Training, A Library Imperative." *Journal of Library Administration* 29, no. 1: 79–93.

"How Do 403(b) Plans Compare to 401(k)s, IRAs and Keoghs?" Available: www.tiaa-cref.org/advisors/403b/403b_compare.html (accessed July 31, 2007).

Howard, Simon. 2003. "The Price of Flexibility." *People Management* 9, no. 6: 59.

Howland, John. 1999. "Beyond Recruitment: Retention and Promotion Strategies to Ensure Diversity and Success." *Library Administration & Management* 13, no. 4 (Winter).

Hussain, Zahid, James Wallace, and Nelarine E. Cornelius. 2007. "The Use and Impact of Human Resource Information Systems on Human Resource Management Professionals." *Information & Management* 44: 74–89.

"Intermittent Leave: The FMLA's Biggest Trouble Spot." 2005. *HRFocus* 82, no. 12 (December): 10–13.

"Is Your Company Ready for e-Learning?" 2002. *IOMA's Corporate e-Learning Buyer's Guide* no. 4: 6–10.

Jackson, Saundra, Diane Lacy, Liz Petersen, and John Sweeney. 2006. "Health Premiums, Raises, Warnings, Contrarians." *HRMagazine* 51, no. 6: 53–56.

Jacobs, Sally J. 1999. "What is the State of Your Organization's Soul?" *Library Mosaics* 10 (November/December): 8-11.

Jex, Steve M. 2002. *Organizational Psychology: A Scientist-Practitioner Approach.* New York: John Wiley & Sons.

Jin, Xudong. 2006. "Human Touch of Library Management in the United States: Personal Experiences of Creating and Developing a Harmonious Environment." 2006. *CLIE*, (December 1) Issue 22.

Johnson, Ben. 2004. "The Case of Performance Appraisal: Deming versus EEOC." *Library Administration & Management* 18, no. 2: 83–86.

Jui, Doris. 1993. "Technology's Impact on Library Operations." ERIC ED 389 333.

Jund-Ming Wang and Brian H. Kleiner. 2004. "Effective Employment Screening Practices." *Management Review News* 27, nos. 4/5: 99–107.

Kahan, Stuart. 2001. "Online Payroll Taking Off." *Practical Accountant* 34, no. 7: 42–44.

Kalev, A., F. Dobbin, and E. Kelly. 2006. "Best Practices or Best Guesses?: Assessing the Efficacy of Corporate Affirmative Action and Diversity Policies." *American Sociological Review* 71, no. 4: 589–617.

Kammeyer-Mueller, John and Hui Liao. 2006. "Workforce Reduction and Job-Seeker Attraction: Examining Job Seekers' Reactions to Firm Workforce Reduction Policies." *Human Resource Management* 45, no. 4: 585–603.

Kane-Urrabazo, Christine. 2006. "Management's Role in Shaping Organizational Culture." *Journal of Nursing Management* 14, no. 3: 188–194.

Kaplowitz, J. 1992. "Mentoring Library School Students: A Survey of Participants in the UCLA/GSLIS Mentor Program." *Special Libraries* 83, no. 4: 219–233.

Kathman, Jane M. and Michael D. Kathman. 1990. "Conflict Management in the Academic Library." *Journal of Academic Librarianship* 16, no. 3: 145–150.

Katz, Judith. 2006. "Tracking Employee Time: A Long-Term Problem." *Nursing Homes Long-Term Management* 55, no. 12: 50–51.

Kaufman, Paula T. 1992. "Professional Diversity in Libraries." *Library Trends* 4 no. 2 (Fall): 214–231.

Keeling, M. 2001. "Issues in Library Management: A Christian Perspective." *Christian Librarian* 25: 49–66.

Keller, Stefan. 2004. "Employee Screening: A Real-World Cost/Benefit Analysis." *Risk Management Magazine* 51, no. 11 (November): 28–32.

Kennedy, R.B. 1994. "The Employment Interview." *Journal of Employment Counseling* 31, no. 3: 110–114.

Kieke, Reba L. 2006. "CIGNA Launches New Solution to Help Patients Pay for Health Care." *Managed Care Outlook* 19, no. 22: 1, 6–7.

King Research. 1983. *Library Human Resources: A Study of Supply and Demand.* Chicago, IL: American Library Association.

Koch, William D. 2006. "Better Hires, Less Waste: A Potential Profit Bonanza." *Financial Executive* 22, no. 4 (May): 29–31.

Kohl, John, Milton Mayfield, and Jacqueline Mayfield. 2004. "Human Resource Regulation and Legal Issues: Web Sites for Instructional and Training Development." *Journal of Education for Business* 79, no. 6: 339–343.

Kohler, S. S. and J. E. Mathieu. 1993. "An Examination of the Relationships between Affective Reactions, Work Perceptions, Individual Resource Characteristics, and Multiple Absence Criteria." *Journal of Organizational Behavior* 14: 515–530.

Kovach, K. A. 1995. "Employee Motivation: Addressing a Crucial Factor in Your Organization's Performance." *Employment Relations Today* 22: 93–107.

Kravitz, Michael S. 1995. *Managing Negative People.* Menlo Park, CA: Crisp Publications.

Krell, Eric. 2002. "Recruiting Outlook: Creative HR for 2003." *Workforce* 81, no. 13 (December): 40–46.

Kuhn, Dennis M. and David E. Stout. 2004. "Reducing your Workforce: What You Don't Know Can Hurt You." *Strategic Finance* 85, no. 11: 41–45.

Kyrillidou, Martha and Kimberly A. Maxwell. 1996. *ARL Annual Salary Survey 1996–97.* Washington, DC: ARL.

Langan, Shelley. 2000. "Finding the Needle in the Haystack: The Challenge of Recruiting and Retaining Sharp Employees." *Public Personnel Management* 29, no. 4 (Winter): 461–464.

Lapointe, Joel. 1998. "People Make the System Go…Or Not." *HRMagazine* 43, no. 10: 28–33.

Lebowitz, Fran. 1996. *The Columbia World of Quotations*. Available: www.bartleby.com (accessed July 7, 2007).

Lehner, John A. 1997. "Reconsidering the Personnel Selection Practices of Academic Libraries." *Journal of Academic Librarianship* 23 (3):199–205,.

"Library Staff Covered by Collective Bargaining Agreements." 2006. *Library Worklife: HR E-News for Today's Leaders* 3, no. 6. Available: www.ala.org/ala/ors/reports/suppl_q's_statististics.pdf (accessed February 5, 2007).

Lipiec, Jacek. 2001. "Human Resources Management Perspective at the Turn of the Century." *Public Personnel Management* 30, no. 2: 137–147.

Lipponen, Jukka and Johanna Leskinen. 2006. "Conditions of Contract, Common In-Group Identity and In-Group Bias Toward Contingent Workers." *The Journal of Social Psychology* 146, no. 6: 671–684.

Lloyd, Joan 2006. "Just Whose Job Is It to Motivate Employees?" *The Receivables Report* 21, no. 8: 9–11.

Locke, E. A. 1976. "The Nature and Causes of Job Satisfaction," In *Handbook of Industrial and Organizational Psychology*, edited by M. D. Dunnette. Chicago: Rand McNally.

Long, Sarah 2004. "Compensation Doesn't Add Up for Library Staff." *Library Mosaics* 15, no. 4: 18.

Losinski, P. 2005. "Trends and Tips for Paraprofessionals in Public Libraries." *Library Mosaics* 16, no. 3: 16–17.

Lubans Jr., John. 1999. "I've Closed My Eyes to the Cold Hard Truth I'm Seeing: Making Performance Appraisal Work." *Library Administration & Management* 13, no. 2:87–89.

Lubans Jr., John. 1999. "She's Just Too Good to Be True, But She Is: Recognition Ceremonies and Other Motivational Rituals." *Library Administration & Management* 13, no. 4 (Fall): 212–215.

Lutgen-Sandvik, Pamela, Sara J. Tracy, and Jess K. Alberts. 2006. "Burned by Bullying in the American Workplace: Prevalence, Perception, Degree and Impact." *Journal of Management Studies* (in press). http://bullyinginstitute.org/res.html (accessed February 21, 2007).

Lutz, Amanda. 2005. "Be Prepared for Changes…Lots of Them!" *Quill Magazine* 93 no. 8: 42.

Lynch, Mary Jo. 2003. "Public Library Staff: How Much Is Enough?" *American Libraries* 34, no. 5: 58–59.

Mamaghani, Farrokh. 2006. "Impact of Information Technology on the Workforce of the Future: An Analysis." *International Journal of Management* 23, no. 4: 845–850.

Marcus, Bruce W. April 24, 2005. "How to Recruit in a Competitive World." *New Jersey Law Journal* 184, no. 4 (April 24): 245.

Marks, Jim. 2001. "Neglect Development of Your Staff at Your Own Risk." *National Underwriter/Life & Health Financial Services* 105, no. 19: 36–38.

Marks, Mitchell Lee. 2003. "Surviving Madness." *HRMagazine* 48, no. 6: 86.

Martin, R. A. 1997. "Recruiting a Library Leader for the 21st Century." *Journal of Library Administration* 24, no. 3: 47–58.

Martin, Theresa. 2005. *Smooth Legal Sailing!: Family Medical Leave Act*. Indianapolis, IN: IUPUI Human Resources Administration.

Martucci, William C. and Brent N. Coverdale. 2004. "Effective Use of Background Checks by Employers." *Employment Relations Today* 31, no. 2: 99–110.

Mason, Florence M. and Louella V. Wetherbee. 2004. "Learning to Lead: An Analysis of Current Training Programs for Library Leadership." *Library Trends* 55, no. 1: 187–217.

Mastrangelo, Paul M., Wendi Everton, and Jeffery A. Jolton. 2006. "Personal Use of Work Computers: Distraction versus Destruction." *CyperPsychology & Behavior* 9, no. 6: 730–740.

Matarazzo, James M. 2000. "Library Human Resources: The Y2K Plus 10 Challenge." *The Journal of Academic Librarianship* 26, no. 4: 223–224.

McClure, Dave. 2005. "Online Payroll: Web-Proven." *Practical Accountant 2005 Year in Review Special Supplement*: 53–56.

McClure, David. 2005. "What to Look for In . . . Payroll." *Accounting Technology* 21, no. 10: 13.

McConnell, John. 2006. "Fighting the Enemy Within." *Personnel Today* (May 9): 30–31.

McKnight, William. 2006. "Managing Change in Information Management." *DM Review* 16, no. 9: 56.

McLean, Carla. 2005. "The Not-So-Odd Couple: Libraries and Unions." *Aliki* 21, no. 2: 11–12.

Meisinger, Susan. 2006. "Workforce Retention: A Growing Concern." *HRMagazine* 51, no. 4: 12.

Melnyk, Andrew. 1976. "Student Aides in Our Libraries." *Illinois Libraries* 58, (Fall): 142.

Meneses, Alicia and Brian H. Kleiner. 2002. "How To Hire Employees Effectively." *Management Research News* 25, no. 5: 39–48.

Mercurio, Nancy. 2006. "Managing Change Successfully." *Canadian Manager* 31, no. 2: 6–7.

Messmer, Max. 2006. "Four Keys to Improved Staff Retention." *CMA Management* 80, no. 1: 14–15.

Milano, Carol. 2005. "Being There: Can Coming to Work Be a Risk?" *Risk Management* 52, no. 11: 30–34.

Miller, Marcus. 2006. "Developing an Effective Mentoring Program." *CMA Management* 80, no. 1: 14–15.

Monroe, John S. 2005. "5 Keys to Better Leadership." *Federal Computer Week* 19, no. 40: 24–30.

Moorman, John A., ed. 2006. *Running a Small Library*. New York: Neal-Schuman Publishers.

Moran Jr., Robert F. 2006. "Meetings: The Bane of the Workplace." *Library Administration & Management* 20, no. 3: 135–139.

Morrow, Paul C. and James C. McElroy. 2001. "Work Commitment: Conceptual and Methodological Developments for the Management of Human Resources." *Human Resources Management Review* 11 (Editorial): 177–180.

Muir, John. 1994. "Dealing with Sickness Absence." *Work Study, London* 43, no. 5: 13–14.

Munde, Gail. May 2000. "Beyond Mentoring: Toward the Rejuvenation of Academic Libraries." *Journal of Academic Librarianship* 28, no. 3: 171–176.

Nadler, Reidan S. 2007. "Are You a Meeting Menace or Master?" *T & D* 61, no. 1: 10–11.

Namie, Gary. 2003. "The Workplace Bullying Institute 2003 Report on Abusive Workplaces." Available: http://bullinginstitute.org/res.html (accessed February 21, 2007).

Nesher, Raviv. 2006. "Employee Misuse Can Put Your Company at Risk." *Central New York Business Journal* 20, no. 25: 22–23.

Oberg, Larry R. 1992. "The Emergence of the Paraprofessional in Academic Libraries: Perceptions and Realities." *College & Research Libraries* 53: 99–112.

Office for Library Personnel Resources, American Library Association. 1986. *Academic and Public Librarians: Data by Race, Ethnicity, and Sex*. Chicago: ALA.

Osif, Bonnie A. and Richard L. Harwood. 1999. "Change: Challenges and Coping." *Library Administration & Management* 13, no. 4 (Fall): 224–228.

Ossi, Gregory J. 2005. "Age Discrimination Protection Is Not Limited to Seniors." *Coal Age* 110, no. 12: 39.

Outlaw, Wayne. 1998. *Smart Staffing: How to Hire, Reward, and Keep Top Employees for Your Growing Company*. Chicago: Upstart Publishing.

Overman, Stephenie. 1992. "Reaching for the 21st Century." *HRMagazine* 37, no. 4: 61–63.

Pergander, Mary. 2006. "Mastering the Group Interview." *American Libraries* 37, no. 2 (February): 44.

Perry, Emma Bradford. 2004. "Let Recruitment Begin with Me." *American Libraries* 35, no. 5 (May): 36–38.

Perry, Phillip M. 2004. "Problem Employees: Get Your Poor Performers Back on Track." *Executive Housekeeping Today* 25, no. 11: 23–28.

Peterson, Robin T. 2005. "An Examination of the Relative Effectiveness of Training in Nonverbal Communication: Personal Selling Implications." *Journal of Marketing Education* 27, no. 2: 143–150.

Poole, Carolyn E. and Emmett Denny. 2001. "Technological Change in the Workplace: A Statewide Survey of Community College Library and Learning Resources Personnel." *College & Research Libraries* 62, no. 6: 503–515.

Poole, Michael and Malcolm Warner, eds. 1998. *The IEBM Handbook of Human Resource Management.* Boston: International Thomson Business Press.

Pulier, Greg. July 2007. "Select the Right Tool for the Job: Video Webcasting Can Reach a Variety of Internal and External Audiences." *Communication News* 44, no. 7: 12, 17.

"Pushing for Higher Library Salaries: Now or Never?" 2003. *American Libraries* 34, no. 1: 55–57.

Pynes, Joan E. 1997. *Human Resources Management for Public and Nonprofit Organizations.* San Francisco: Jossey-Bass.

Raghuram, Sumita and Batia Wiesenfeld. 2004. "Work-Nonwork Conflict and Job Stress Among Virtual Workers." *Human Resources Management* 43, no. 2/3: 259–277.

Ragsdale, Mary Alice and John Mueller. 2005. "Plan, Do, Study, Act, Model to Improve an Orientation Program." *Journal of Nursing Care Quality* 20, no. 3: 268–272.

Rainham, David. 2003. "How to Deal with a Violent Employee." *The Record (Kitchner-Waterloo, Ontario),* June 27 (Life): D-2.

Rajesh, Saundarya. 2004. "Does This One Fit? Recruiting the Right Talent for Your Company Can Be a Traumatic Experience. Here's Insight into Factors that Drive the Recruitment Process." *Businessline* (April 14): 1.

Ramsay, Martin L. and Howard Lehto. 1994. "The Power of Peer Review." *Training & Development* 48, no. 7: 38–41.

Raschke, Gregory K. 2003. "Hiring and Recruitment Practices in Academic Libraries: Problems and Solutions." *Libraries and the Academy* 3, no. 1:53–67.

Ribbink, Kim. 2002. "Seven Ways to Better Communicate in Today's Diverse Workplace." *Harvard Management Communication Letter* 5, no. 11: 3–5.

Robbins, Stephen P. 2000. *Essentials of Organizational Behavior,* 6th ed. Upper Saddle River, NJ: Prentice-Hall.

Rogelberg, Steven G., Cliff Scott, and John Kello. 2007. "The Science and Fiction of Meetings." *MIT Sloan Management Review* 48, no. 2: 17–21.

Rogers, Michael and Peter Shepherd. 2003. "Tackling Recruitment." *Library Journal* 128, no. 2 (February): 40-43.

Rosenthal, Roseanne. 2006. "Stand and Think Tall: 93% of Communication Is Nonverbal." *Illinois Music Educator* 66, no. 3: 58–59.

Rubin, Richard. 1993. *Hiring Library Employees.* New York: Neal-Schuman.

Russell, Carrie. 1998. "Using Performance Measurement to Evaluate Teams and Organizational Effectiveness." *Library Administration & Management* 12, no. 3 (Summer):156–158.

Safran, Gerson. 2006. "Making the Case for an HRMS." *Canadian HR Reporter* 19, no. 7: 13.

Sampson, Eleri. 1995. "First Impressions: The Power of Personal Style." *Library Management* 16, no. 4: 25–28.

Schachter, Debbie. 2006. "An Essential Function for Special Librarians." *Information Outlook* 10, no. 10: 8–9.

Schneider, Karen G. 2003. "Managing the Virtual Workplace." *Library Journal* 128, no. 1: 24–25.

Sebastian, Don. 2004. "Effective Communication in the Workplace." *Executive Housekeeping Today* 25, no. 12: 16–17.

Sherer, Pamela D. and Lori A. Coakley. 1999. "Questioning and Developing Your Part-Time Employee Practices." *Workforce* (October Supplement): 4.

Shiparksi, L. 1996. "Successful Interview Strategies." *Nursing Management* 27, no. 7: 32F–32H.

Shore, Ted H., Armen Tashchian, and Janet S. Adams. 1997. "The Role of Gender in a Developmental Assessment Center." *Journal of Social Behavior and Personality* 12, no. 5: 191–203.

SHRM (Society for Human Resources Management). 2007. "By the Numbers: Surf, Sand and a Cell Phone." *Employee Benefit News* 21, no. 10: 66.

Sigel, Randy. 1992. "Seven Steps to Keep Top Perfomers." *Public Relations Journal* 48, no. 2: 12.

Simmons-Welburn, Janice. 1999. "Using Culture as a Construct for Achieving Diversity in Human Resources Management." *Library Administration & Management* 13, no. 1 (Winter): 4–13.

Singer, Paula and Jeanne Goodrich. 2006. "Retaining and Motivating High-Performing Employees." *Public Libraries* 45, no. 1: 58–63.

Sloboda, Brian. 1999. "'Netiquette'—New Rules and Policies for the Information Age." *Management Quarterly* 40, no. 4: 9–33.

Smith, Shawn and Rebecca Mazin. 2004. *The HR Answer Book*. New York: AMACOM.

Spector, Paul E. 1997. *Job Satisfaction: Application, Assessment, Causes and Consequences*. Thousand Oaks, CA: Sage Publications.

Spinelli, Lisa. 2006. "Accentuate the Positive." *Accounting Technology* 20 (Fall Supplement): 6.

Sreenivasulu, V. 2000. "The Role of a Digital Librarian in the Management of Digital Information Systems (DIS)." *The Electronic Library* 18, no. 1: 12–20.

Stanley, Mary J. 2001. "Taking Time for the Organization: How IUPUI University Library Is Building Teams." *C&RL News* 62, no. 9: 900–908.

Stanley, Mary J. 2007. "Where Is the Diversity: Focus Groups on How Students View the Face of Librarianship." *Library Administration & Management* 21, no. 2: 20–35.

Stanton, E. S. 1977. *Successful Personnel Recruiting and Selection.* New York: AMACON.

Strebler, Marie. 2006. "Why Motivation Holds the Key to an Engaged Age-Diverse Workforce." *People Management* 12, no. 23: 48.

Stueart, Robert D. and John Taylor Eastlick, 2nd. ed. 1981. *Library Management.* Littleton, CO: Libraries Unlimited.

"Survey Reports Increased Salaries." 2007. *American Libraries* 38, no. 1: 10.

"The Labor Union Movement in America." Available: www.socialstudies help.com/Eco_Unionization.htm (accessed February 5, 2007).

Sweeney, John, Angela Stone, and Naomi Cossack. 2007. "Skills Data, Retirement Benefits, Difficult Employees." *HRMagazine* 52, no. 1: 49–50.

Taber, Tom D. and George M. Alliger. 1995. "A Task-Level Assessment of Job Satisfaction." *Journal of Organizational Behavior* 16, no. 2: 101–121.

Tennant, Roy. 2002. "The Digital Librarian Shortage." *Library Journal* 127, no. 5: 32.

Tenopir, Carol. 2006. "What Chat Transcripts Reveal." *Library Journal* 131, no. 4: 34.

Terwilliger, Michael S. 2005. "A Supervisor's Guide to Progressive Discipline, Part 1." *Fire Engineering* 158, no. 5: 105–109.

Terwilliger, Michael S. 2005. "A Supervisor's Guide to Progressive Discipline, Part 2." *Fire Engineering* 158, no. 6: 97–102.

Terwilliger, Michael S. 2005. "A Supervisor's Guide to Progressive Discipline, Part 3." *Fire Engineering* 158, no. 7: 85–92.

"To Become Critical for F/S: Job-Seekers Turning to Web as Online Recruiting Grows." 2001. *FoodService Director* 14, no. 4 (April 15): 6.

Tonidandel, Scott, Derek R. Avery, and McKensy G. Phillips. 2007. "Maximizing Returns on Mentoring: Factors Affecting Subsequent Protégé Performance." *Journal of Organizational Behavior* 28: 89–110.

"Training or Punishment: Which Path Should You Take?" 2001. *Fair Practice Guidelines.* Issue 535 (February 1): 5–6.

Turnbull, Claire. 2003. "Online and Flexible: HR in 2003." 2, no. 3 (January/February): 12–13.

Turner, Anne M. 2004. "It Hurts to Ignore Work Injury Roots." *Library Journal* 120, no. 1: 64.

Tyler, Kathryn. 2005. "Performance Art." *HRMagazine* 50, no. 8: 58–63.

US Bureau of the Census. 1983. *The 1980 Census of Population.* Washington, DC: The Bureau of the Census.

US Bureau of the Census. 1984. "Earnings by Occupation and Education" in 1980 Census Population, vol. 2. Washington, DC: The Bureau of the Census: 54.

US Bureau of Labor Statistics. 1975. *Library Manpower: A Study of Demand and Supply*. Washington, DC: The Bureau.

Varner, Iris I. 2001. "Teaching Intercultural Management Communication: Where Are We? Where Do We Go?" *Business Communication Quarterly* 64, no. 1: 99–111.

Vaughan, Jason. 2005. "Lied Library @ Four Years: Technology Never Stands Still." *Library Hi Tech* 23, no. 1:34–49.

Von Dran, Gisela. 2005. "Human Resources and Leadership Strategies for Libraries in Transition." *Library Administration & Management* 19, no. 4: 177–184.

Ward, Patricia Layzell. 2000. "Trends in Library Management." *Library Review* 49, no. 9: 436–441.

Weingart, Sandra, Carol A. Kochan, and Ann Hedrich. 1998. "Safeguarding Your Investment: Effective Orientation for New Employees." *Library Administration & Management* 12, no. 3 (Summer): 156–158.

Weitzel, Thomas Q. 2004. "Managing the Problem Employee: A Road Map for Success." *FBI Law Enforcement Bulletin* 73, no. 11: 25–32.

"When Does COBRA Coverage Begin Under the New Regulations?" 1999. *COBRA Advisory* 3, no. 1: 4–5.

White, Herbert S. 1989. "The 'Quiet Revolution': A Profession at the Crossroads." *Special Libraries* 80, no. 1: 24–31.

Whitnery, Jo Ellen. 2002. "Documentation 101: Mastering the 7 C's and Other Helpful Hints." *Rural Telecommunications* 21, no. 3 (May/June): 42–44.

Wilson, Jennifer. 2006. "Motivating Your Team by Putting 'The Six' Into Action." *Accounting Today* 20, no. 21: 22–28.

Wollenhaupt, G. 2007. "Diversity Strengthens Companies and Employees." *The Indianapolis Star* (January 15), Supplement: G2.

Wood, John Andy. 2006. "NLP Revisited: Nonverbal Communications and Signals of Trustworthiness." *Journal of Personal Selling & Sales Management* 26, no. 2: 197–204.

Worrall, Les and Cary Cooper. 2006. "Short Changed." *People Management* 12, no. 13: 36–38.

Youngman, Daryl C. 1999. "Library Staffing Considerations in the Age of Technology: Basic Elements for Managing Change." *Issues in Science and Technology Librarianship* (Fall): 24.

Zatzick, Christopher D. and Roderick D. Iverson. 2006. "High-Involvement Management and Workforce Reduction: Competitive Advantage or Disadvantage?" *Academy of Management Journal* 49, no. 5: 999–1015.

Zimmerer, Thomas W. 1973. "Increasing Productivity Among Marginal Employees." *Industrial Management* 15, no. 1: 1–3.

WEB SITES

www.bls.gov (accessed January 22, 2007).
www.dol.gov/esa/regs/compliance/whd/fiarpay/fact_exemption.htm
(accessed January 22, 2007).

INDEX

ABOUT THE AUTHOR

Mary J. Stanley is Associate Dean at the IUPUI (Indiana University Purdue University Indianapolis) University Library. As part of her responsibilities as Associate Dean, she serves as Director of Human Resources, which she has done for the past 12 years. She has been with the library for over 20 years and a part of the IUPUI campus for 27 years. Professional interests include library human resources, diversity, and combined social work/library collaboration. She has done statewide workshops on conflict resolution and problem employees. She has worked in public, academic, and special libraries during her library career. She holds an MLS from Indiana University and is certified as a Birkman consultant and a Stephen Covey consultant. She is married to Michael H. Stanley and has two children and two grandchildren.